Fundamentals of
Database Indexing
and Searching

Fundamentals of Database Indexing and Searching

Arnab Bhattacharya

Indian Institute of Technology (IIT), Kanpur
India

CRC Press
Taylor & Francis Group
Boca Raton London New York

CRC Press is an imprint of the
Taylor & Francis Group, an **informa** business

A CHAPMAN & HALL BOOK

CRC Press
Taylor & Francis Group
6000 Broken Sound Parkway NW, Suite 300
Boca Raton, FL 33487-2742

First issued in paperback 2016

© 2015 by Taylor & Francis Group, LLC
CRC Press is an imprint of Taylor & Francis Group, an Informa business

No claim to original U.S. Government works

Version Date: 20140930

ISBN 13: 978-1-138-03395-5 (pbk)
ISBN 13: 978-1-4665-8254-5 (hbk)

Visit the Taylor & Francis Web site at
http://www.taylorandfrancis.com

and the CRC Press Web site at
http://www.crcpress.com

To
my parents,
my children,
and my wife

Summary

Contents

List of Figures

List of Tables

List of Key Concepts

List of Examples

Preface

Currently, we are living in a "data world" where we are regularly deluged with an immense amount of data, both personal and otherwise. The range of personal data varies from digital news feeds and Web browsing history to emails and mobile phone data. We are also witnessing unprecedented growth in the amount of scientific data, from protein sequences and structures to biomedical images, sensor readings, discovery of chemical compounds, and astronomical data. With the improvement in data acquiring technologies, digital databases are becoming a necessity for every scientific discipline.

Although databases have become an integral part of any large computer system, in many cases, they are still used simply as a data repository. In order to render the databases more useful than just a digital data store, the ability to search for data objects similar to a query must be supported. The prospect of success, thus, lies critically in the ability to efficiently handle the massive amount of data that is produced on a regular basis, as well as the improved ways of retrieving the required information from such massive collections. The indexing techniques developed over decades aim to provide just that capability.

This book covers the well-known database searching and indexing techniques. It focuses mostly on similarity search queries where, given a query object, it is required to return objects from the database that are "similar" to it, and not just exactly matching it. Generally, a distance function is used to measure the notion of dissimilarity. Objects that are not dissimilar by more than a range threshold, or, are least dissimilar to the query, are then sought.

The idea of this book came to my mind when I taught a very similar course for the first time. While teaching the subject, I realized how difficult it was to translate any description into an explanation. Thus, instead of trying to be a compendium of all the indexing and searching methods in the literature, the focus of this book is to organize the most common and representative index structures according to their characteristics and to understand them using examples and concepts. The setting does not refer to a relational database or any other special kind of database (such as graph, object-oriented, key-value store, etc.); it applies uniformly to all of them and is valid no matter what the internal structure of a database is.

The book is organized into six parts.

The first part covers the basics and includes a chapter on what database queries are and what similarity search queries mean. Although the most important criterion of judging an indexing scheme is the time it requires to answer a query, it is sometimes useful to design practical heuristics. The chapter also discusses how these approximate methods can be evaluated.

In the second part, the low-dimensional index structures are described. The first chapter in this part discusses hashing where mostly single-dimensional keys are used. The second chapter describes the index structures that are suitable for main memory applications. Strictly speaking, many of these structures can be applied, at least theoretically, to higher dimensions. However, in such cases, they become ineffective due to the complexity of the design, the explosion in the structure, or the increase in storage requirements. Thus, they are mostly viewed as memory-resident, low-dimensional structures.

The sole chapter in the third part of the book contains the hierarchical disk-based index structures. It assumes that the database objects are represented in a vector format in a fixed dimensional space and the dissimilarity between the objects is measured using the Euclidean distance. These structures work with feature vectors of any dimensionality.

The next part removes the limitation of working with object vectors. The database objects may not have a vector-based representation (for example, images or text). The requirement is that given any two objects, it is always possible to compute a distance measure between them. The distance need not be Euclidean, and the first chapter in this part discusses several useful distance measures. The second chapter describes the index structures that use the distance information to efficiently solve similarity search queries. It mostly relies on the metric properties of the distance function.

The fifth part deals with the infamous curse of dimensionality phenomenon. A whole chapter is dedicated to discussing what the phenomenon is and why indexing becomes almost useless in very high-dimensional spaces. The following chapter describes several indexing methods that specifically deal with high-dimensional spaces.

The final part of the book describes several data reduction methods. The first chapter in this part discusses dimensionality reduction techniques that help in softening the curse of dimensionality. It also discusses several embedding methods that transform object descriptions into suitable object vectors which can then be indexed using the hierarchical structures. The last chapter describes various data representation and histogram techniques that transform different datasets into a common framework, thereby enabling their comparison and unified representation.

The book has been written mostly for postgraduate and advanced undergraduate studies. It has been prepared to not depend on any prerequisites, except very basic computer science fundamentals. Thus, the book can be studied mostly on its own. Some useful background information has been included in the appendices to help review some of the fundamentals if needed.

I hope the students and the teachers find it useful. Even if one of them benefits from reading this book, I will consider this endeavor to be successful.

Arnab Bhattacharya

Acknowledgments

The biggest motivation for this book has come from my parents. They have been extremely excited about this project from the time it was just an idea. Their excitement is what drove me thinking and planning the book even at times of inaction. It is a wonderful feeling to finally finish this book and to make them happy.

My two children and my wife have also played stellar roles in the entire journey. In times of writer's block, playing with my small kids helped remove the cobwebs from my mind and to concentrate again. And, in times when writing consumed me, my wife covered for me and took care of them.

I am also indebted to the numerous students who sat through the course that largely shaped this book. Very often their quizzical looks made me think afresh about how a particular structure should be explained, and their questions urged me to explore the topics further.

I gratefully acknowledge several of my teachers and friends in both my undergraduate and postgraduate studies as well as my colleagues from whom I have learned many concepts and ideas in computer science, some of which have been relevant to the ones I have mentioned in this book. A special thanks goes to my former thesis advisor who introduced me to this topic.

Finally, I am grateful to Taylor & Francis for approving this project and for allowing me the time to create the book I envisioned.

Arnab Bhattacharya

Part I

Basics

Chapter 1

Database Queries

The primary purpose of databases is to store data objects along with their attributes. However, a necessary function is to also enable retrieving one or more data objects that pertain to some conditions. The querying mechanism is greatly supported by the ability to "search" for the objects that satisfy the query conditions. These are, therefore, often referred to as *search queries*.

This chapter explains what a similarity search query is and defines the different types of such queries. It assumes a general setting of the database and not any particular form, such as relational systems, graph databases, or key-value stores. It also discusses the various error metrics that a search algorithm may encounter.

1.1 Basic Setting

A DATABASE D consists of n objects. Each object has t *fields* or *attributes* or *dimensions*. Thus, the database can be represented as

$$D = \{O_1, \ldots, O_n\} \tag{1.1}$$

where each object $O_i \in D$ can be represented as

$$O_i = \{O_{i,1}, \ldots, O_{i,t}\}. \tag{1.2}$$

While some of these attributes of the objects can be numerical (either integers or real numbers), some others can be categorical (i.e., they can take values only from a pre-defined set), or even boolean (simply *true* or *false*).

An object that is posed as a QUERY to the database can be represented in the same consistent manner, i.e., as an object Q with t dimensions:

$$Q = \{Q_1, \ldots, Q_t\} \tag{1.3}$$

Using this setting, we next describe some important types of queries.

3

1.2   Exact Search

An EXACT SEARCH query tries to find a database object that *exactly* matches the query. It is also known as a POINT QUERY or an EXACT MATCH QUERY.

Definition 1.1 [Point Query]. *Given a database D and a query object Q, return all objects $O_i \in D$ such that $O_i = Q$.*

The most common definition of the equality operator $(=)$ is that all the dimensions match, i.e.,

$$O_i = O_j \iff \forall a = 1, \ldots, t, \; O_{i,a} = O_{j,a} \tag{1.4}$$

However, for a particular application, two objects may be considered to be equal if only some of the pre-defined dimensions match.

1.3   Similarity Search

It is not always possible to find the query object exactly in the database. It is rather more appropriate to look for objects that are "similar" to the one that is queried. SIMILARITY SEARCH addresses this issue by defining a notion of similarity between two objects.

It is often easier to define the notion of DISTANCE between a pair of objects. The distance function measures the *dissimilarity* between objects. Thus, retrieving an object that is more similar is equivalent to retrieving an object that has a lesser distance. A common example is the Euclidean distance or the L_2 norm.

The basic database setting (Section 1.1) can be then endowed with a distance function $d(O_i, O_j)$ between any two objects to yield the *extended setting*. It is on this extended setting that the similarity search queries are asked.

There are two important similarity search queries that are defined next.

Definition 1.2 [Range Query]. *Given a database D, a query object Q, a distance function d, and the range of distance r, return all objects $A = \{O_i \in D\}$ such that $d(O_i, Q) \leq r$.*

Definition 1.3 [Nearest Neighbor Query]. *Given a database D, a*

Table 1.1: Distances from query $Q = (4, 5)$.

Object	Coordinates	$d(Q, O_i)$
O_1	3, 7	2.24
O_2	3, 6	1.41
O_3	5, 8	3.16
O_4	9, 2	5.83

query object Q, a distance function d, and the number of nearest neighbors k, return all objects $A = \{O_i \in D\}$ such that $|A| = k$ and for any $O_i \in A$ and $O_j \notin A$, $d(O_i, Q) \leq d(O_j, Q)$.

When there are more than k objects with the same distance as the kth object, any one of them can be returned as part of the answer set. Alternatively, all of them can be returned and the first condition is then relaxed to $|A| \geq k$.

A different type of similarity search query that does not use a distance function is defined next.

Definition 1.4 [Window Query]. *Given a database D and query ranges Q_j^{low}, Q_j^{high} in each dimension $j = 1, \ldots, t$, return all objects $A = \{O_i \in D\}$ such that $\forall j = 1, \ldots, t$, $Q_j^{low} \leq O_{i,j} \leq Q_j^{high}$.*

A point query can be represented as a range query with range $r = 0$ or as a window query with both the low and high values equal to the point value in each dimension.

Example 1.1 [Similarity Search]. Consider the following database of 2-dimensional objects:

$$O_1 = (3, 7), O_2 = (3, 6), O_3 = (5, 8), O_4 = (9, 2)$$

Using the Euclidean distance (see Section 5.2 for the definition) for the query $Q = (4, 5)$, find the answers for the range query with $r = 2$ and nearest neighbor query with $k = 2$.

The distances from the query to all the database objects are given in Table 1.1. The answer to the range and nearest neighbor queries are, therefore, $\{O_2\}$ and $\{O_2, O_1\}$ respectively. $\quad\square$

Table 1.2: Distance matrix between objects.

Distances	O_{21}	O_{22}	O_{23}
O_{11}	2.24	3.61	2.24
O_{12}	3.16	2.83	1.42
O_{13}	3.16	5.66	3.16

1.4   Join

In many situations, it is not enough to retrieve only single objects as answers. Rather, similar pairs of objects need to be found between two datasets. A common example is finding pairs of hotels and shopping malls that are close to each other. The JOIN query addresses this issue by searching for object pairs from both the datasets such that they satisfy the range or nearest neighbor conditions.

Definition 1.5 [Join Query (Range)]. *Given two databases D_1, D_2, a distance function d, and the range of distance r, return all object pairs $J = \{O_i \in D_1, O_j \in D_2\}$ such that $d(O_i, O_j) \leq r$.*

Definition 1.6 [Join Query (Nearest Neighbor)]. *Given two databases D_1, D_2, a distance function d, and the number of nearest neighbors k, return all object pairs $J = \{O_i \in D_1, O_j \in D_2\}$ such that $|J| = k$ and for any $(O_i, O_j) \in J$ and $(O_p, O_q) \notin J$, $d(O_i, O_j) \leq d(O_p, O_q)$.*

If D_1 and D_2 are the same database, then it is called a SELF-JOIN.

Example 1.2 [Join]. Consider the following two databases of 2-dimensional objects:

$$O_{11} = (3,7), O_{12} = (3,6), O_{13} = (5,8)$$

$$O_{21} = (2,9), O_{22} = (1,4), O_{23} = (4,5)$$

Using the Euclidean distance (Section 5.2), find the answers for the join query with range $r = 2$ and number of nearest neighbors $k = 2$.

The distance matrix between the objects of the two databases is given in Table 1.2. The answer to the range and nearest neighbor join queries are, therefore, $\{(O_{12}, O_{23})\}$ and $\{(O_{12}, O_{23}), (O_{11}, O_{21})\}$ (or $\{(O_{12}, O_{23}), (O_{11}, O_{23})\}$) respectively.   □

1.5   Errors

In this section, we describe the different error measures that are associated with queries. Although the book deals with search algorithms that always deliver the correct answer, the notion of errors is useful for understanding how heuristics work.

For any search, the set of objects that are sought is denoted by POS-ITIVES, P. The rest of the database objects, i.e., the ones that are not sought, form the NEGATIVES set, $N = D \setminus P$.

For a particular query algorithm $\mathcal{A}$, assume that the set of objects it returns as answers is denoted by P' and the rest is $N' = D \setminus P'$. The following sets define its performance:

- TRUE POSITIVES, TP: Objects in the positive set *and* $\mathcal{A}$ has returned: $P \cap P'$.

- TRUE NEGATIVES, TN: Objects in the negative set *and* $\mathcal{A}$ has not returned: $N \cap N'$.

- FALSE POSITIVES, FP: Objects in the negative set *but* $\mathcal{A}$ has returned: $N \cap P'$.

- FALSE NEGATIVES, FN: Objects in the positive set *but* $\mathcal{A}$ has not returned: $P \cap N'$.

Thus,

$$P = TP \cup FN \qquad N = TN \cup FP \tag{1.5}$$
$$P' = TP \cup FP \qquad N' = TN \cup FN \tag{1.6}$$

The "errors" of the querying algorithm $\mathcal{A}$ are captured by *false positives* since they denote objects that have been wrongly designated as answers as well as by *false negatives* since they denote objects that are correct answers but have not been returned by $\mathcal{A}$. Consequently, these two measures are also known as TYPE I ERRORS and TYPE II ERRORS respectively.

The CONFUSION MATRIX provides a visual way of presenting the information (Table 1.3). The rows indicate the true answers while the sets returned by the querying algorithm are shown in the columns.

Example 1.3 [Positives and Negatives]. Consider the database:

$$D = \{O_1, O_2, O_3, O_4, O_5, O_6, O_7, O_8\}$$

Table 1.3: Confusion matrix.

		Returned by algorithm	
		Positives P'	Negatives N'
True answers	Positives P	TP	FN
	Negatives N	FP	TN

Suppose for a search query, the correct answer is $\{O_1, O_5, O_7\}$ but a particular querying algorithm has returned $\{O_1, O_3, O_5, O_6\}$. Find the associated error metrics. Also, draw the confusion matrix.

- Positives $P = \{O_1, O_5, O_7\}$

- Negatives $N = \{O_2, O_3, O_4, O_6, O_8\}$

- True positives $TP = \{O_1, O_5\}$

- True negatives $TN = \{O_2, O_4, O_8\}$

- False positives $FP = \{O_3, O_6\}$

- False negatives $FN = \{O_7\}$

- Confusion matrix

	P'	N'	Total
P	2	1	3
N	2	3	5
Total	4	4	8

□

1.5.1 Error Parameters

For measuring the performance of a querying algorithm $\mathcal{A}$, various *error parameters*, *error metrics*, or *performance metrics* based on the previous measures have been defined.

- RECALL, or SENSITIVITY, or TRUE POSITIVE RATE: Proportion of positives returned by $\mathcal{A}$.

- PRECISION: Proportion of positives in those returned by $\mathcal{A}$.

- SPECIFICITY or TRUE NEGATIVE RATE: Proportion of negatives not returned by $\mathcal{A}$.

- FALSE POSITIVE RATE: Proportion of negatives returned by $\mathcal{A}$.

- FALSE NEGATIVE RATE: Proportion of positives not returned by $\mathcal{A}$.

- ACCURACY: Proportion of positives returned and negative not returned by $\mathcal{A}$.

- ERROR RATE: Proportion of positives not returned and negatives returned by $\mathcal{A}$.

The definitions can be summarized as:

$$\text{recall} = \frac{|TP|}{|P|} \tag{1.7}$$

$$\text{precision} = \frac{|TP|}{|P'|} \tag{1.8}$$

$$\text{specificity} = \frac{|TN|}{|N|} \tag{1.9}$$

$$\text{false positive rate} = \frac{|FP|}{|N|} \tag{1.10}$$

$$\text{false negative rate} = \frac{|FN|}{|P|} \tag{1.11}$$

$$\text{accuracy} = \frac{|TP \cup TN|}{|D|} \tag{1.12}$$

$$\text{error rate} = \frac{|FP \cup FN|}{|D|} \tag{1.13}$$

Some of these error metrics are related to each other, such as

$$\text{false positive rate} = 1 - \text{true negative rate} \tag{1.14}$$

$$\text{false negative rate} = 1 - \text{true positive rate} \tag{1.15}$$

$$\text{error rate} = 1 - \text{accuracy} \tag{1.16}$$

The most commonly used metrics for comparison of different query algorithms are *precision* and *recall*. Two algorithms may be such that one has a better precision but a worse recall than the other. In order to provide a convenient way of deciding which is better, a simple metric, F-SCORE, F1-SCORE, or F-MEASURE, is used. F-score is defined as the *harmonic mean* of precision and recall, i.e.,

$$\text{F-score} = \frac{2 \times \text{precision} \times \text{recall}}{\text{precision} + \text{recall}} \tag{1.17}$$

In terms of the four major performance metrics, the F-score is defined as:

$$\text{F-score} = \frac{2 \times TP}{2 \times TP + FN + FP} \tag{1.18}$$

Precision and recall can also be weighted when defining the F-score [van Rijsbergen, 1979]. If recall is β times more important than precision, then

$$\text{F-score} = \frac{(1 + \beta^2) \times \text{precision} \times \text{recall}}{\beta^2 \times \text{precision} + \text{recall}} \tag{1.19}$$

The simple F-measure is when $\beta = 1$, i.e., when precision and recall are equally important.

Another measure that takes into account both precision and recall is the G-MEASURE which is the *geometric mean* of the two error metrics:

$$\text{G-measure} = \sqrt{\text{precision} \times \text{recall}} \tag{1.20}$$

Example 1.4 [Error Metrics]. Find the rest of the error metrics for the algorithm in Example 1.3.

- Recall or Sensitivity $= 2/3 = 0.67$

- Precision $= 2/4 = 0.50$

- Specificity or True negative rate $= 3/5 = 0.60$

- False positive rate $= 2/5 = 0.40$

- Accuracy $= 5/8 = 0.625$

- Error rate $= 3/8 = 0.375$

- F-score $= 4/7 = 0.571$

- G-measure $= \sqrt{1/3} = 0.577$

□

In biometrics applications, the false positive rate is also known as FALSE ACCEPTANCE RATE (FAR) or FALSE MATCH RATE (FMR) as this denotes the rate of wrong objects being accepted by the algorithm. Conversely, the false negative rate is also known as FALSE REJECTION RATE (FRR) or FALSE NON-MATCH RATE (FNMR) as this denotes the rate of correct objects being rejected by the algorithm.

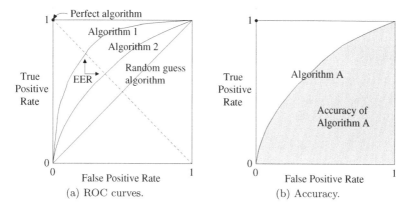

(a) ROC curves. (b) Accuracy.

Figure 1.1: ROC curve and its accuracy.

1.5.2 ROC Curve

In general, any query algorithm requires some parameters, depending on the values of which, its performance changes. Thus, while one set of parameters may result in a high recall but low precision, another set may lead to low recall and high precision. Hence, to assess the performance of the algorithm over different sets of parameters, the RECEIVING OPERATING CHARACTERISTIC (ROC) curve is used. It plots true positive rate (as the y-axis) versus false positive rate (as the x-axis) for different runs of the algorithm. Equivalently, it is a plot of sensitivity versus 1 - specificity. The area under the ROC curve measures the *discrimination* for the algorithm. Sometimes this is also called *accuracy* although it is different from what is defined in terms of positive and negative sets.

For an algorithm that simply makes random guesses about whether a database object is part of the answer set or not, the ROC curve is the 45° diagonal. Thus, its discrimination is only 0.5. A perfect query algorithm, on the other hand, always has a true positive rate of 1 and a false positive rate of 0. Consequently, its discrimination is 1.

Figure 1.1a shows ROC curves of two algorithms along with those of the random guess algorithm and the perfect algorithm. Figure 1.1b shows how the accuracy is measured as the area under the ROC curve. In Figure 1.1a, Algorithm 1 has a better accuracy than Algorithm 2.

A simpler way of comparing two algorithms is by using the EQUAL ERROR RATE (EER). EER denotes the point in the ROC curve where the false positive rate is equal to the false negative rate. The EER points of Algorithm 1 and Algorithm 2 are marked in Figure 1.1a.

Part II

Low-Dimensional Index Structures

Chapter 2

Hashing

HASHING is a mathematical function that transforms a key k to be searched to a location $h(k)$ where the contents corresponding to the key can be found. An example of a very simple hash function with m locations is $h(k) = k \bmod m$.

A good hash function should exhibit the following two properties:

- *Uniform*: The total domain of keys should be distributed uniformly over the range.

- *Random*: The hash values should be distributed uniformly irrespective of the distribution of the keys.

It is easy to see that more than one key can hash to the same location for a hash function. This phenomenon is called *collision* and the ways to handle collisions are called *collision resolution* mechanisms.

In a database context, the hash locations are disk pages or buckets that can contain a multiple number of keys and the corresponding objects. Hence, the hash function maps a key to a bucket. The searching of a key within a bucket is a simple linear scan. Hence, the concept of collision is replaced by that of *overflow*, which happens when there is no more space in a hash bucket to store any more keys.

Overflow can happen either due to a skew in the distribution of the keys or due to the non-uniformity of the hash function. The chances of overflowing can only be reduced, but can never be eliminated completely.

Hash functions strive to complete searching for *any* key in $O(1)$ time, i.e., within a constant number of steps. Thus, in a database querying context, hash functions are desirable for point queries. However, they cannot support range and kNN queries well.

This chapter describes the various static and dynamic hashing techniques in the context of database queries.

2.1   Static Hashing

The simplest kind of hashing technique is that of STATIC HASHING where the number of locations for the hashed values is fixed (i.e., static) irrespective of the number of keys. The function $h(k) = k \bmod m$ shows a simple example with m locations.

The *overflow handling* mechanisms follow two broad categories as described next.

2.1.1   Chaining

CHAINING (also known as SEPARATE CHAINING, CLOSED ADDRESS-ING, or OPEN HASHING) observes a simple method of overflow resolution. Once the primary hash bucket is full, additional disk pages called *overflow buckets* or *chains* are employed to store the additional keys.

Thus, to search for a key k, it is first hashed, and the primary bucket in $h(k)$ is searched. If it is not found there, the overflow buckets are searched in sequence till it is either located in one of them or it is not found at all.

If the hash function is quite non-uniform, a large number of keys may hash to the same location and the length of the overflow buckets may be large. This increases the searching time.

2.1.2   Open Addressing

OPEN ADDRESSING (or CLOSED HASHING) does not employ overflow buckets. For a key k, if the primary bucket at $h(k)$ is full, it *probes* for another location by utilizing a *probe sequence*. The probe sequence produces an *offset* or *interval* from the current location. Thus, if the interval at the ith attempt is o_i, the new location for key k is $h(k, i) = (h(k)+o_i.i) \bmod m$, assuming a total of m locations. If even that location is full, the next number from the probe sequence is utilized to get to a newer location, and so on.

There are three main ways of producing the intervals:

1. LINEAR PROBING: The intervals remain fixed, i.e., $o_i = c$ where c is a constant (generally, 1). The new locations, thus, change *linearly* from the original one: $h(k, i) = (h(k) + c.i) \bmod m$.

2. QUADRATIC PROBING: The intervals change linearly, i.e., $o_i = c.i$ so that the effect is *quadratic*. Thus, $h(k, i) = (h(k)+c.i^2) \bmod m$. Again, the constant c is generally maintained as 1.

3. DOUBLE HASHING: The intervals change according to another hash function h', i.e., $h(k, i) = (h(k) + h'(k).i) \bmod m$.

Linear probing tends to cluster the keys more, since if more keys hash to the same location, they are spread contiguously. Since double hashing spreads the keys according to the key value which is not fixed, it displays the least clustering and overflowing effects.

2.1.3   Problems of Static Hashing

The most vital problem for static hashing is the estimate of the number of locations which depends on the estimate of the number of keys. If the number of keys are quite less than the estimate, a large amount of space is wasted. More importantly, if the estimate is low, at some point, the hash table becomes full. Consequently, a new hash function needs to be generated, a correspondingly larger hash table needs to be allocated, and *all* the entries need to be re-hashed. This is a large overhead. Also, while this re-organization operation is going on, all database accesses through the hash table need to be suspended.

2.2   Dynamic Hashing

The DYNAMIC HASHING techniques address the issues of static hashing by modifying the hash function *dynamically* as the number of hashed keys increases or decreases. However, the modifications are not random and follow certain patterns so that finding the key remains a deterministic problem. In the next couple of sections, three different techniques differing in how these modifications are performed, are described.

2.2.1   Dynamic Hashing

The earliest method on dynamic hashing [Larson, 1978] organized the overflow buckets as binary search trees (the method did not have a specific name). The first hash function $h_0(k)$ produces an integer between 0 and $m - 1$ which acts as the index of the *primary page*. So, it can be as simple as the $k \bmod m$ function. For each primary page, there is a binary search tree for handling the overflow.

The binary search trees are constructed using a series of subsequent hash functions $g(k) = \{h_1(k), \ldots, h_i(k), \ldots\}$ where each $h_i(k)$ produces a single bit. At level i of the tree, if $h_i(k) = 0$, the left branch is traversed;

otherwise, the right branch is accessed. In this way, any key can be stored and retrieved. A simple and effective example of $g(k)$ is the bit representation of the key.

Key Concept 2.1 [Dynamic Hashing]. The overflow buckets are organized as a binary search tree. The successive bits of the key guide the path.

While this technique successfully handles the insertion of many keys, it does not perform elegantly when the space of keys are reduced, i.e., when many keys are deleted. Essentially, deleting a key requires adjusting the binary search tree, which may suffer from performance degradation.

More importantly, the method is not at all suited for database applications, since the binary search tree is not organized in a disk-page manner. Traversing multiple nodes may require multiple disk accesses.

2.2.2   Extendible Hashing

The EXTENDIBLE HASHING [Fagin et al., 1979] technique handles the change in the number of keys, both increments and decrements, by maintaining two *depth* parameters. The first-level structure consists of a *directory* of pointers to buckets (or leaf pages) and is characterized by a *global depth* parameter. If the global depth is d, then there are 2^d pointers to buckets. The bucket pointed to by pointer i contains all keys *starting* with the bit string i, i.e., whose d most significant bits represent i.

Each of the buckets has a *local depth* l where $l \leq d$. Similar to the directory cells, the bucket j is responsible for all keys starting with the bit string j.

While the number of pointers is 2^d, the number of buckets can be much less than that. A single leaf bucket or a leaf page can be pointed to by many pointers. This is designed specifically to re-use the space when the local depth is less than the global depth.

A bucket j with local depth $l < d$ is pointed to by all directory cells i that share the same prefix $j \in [0, 2^l - 1]$ where $i \in [0, 2^d - 1]$. The rest of the bit string of i, i.e., the last $d - l$ bits, does not matter.

Key Concept 2.2 [Extendible Hashing]. A global directory of bit values up to a certain length is maintained as primary hash buckets. One or more directory pages point to local pages. When a local page overflows, the number of directory pages is doubled and one more bit is used to hash a key.

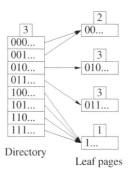

Figure 2.1: Example of an extendible hashing structure.

Figure 2.1 shows an example. The global depth is 3 and, thus, all keys are hashed by the 3 most significant bits. The first leaf page has a depth of 2 and contains all keys pointed to by 000... and 001.... Hence, essentially, its signature becomes 00.... Similarly, the effective hash function for the other leaf pages are shown.

2.2.2.1 Searching and Insertion

To search for a new key in an extendible hashing structure with global depth d, the pointer in the directory corresponding to its most significant d bits is traversed. In the leaf page thus arrived, the key is then searched.

The procedure for insertion is similar. However, when a leaf page overflows, due to its dynamic nature, the structure re-organizes itself in the following manner.

First, assume that the leaf page that is overflowing has a local depth $l < d$. It splits into two new leaf pages, both having local depth $l+1$. The contents in the leaf are then distributed according to the $(l + 1)^{\text{th}}$ most significant bit to the new leaves. The pointers from the global directory are also updated accordingly. Note that since $l < d$, there must have been at least 2 directory pointers that pointed to the old leaf page.

Figure 2.2a shows an example when the bottom-most leaf in Figure 2.1 overflows. The local depths are increased to 2 for the two new pages. The contents are re-hashed according to the new hash functions that now use the 2nd bit as well. The pointers from the directory are adjusted accordingly.

Except for the extremely pathological case when all the keys have the same starting $(l + 1)$ bits, this technique handles the overflow quite elegantly. For the case when it does not, the local depth is again

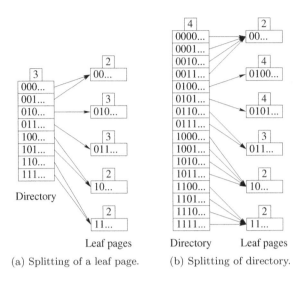

(a) Splitting of a leaf page.   (b) Splitting of directory.

Figure 2.2: Insertion in an extendible hashing structure.

incremented and the process goes on till the local depth becomes equal to the global depth.

When a leaf page that needs to be split due to an overflow has the same local depth as the global depth of the structure, i.e., $l = d$, the global depth is incremented by one. As a result, the entire global directory size is *doubled*. The overflowing leaf page is then split similarly as earlier, and all the directory pointers are updated.

Figure 2.2b depicts such a situation for Figure 2.2a. The leaf page corresponding to $010\ldots$ splits. Two new leaf pages $0100\ldots$ and $0101\ldots$ with local depth 4 are allocated. As a result, the global depth also becomes 4 and the directory doubles. The new pointers are updated to point to the correct leaf pages.

2.2.3   Linear Hashing

While the extendible hashing technique can handle overflow of keys quite nicely, the periodical doubling of the entire directory size can be very inefficient. To handle this, the LINEAR HASHING technique was proposed [Litwin, 1980, Larson, 1988].

Similar to extendible hashing, the linear hashing structure also has *primary buckets* and *overflow buckets*. When there are n primary buckets, a family g of hash functions $\{h_0, \ldots, h_i, \ldots\}$ is used where $h_i(k) = h(k) \bmod (2^i n)$. The hash function h_0 is used to index into the primary buckets. The nature of the hash functions is similar to that of extendible hashing in that h_{i+1} doubles the range of h_i.

However, the key difference lies in the way the primary buckets are split. For any insertion, *at most one* primary bucket is added. This linear growth has lent the name *linear* hashing to the structure.

A global level i is maintained for the structure. When a primary bucket addressed by h_0 becomes full, another new bucket is chained to it. Since this amounts to an overflow, a split needs to be done. A specialized *split pointer* is maintained that addresses the bucket that will be split. The contents of the bucket that are split are re-hashed using h_{i+1}. Interestingly, this is *independent* of the bucket that has overflown. The split pointer is incremented after this operation and it goes around in a round-robin fashion. The global level i incremented only when the split pointer returns to the first primary bucket.

Key Concept 2.3 [Linear Hashing]. For every overflow, only one primary bucket is split. The bucket that is split is not necessarily the one that overflows. It is controlled by the split pointer which cycles among all the primary buckets.

Suppose there are n primary buckets. The split pointer s and the level l of a linear hashing structure are initially at 0. Every time a split occurs, s is incremented till it advances to $2^l.n$. It then gets reset to 0, and the level of the structure gets incremented to $l + 1$.

Thus, in a linear hashing scheme, full buckets are not necessarily split, and buckets that are split are not necessarily full. While this seems counter intuitive, the success of the method lies in the principle that every (primary) bucket will be split sooner or later and, so, all overflows will be eventually reclaimed and re-hashed.

2.2.3.1 Searching

For searching a key k, first the primary bucket $b = h_l(k)$ is compared with the split pointer s. If $b \geq s$, then it means that the bucket b has not yet been split, and therefore, k must be found here if it is at all present. Otherwise, i.e., when $b < s$, it indicates that the split pointer has advanced beyond b, and hence, the bucket b must have been split. Therefore, the key k is either in this bucket b or in $b + 2^l.n$. Hence, k is hashed according to h_{l+1} and *not* h_l, and the bucket $h_{l+1}(k)$ is searched.

2.2.3.2 Insertion

The insertion procedure is similar. The appropriate bucket b' is first identified using either $h_l(k)$ (if $b \geq s$) or $h_{l+1}(k)$ (if $b < s$). If b' does *not* overflow, the insertion procedure ends.

However, if it overflows, a new bucket is created and is chained to it to accommodate the overflowing key k. Also, the bucket pointed to by s is split, and it contents are re-hashed according to h_{l+1} into old, i.e., s and new, i.e., $(s + 2^l.n)$ buckets. The split pointer s is incremented as well. If s reaches $2^l.n$, the level of the entire structure is incremented to $l + 1$ and s is reset to 0.

Example 2.1 [Linear Hashing]. Insert the following keys in order in an empty hash table using linear hashing:

$$3, 12, 1, 7, 8, 4, 11, 2, 10, 13$$

Assume $n = 3$ primary buckets.

Figure 2.3 outlines the steps.

Figure 2.3a shows the initial state with $l = 0$ and $s = 0$.

Assuming a capacity of 2 keys per bucket, the first couple of insertions (using the hash function $h_0 = k \bmod 3$) do not result in any overflow (Figure 2.3b). However, when 4 is inserted next, bucket 1 overflows. A new bucket is chained to it, and 4 is stored there (Figure 2.3c). The bucket $s = 0$ is split creating a new bucket $s + 2^0.3 = 3$ out of it, and its contents (keys 3 and 12) are re-hashed according to the function $h_1 = k \bmod 2^1.3$ (Figure 2.3d). Also, s is incremented to 1. The level remains at $l = 0$.

The next couple of insertions (keys 11 and 2) are made in bucket 2 according to h_0 since $2 \geq s$ (Figure 2.3e). The last insertion leads to splitting of bucket 1 (Figure 2.3f) resulting in bucket 4 and $s = 2$.

The next keys 10 and 13 are inserted according to $h_1 = k \bmod 6$ as their primary hash values according to $h_0 = k \bmod 3 = 1 < s$ (Figure 2.3g). When 13 is inserted, bucket 2 is split, s is reset to 0, and the level of the structure is incremented to $l = 1$ (Figure 2.3h).   □

2.3 Locality Sensitive Hashing (LSH)

The biggest problem with hashing is the fact that while it allows for fast point queries, it does not support similarity searches such as range query or kNN query. LOCALITY SENSITIVE HASHING (LSH) [Indyk and

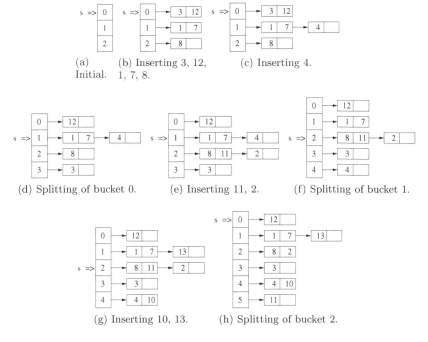

(a) Initial. (b) Inserting 3, 12, 1, 7, 8. (c) Inserting 4.

(d) Splitting of bucket 0. (e) Inserting 11, 2. (f) Splitting of bucket 1.

(g) Inserting 10, 13. (h) Splitting of bucket 2.

Figure 2.3: Example of linear hashing.

Motwani, 1998] handles this by using the idea of *randomized algorithms* [Motwani and Raghavan, 1995]. It is a *Monte Carlo* algorithm since it produces results in bounded time that are only probabilistically correct, with bounded errors. Further, allowing the algorithm more time results in improved accuracy.

The main philosophy of LSH techniques is the following: if two objects are closer in space, then they hash to the same bucket with high probability; and, if two objects are far apart, then they are very unlikely to hash to the same bucket. The goal, thus, is to design a hash function that is *approximately distance-preserving* within some tolerance. It is then easy to see how such a function can be useful for similarity search queries.

Key Concept 2.4 [Locality Sensitive Hashing (LSH)]. If two objects are closer in space, then they hash to the same bucket with high probability. If two objects are far apart, then they are very unlikely to hash to the same bucket.

Formally, a locality sensitive hash function family $H = \{h\}$ is said to be (r_1, r_2, p_1, p_2)-*sensitive* for distance thresholds r_1 and r_2 and probability thresholds p_1 and p_2 ($p_1, p_2 \in [0, 1]$) if for any object pair x, y,

- If $d(x, y) \le r_1$, then $P[h(x) = h(y)] \ge p_1$
- If $d(x, y) \ge r_2$, then $P[h(x) = h(y)] \le p_2$

In other words, objects that are closer than r_1 distance hash to the same bucket with at least a probability of p_1, and objects that are farther apart by more than r_2 distance hash to the same bucket with at most a probability of p_2. Obviously, the conditions make sense when $r_1 < r_2$ and $p_1 > p_2$. Since the hashed values lie in a space where indexing or distance computation is easier, and has generally a lesser number of dimensions, LSH can also be viewed as a *dimensionality reduction* technique.

LSH operates with two important parameters:

1. *Number of hash tables* used, l.

2. *Number of hash functions* that are concatenated to get a particular hash value (also called the *width parameter*), k.

The k hash functions $h_1, \ldots, h_k$ are chosen randomly from the LSH family H. Therefore, a hash instance of a particular object O is

$$g_j(O) = (h_1(O) \odot \cdots \odot h_k(O)) \qquad (2.1)$$

where $\odot$ denotes concatenation. The complete hash representation of the object O is

$$LSH(O) = \langle g_1(O), \ldots, g_l(O) \rangle \qquad (2.2)$$

2.3.1 Hamming Space

The following example shows how LSH works when data is mapped to a Hamming space from which bits are sampled to construct the hash. In a Hamming space, the distance between objects is measured by Hamming distance (see Section 5.8.1 for the definition).

Example 2.2 [LSH in Hamming Space]. Consider the following data points:

$$(25, 32), (42, 1), (46, 67), (62, 55), (7, 34), (27, 25), (65, 15), (71, 5)$$

Solve the 1-NN query for $Q = (5, 45)$ using LSH in Hamming space.

The data points are first mapped to a Hamming space by quantization (division by 10) and subsequent concatenation of the *unary* bit

Table 2.1: Mapping to Hamming space using quantization.

O_i	x, y	Quantized x', y'	Hamming Space
O_1	25, 32	2, 3	1100000 1110000
O_2	42, 1	4, 0	1111000 0000000
O_3	46, 67	4, 6	1111000 1111110
O_4	62, 55	6, 5	1111110 1111100
O_5	7, 34	0, 3	0000000 1110000
O_6	27, 25	2, 2	1100000 1100000
O_7	65, 15	6, 1	1111110 1000000
O_8	71, 5	7, 0	1111111 0000000
Q	5, 45	0, 4	0000000 1111000

strings (maximum 7 bits) of the two quantized dimensions. This produces Table 2.1.

Next, LSH is applied with $l = 4$ and $k = 3$ where each h_i extracts a *single* bit. Thus, for each object, 4 hash values are formed, where each hash value is an extraction of 3 random bits from the total of 14 bits. The same hashing is also applied on the query Q whose quantized values are $(0, 4)$. The hashed values are captured in Table 2.2.

A 1-NN query for Q, thus, produces the following collision sets:

- $l = 1$ (bits 2,9,13): O_5

- $l = 2$ (bits 7,10,14): O_1, O_3, O_4, O_5

- $l = 3$ (bits 1,5,11): Φ

- $l = 4$ (bits 8,12,14): O_1, O_5, O_6, O_7

A *majority counting* of the collision sets produces O_5 which can be verified to be the *true answer*. □

The above example highlights the fact that while using only one hash table may produce erroneous results, using the majority tends to produce the correct result. There are provable bounds on the error factor and the running time of the LSH algorithms [Indyk and Motwani, 1998].

The time required to hash the query is $O(k.l)$ since it is hashed to l tables, and for each table, k hash functions are used.

With an increase in the number of hash tables l, the probability of obtaining the correct answer increases, although it increases the running time as well. The width of LSH, i.e., k, controls the accuracy of each hash instance. With more k, the difference in the probabilities with which a

Table 2.2: LSH in Hamming space.

O_i	Hamming space	Bits			
		$2, 9, 13$	$7, 10, 14$	$1, 5, 11$	$8, 12, 14$
		$l = 1$	$l = 2$	$l = 3$	$l = 4$
O_1	1100000 1110000	110	010	100	100
O_2	1111000 0000000	100	000	100	000
O_3	1111000 1111110	111	010	101	110
O_4	1111110 1111100	110	010	111	110
O_5	0000000 1110000	010	010	000	100
O_6	1100000 1100000	110	000	100	100
O_7	1111110 1000000	100	000	110	100
O_8	1111111 0000000	100	100	110	000
Q	0000000 1111000	010	010	001	100

pair of close and a pair of far points collide, i.e., $p_2 - p_1$, increases. In other words, the locality preserving property becomes more effective.

2.3.2 E2LSH

The original LSH algorithm was intended for Hamming space. However, most applications are in a vector space equipped with the Euclidean (L_2) norm. It is possible to extend the LSH algorithm by embedding the objects from L_2 space to L_1 space and in turn to a Hamming space. However, as shown in [Datar et al., 2004], it is easier to work directly in the L_2 space. The special name given to such a scheme is E2LSH.

E2LSH algorithms use the idea of p-stable distributions [Datar et al., 2004]. Essentially, it chooses a random vector a of the same dimensionality d that the objects have. The elements of a are sampled independently from a p-stable distribution. For a real number b in the range $[0, r]$, the hash value of an object v is given by $h_{a,b}(v) = \lfloor (a.v + b)/r \rfloor$. Thus, for each choice of a, b, the hash function $h_{a,b}$ maps the object onto a set of integers.

For two vectors v_1, v_2, the p-stability property of a guarantees that the distance between their projections, i.e., $a.v_1 - a.v_2$, is distributed as the p-norm distance between the original vectors, i.e., $L_p(v_1, v_2)$ [Datar et al., 2004]. This intuitively shows how the locality sensitivity property is preserved. For Euclidean (i.e., L_2) space, the standard normal distribution $N(0, 1)$ is generally used since it is 2-stable.

2.4   Multi-Dimensional Hashing

While hashing has always been intended to index single-dimensional keys to a range of buckets, it is sometimes necessary to hash keys with multiple dimensions. One standard approach is by concatenation (or some similar aggregation operation) of dimensions to form a single key. The next structure treats the dimensions separately, or in other words, the data point is treated as having a multi-dimensional key.

2.4.1   Grid File

The GRID FILE structure successfully implements a multi-dimensional hashing scheme with the aim of retrieving any object with at most two disk accesses [Nievergelt et al., 1984]. It consists of two main components: the *grid directory* and the buckets (or disk pages) to store the data.

The entire data space of d-dimensional objects is broken into grid cells. The grid directory itself is broken into two parts:

1. A d-dimensional array, called the *grid array*, that contains the pointers from every grid cell, and

2. d number of one-dimensional *linear scales*, that stores the grid partitions for each dimension.

Key Concept 2.5 [Grid File]. The entire multi-dimensional space is divided into grid cells. The keys are stored in disk pages. Each disk page is pointed to by one or more grid cells.

Figure 2.4 shows a grid file structure for a 3-dimensional space. The linear scales are shown below the grid array. The linear scale corresponding to dimension X shows that the entire range from $[x_0, x_3]$ is divided into three partitions using the values x_1 and x_2. Similarly, the other two dimensions are partitioned. The partitions are labeled using integers, which serve as the index of the partition.

Similar to the extendible hashing scheme, each data bucket corresponds to exactly one disk page, although multiple grid cell pointers may point to the same bucket. For example, while bucket 7 contains data only from the cell $(1, 0, 0)$, bucket 3 contains data corresponding to two grid cells, $(2, 0, 1)$ and $(2, 1, 1)$.

The size of the grid array grows exponentially with the number of

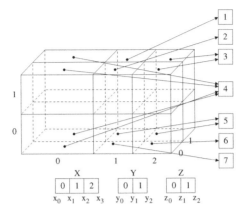

Figure 2.4: Grid file.

dimensions d. If there are m partitions in each dimension, the number of cells is m^d. Thus, it may be too large to fit in the main memory, especially for high values of d. However, the linear scales take up much less space (only $m.d$) and are, therefore, always stored in the memory.

2.4.1.1   Searching

When a key k is searched, first the grid cell in which it lies is found. For each dimension of the key, the linear scales are searched to find the corresponding index of the cell along that dimension. The combination of all these indices provides the location of the grid cell in the grid array. Following the pointer from the grid cell, the key is then searched in the bucket.

This requires one disk access for the bucket and at most one more disk access for accessing the cell of the grid array, if it does not fit in the memory.

2.4.1.2   Insertion

The size of the grid is controlled by the dynamic growth of the number of keys. If a particular bucket becomes full, it needs to be split. The split dimension is chosen in a round-robin fashion. If the split needs to happen along dimension i, the range of the bucket is split mid-way through that dimension.

For example, if bucket 5 which corresponds to the ranges (x_1, x_3), (y_1, y_2) and (z_0, z_1) needs to be split along the x-dimension, the split point will be $(x_1 + x_3)/2$. A new bucket 8 will be formed and the contents of 5 will be re-hashed between the old and the new buckets.

2.5   Space-Filling Curves

SPACE-FILLING CURVES are transformations from higher dimensional locations to 1-dimensional points, and is, thus, in a sense, a hashing technique. Essentially, it is a ONE-DIMENSIONAL ORDERING of the grid points of a d-dimensional matrix. Since accessing a hard disk is logically uni-dimensional (see Appendix A), ordering multi-dimensional points that are closer to each other is useful as it increases the *data locality*.

Key Concept 2.6 [Space-Filling Curve]. A space-filling curve is a mapping of multi-dimensional points into a single-dimensional ordering. The multi-dimensional space is divided into grid cells and a curve passes through the grid cells in a systematic manner generating the order.

2.5.1   Desirable Properties

A space-filling curve should have the following desirable properties:

1. The curve should pass through each high-dimensional location *once and only once*.

2. Both the transformation and its inverse should be *simple* operations.

3. The curve should be *stable*, i.e., the relative ordering between points should not change when the resolution (i.e., the number of divisions across each dimension) of the grid changes.

4. The *degree of locality* should be high, i.e., locations that are neighbors in the high dimension should be close to each other in the one-dimensional ordering.

5. The curve should be *admissible*, i.e., for each dimension, if a particular direction is encountered earlier for a point, it should be encountered earlier for all points; e.g., for a two-dimensional curve, it may be the case that points that are towards the left and top are always encountered earlier.

2.5.2   Examples

Most conversions are from two-dimensional regular grids of size $2^g \times 2^g$ (i.e., a factor of two). This results in a curve of order g. While it works

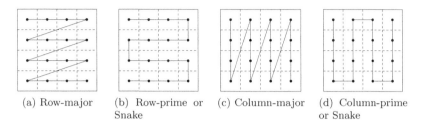

(a) Row-major   (b) Row-prime or   (c) Column-major   (d) Column-prime
                       Snake   or Snake

Figure 2.5: The row and column order space-filling curves.

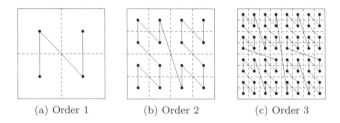

(a) Order 1   (b) Order 2   (c) Order 3

Figure 2.6: The Z-order (or Morton-order or Bit interleaving or N-order) space-filling curve.

for any grid, the other conversions are harder to specify and sometimes ambiguous as well. Figures 2.5 through 2.8 show examples of the major space-filling curves.

For space-filling curves that are not row- or column-orders, a curve of order g is generated by replacing each vertex of the basic curve (i.e., of order 1) by the curve of order $g - 1$ after appropriate rotation and/or reflection. When the order tends to infinity, the curve is called a *fractal*.

2.5.3   Properties

Table 2.3 shows the properties of the space-filling curves.

Although the Hilbert curve is not simple and does not enjoy the admissible property, due to its stability, very high degree of locality, and the fact that the distance between successive locations is the ideal (1.0), it is considered to be the most appropriate space-filling curve for indexing purposes [Faloutsos and Roseman, 1989], and has consequently found usage in R-trees (the Hilbert R-tree [Kamel and Faloutsos, 1994] in Section 4.7).

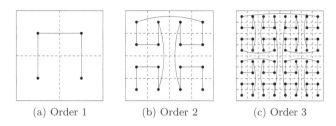

(a) Order 1   (b) Order 2   (c) Order 3

Figure 2.7: The Gray code space-filling curve.

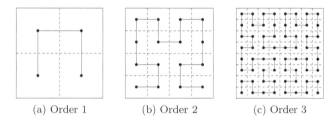

(a) Order 1   (b) Order 2   (c) Order 3

Figure 2.8: The Hilbert-order (or Peano-Hilbert-order) space-filling curve.

Table 2.3: Properties of space-filling curves.

Property	Space-filling curve				
	Row or Column	Row-prime or Column-prime	Z	Gray	Hilbert
Once and only once	Yes	Yes	Yes	Yes	Yes
Simple	Yes	Yes	Yes	Yes	No
Stable	No	No	Yes	Yes	Yes
Degree of locality	Low	High	Low	Low	High
Admissible	Yes	No	Yes	No	No
Distance between successive locations	2.00	1.00	1.67	1.50	1.00

Chapter 3

Memory-Based Index Structures

Most databases are designed to hold data at the secondary storage medium, i.e., the disk. Consequently, the majority of the index structures are disk-based in the sense that they fetch data from the disk directly. However, with the increase in sizes of main memory storage in recent years, the concept of "in-memory" databases has become very important. In such databases, it is assumed that the entire data fits in the main memory. As a result, the index structure should be memory-based as well.

This chapter describes the most important memory-based index structures. Although most of these structures can be extended in theory to any dimensionality, they work best in one or two dimensions, and are rarely used for any higher dimension.

We first describe the binary search trees that work for single-dimensional keys. The three hierarchical structures—quadtree, K-d-tree, and range tree—generalize the binary search tree in multiple dimensions. The next structure, Voronoi diagram, is quite useful in nearest neighbor searches and in computational geometry applications. The trie structure and its variants (most notably, the suffix tree) find multiple usage in string applications. The last index, the bitmap index, leverages the efficiency of bit-wise operations by organizing the objects into bit vectors.

However, before we describe any index structure, we first discuss briefly what exactly is meant by the term and what are its properties.

3.1 Index Structures

INDEX STRUCTURES are data structures (with their associated algorithms) that organize database objects for efficient searching and retrieval. Thus, according to this definition, hash tables (along with the hash functions) are also index structures. An index structure has certain desirable properties, and based on them, there are several possible classifications.

3.1.1 Properties of Index Structures

An index structure helps in identifying the relevant objects from a database. There are four desirable properties of an index structure:

1. *Efficient access*: The index structure should enable efficient searching and querying. In particular, it must be faster than a linear scan of the entire database; otherwise, there is little point in using it.

2. *Small update overhead*: If the index structure is used for dynamic databases, it should support easy insertion and updating of objects. If the update overhead is too high (e.g., if the index needs to be entirely re-built), then it is suitable only for static datasets where the data objects do not change.

3. *Small size*: The index structure itself should be small in size, i.e., the space overhead of indexing should be low. Preferably, it should fit in the memory itself, so that the pointers to the actual database objects from the structure can be accessed quickly.

4. *Correctness*: The last but probably the most important property of an index structure is the correctness, i.e., the objects retrieved using the structure should correctly answer the query. In other words, if no indexing scheme was used, and the database was scanned linearly to retrieve the answers, there should not be any difference in the set of objects retrieved when using the index structure.

3.1.2 Classification of Index Structures

Depending on the property of an index structure, there are different ways of classifying it. Based on where the index structure is stored, they can be classified into two broad groups:

1. Memory-based index structures

2. Disk-based index structures

MEMORY-BASED INDEX STRUCTURES assume that the entire dataset fits into the main memory and, therefore, no I/O cost needs to be paid. The cost of querying is composed mostly of the CPU cost needed for processing data objects already in memory. DISK-BASED INDEX STRUCTURES, on the other hand, are used when the data does not fit into the memory, and disk accesses are required. The aim of such structures is to reduce the number of random I/Os as much as possible. They generally ignore the cost of computation once an object is brought into memory. (See the discussion in Appendix A for why this happens.)

The fanout (i.e., the number of children) in hierarchical disk-based structures, e.g., R-tree (Section 4.4) [Guttman, 1984] and K-d-B tree (Section 4.2) [Robinson, 1981] depend mostly on the *disk page size* (or *block size*) of the system. Generally, the page is packed such that when it is accessed as many data objects as possible are brought into memory. In contrast, the fanout in memory-based hierarchical structures, e.g., K-d-tree (Section 3.4) [Bentley, 1975] and quadtree (Section 3.3) [Finkel and Bentley, 1974] do not depend on such parameters. They are determined by the type of indexing scheme used and the dimensionality of the data indexed.

Although *one-dimensional indexing method* can be classified into memory-based, e.g., binary search tree (Section 3.2) [Cormen et al., 2009] or disk-based structures, e.g., B+-tree (Section 4.1) [Comer, 1979], they are generally considered to be important enough to be studied as a separate class. Hashing and space-filling curves described earlier are some of the important examples in this class.

The second way of classifying hierarchical tree-based index structures is based on the partitioning scheme:

1. Space-partitioning methods

2. Data-partitioning methods

SPACE-PARTITIONING METHODS divide the entire data space (assuming it to be a vector space) into different partitions, each one of which is handled by a child at the next level. The partitioning scheme ignores the amount of data that each child is assigned. It may happen that all the actual data falls in the partition of only one child and the rest of the children index the *dead space*, i.e., the space where there is no data. K-d-trees (Section 3.4) [Bentley, 1975] and quadtrees (Section 3.3) [Finkel and Bentley, 1974] are typical examples of such structures. The disk-based space-partitioning structures, thus, do not provide any guarantee on the space usage of each node (or disk block).

DATA-PARTITIONING STRUCTURES, on the other hand, concentrate on the data and not the space. Consequently, the amount of data handled by each child is typically balanced. The problem of dead space indexing is greatly reduced and a guarantee is provided on the space usage in each node (or disk block) for disk-based structures. R-tree (Section 4.4) [Guttman, 1984] is the most well-known example of this kind of structure.

The third classification of index structures is into two groups:

1. Point access methods (PAM)

2. Spatial access methods (SAM)

PAM structures can index only points (e.g., quadtree [Finkel and Bentley, 1974]) while *SAM* structures can index spatial objects in addition to points (e.g., R-tree [Guttman, 1984]). Even though, in theory, arbitrary object shapes can be indexed, in reality, most of the SAM structures enclose the objects in a *minimum bounding rectangle* (MBR) and index the MBRs only. The refinement using the actual object geometry is done later.

The book by [Samet, 2006] contains an exhaustive overview of all the index structures.

3.2   Binary Search Tree (BST)

The simplest binary tree that can be used for efficient searching is a BINARY SEARCH TREE (BST) [Cormen et al., 2009]. A BST is a rooted tree with at most two children. Each child is a BST itself. It can be empty or may contain a single node as well.

For any node, a BST maintains the invariant that all the values in the left child are less than or equal to the value maintained at the node, while all the values in the right child are greater than the value at the node. In other words, if a node has value v, then every value l in the left subtree (i.e., the tree rooted at the left child) and every value r in the right subtree follow the properties:

1. $l \leq v$

2. $r > v$

Key Concept 3.1 [Binary Search Tree (BST)]. All keys in the left subtree of a node are less than or equal to the key at the node while all keys in the right subtree are greater.

In the context of databases, each node, in addition to the key, maintains a *data pointer* that points to the data object associated with the

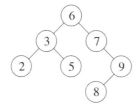

Figure 3.1: A binary search tree (BST).

key. While the key is used for indexing and ordering, the values of the other attributes of an object are referenced using data pointers.

Figure 3.1 shows an example of a binary search tree. Since the root is 6, all keys less than that are in the left subtree while the rest of them are in the right subtree.

3.2.1 Searching

Searching a key starts from the root. Suppose, key q is searched. If q is equal to the value at the root, the search terminates successfully right there. If it is less, then only the left child of the root needs to be searched; otherwise, only the right child is searched. The advantage is that at any time, the properties of a BST guarantee that only one side of the tree can contain the key. The other half gets pruned. The searching proceeds recursively till the key is found or till it reaches a leaf, in which case, the search is returned as unsuccessful.

Suppose the key 5 is searched in the example tree of Figure 3.1. First, it is compared with the value at the root, 6. Since the search key is smaller, the search proceeds only with the left child. It is compared to the root of this subtree, i.e., 3. Now, since the key is greater, only the right child is searched. As the value matches 5, it is returned as the answer.

Searching for a particular value in a BST with n values requires $O(\log_2 n)$ time on average. However, since a BST can be unbalanced, searching may require $O(n)$ time in the worst case (when the tree degenerates to a chain of nodes).

3.2.2 Insertion

Inserting a key essentially follows the same strategy as in searching. The procedure starts by comparing the key value with that in the root. Suppose, the value at the root is greater. The key, hence, should be

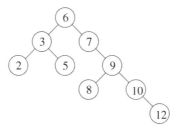

Figure 3.2: The BST of Figure 3.1 after insertion of 10 and 12.

inserted in the left child. If the left child is absent, a new node is allocated as the left child and the value is inserted. Otherwise, the process is recursively conducted in the appropriate subtree. Finally, a new leaf is created to accommodate the new key.

Figure 3.2 shows the BST after the keys 10 and 12 are inserted.

3.2.3   Discussion

While the search strategy for a BST is simple, and the average running time of a search is low, the worst-case running time is linear which can be impractical. The problem stems from the fact that a BST can be highly unbalanced (as in Figure 3.2).

The *balance factor* (or *height balance*) of a node is defined as the difference in heights of its right and left subtrees. The balance factor of a tree is that of its root. Roughly, a tree (or a subtree) is said to be balanced if the balance factor is between -1 and $+1$. The next section describes balanced binary search trees.

3.2.4   Balanced Binary Search Tree

Consider the BST shown in Figure 3.2. There are substantially more nodes in the right subtree than the left subtree. The search performance in such unbalanced trees can degrade significantly. In the worst case, consider a binary search tree where the keys are inserted in a sorted order. The tree then degenerates to a single path. Consequently, the searching time becomes $O(n)$. Efforts, therefore, have been made to restrict the imbalance in a BST by constraining the heights of the left and right subtrees from any node to be within ± 1 of each other. This guarantees the running time of a search to be within $O(\log_2 n)$, albeit with an increase in the complexity of the structure.

Two of the most important balanced binary search structures are

AVL TREES [Adelson-Velskii and Landis, 1962] and RED-BLACK TREES [Bayer, 1972]. They are not *perfectly balanced* in the sense that the leaves are not all at the same level. However, the height remains within the $O(\log_2 n)$ bound.

Searching in a balanced BST follows the same procedure as in a normal BST. Only during insertion and deletion, the tree may become unbalanced, and remedial actions may need to be taken. The AVL tree does this by invoking one or more "rotation" operations that restore the height balance to within ± 1. The red-black tree puts constraints in how the nodes can be structured, and is generally less balanced overall. The textbooks by [Sedgewick and Wayne, 2011] and [Cormen et al., 2009] contain excellent descriptions of these two structures along with the searching and other procedures.

In general, the search operations in AVL trees are faster than the red-black trees due to lesser overall height while the insertion and deletion operations are slower due to a greater number of rotation operations.

3.3 Quadtree

A QUADTREE can be considered as a generalization of the binary search tree in two dimensions [Finkel and Bentley, 1974]. Recall that the value v of the key (henceforth referred to as a point) at a node partitions the entire range of values (i.e., the entire number line) into two halves, lesser than or equal to v and greater than v.

If, however, the point is in two dimensions (say (x, y)), the partition needs to be done into four parts:

1. $(\leq x, \leq y)$
2. $(\leq x, > y)$
3. $(> x, \leq y)$
4. $(> x, > y)$

The structure of a quadtree follows this pattern: each node has four children corresponding to the four quadrants obtained by considering the two-dimensional point in the node as the origin.

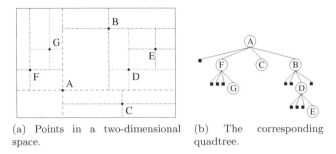

(a) Points in a two-dimensional space.

(b) The corresponding quadtree.

Figure 3.3: An example of a quadtree.

Key Concept 3.2 [Quadtree]. Every two-dimensional key in a node acts as the origin and divides the space into four quadrants. The points in each of these quadrants are, in turn, indexed by a child node.

Figure 3.3b shows a quadtree corresponding to the two-dimensional points in Figure 3.3a. For illustration purposes, non-existent children are shown as small squares.

3.3.1   Insertion

To illustrate how points are inserted in a quadtree, consider the example in Figure 3.3a and assume that the points are inserted in alphabetical order. The first point A is made the root. The next point B is made the child of A (at position 4 since both its coordinates are greater than A). Similarly, C is made another child of A. However, when D arrives, it is in the same quadrant as B. Since B is already a child of A, D is made a child of B. Similarly, the other nodes are inserted. The complete tree is shown in Figure 3.3b.

Though the procedure is simple, the structure of the final quadtree depends heavily on the *order* of insertion of the points. An important effect of this is the fact that, similar to a BST, a quadtree is also unbalanced, as no attempt is made to balance the structure during insertion.

3.3.2   Searching

Searching a point is also simple, and it follows the same principle as insertion. First, the root is searched to determine the quadrant the query point lies. Correspondingly, the appropriate child is next searched and so on.

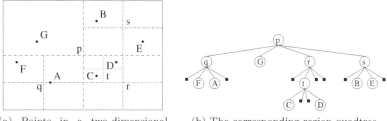

(a) Points in a two-dimensional space.

(b) The corresponding region quadtree.

Figure 3.4: An example of a region quadtree.

Though the average running time for searching is $O(\log n)$ for a dataset of n objects, the worst-case running time, even for balanced quadtrees, can be $O(\sqrt{n})$ [Lee and Wong, 1977].

3.3.3 Variants and Extensions

The most common quadtrees are the ones described above, known as POINT QUADTREES, since the points divide the two-dimensional space into quadrants. In another form of quadtrees, known as REGION QUADTREES [Samet, 2006], the division is always done at the *geographical center* of the space. For points that are uniformly distributed over the space, region quadtrees tend to be more balanced than point quadtrees. Figure 3.4b shows a region quadtree built on the points shown in Figure 3.4a. Note that the points shown in lowercase are not the original points, but they become nodes as they are geographical centers. All the data points are stored as leaves. Also note that when a point is the only one in a quadrant (e.g., G), it is made a node, and no further division is performed.

3.3.4 Discussion

Although quadtrees are designed for two-dimensional spaces, it can be extended to multiple dimensions. In d dimensions, the point at the root divides the entire space into 2^d sub-spaces. The fanout, therefore, quickly becomes impractical. The search time also degenerates rapidly: in d dimensions, the worst-case time for balanced quadtrees is $O(d.n^{(1-1/d)})$ [Lee and Wong, 1977]. When d is large, this can become worse than a simple linear scan of the database due to the overheads.

As a special case in three dimensions, these structures have been named as OCTREES [Samet, 1990]. Octrees are quite useful for three-dimensional video applications such as computer graphics [Puech and Yahia, 1985].

3.4   K-D-Tree

One of the main problems of the quadtree is its impractically high fanout in high-dimensional spaces. The number of children grows to 2^d for d dimensions. The problem stems from the fact that at each node, all the d dimensions are taken into account while splitting the space.

K-D-TREES [Bentley, 1975] attempt to solve this problem by focusing on only one dimension at a time while splitting a node. Unlike a quadtree, it is a binary tree, and the structure is exactly the same as an unbalanced binary search tree. While in a BST, there is only a single dimension on which all the levels of the tree are split, in a K-d-tree, the dimension on which the split is done is cycled. The first split, i.e., the split at the root is based on the first dimension of the points. The immediate children of the root are split based on the second dimension and so on. If there are k dimensions, the split at level i is based on the $(i \bmod k)^{\text{th}}$ dimension.

If a node at level i stores object v, its two children are split based on the value $v[i \bmod k]$. In particular, every node l in the left subtree and every node r in the right subtree follow the invariants:

1. $l[i \bmod k] \leq v[i \bmod k]$

2. $r[i \bmod k] > v[i \bmod k]$

Key Concept 3.3 [K-D-Tree]. In every level, a node is divided into two children based on only one dimension of the key. The dimensions are cycled among the levels.

3.4.1   Insertion

Consider the set of two-dimensional points in Figure 3.5a. When the points are inserted in an alphabetical order, the corresponding K-d-tree that is built is shown in Figure 3.5b.

The first split is based on dimension 0 with A as the root. The splits

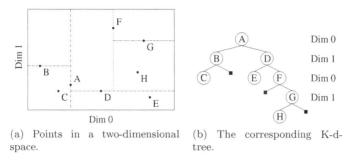

(a) Points in a two-dimensional space.

(b) The corresponding K-d-tree.

Figure 3.5: An example of a K-d-tree.

for the children of A, i.e., B and D are based on dimension 1. The next split is again on dimension 0 and so on.

The insertion procedure suffers from the fact that the structure of the final tree depends heavily on the choice of the dimensions and the order of insertion. For example, if the root was split according to dimension 1, etc., then the resulting tree would have been very different. Note that the tree can be heavily imbalanced, as in the current example.

3.4.2 Searching

Searching a point follows the same principle as in insertion. Within each node, the dimension on which it is split is recorded. Thus, when a query comes, only its first dimension is checked against that of the root A in the example, and so on.

Similar to quadtree, if a K-d-tree is balanced, although the average performance of a search is $O(\log n)$ for n objects, the worst case can be $O(\sqrt{n})$ for 2-dimensional and $O(d.N^{(1-1/d)})$ for d-dimensional spaces [Lee and Wong, 1977].

3.4.3 Variants

The variant described above, where the splits are based on the actual data points, is known as the POINT K-D-TREES. Similar to quadtrees, there is another important version where the splits are done at the middle of the range for a dimension, and not necessarily at a data point. The space is divided into regions, and the data points form the leaves of the tree. This is known as the REGION K-D-TREE [Samet, 2006]. Once more, for points that are uniformly distributed over the space, region K-d-trees tend to be more balanced than point K-d-trees.

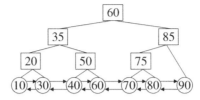

Figure 3.6: A one-dimensional range tree.

3.5   Range Tree

Binary search trees, quadtrees, and K-d-trees perform well when the query is for a point. However, if the query is for a range, i.e., when the objective is to retrieve all points that fall within a range (e.g., find all points between 2 and 4), then the above structures fail. For example, for the above query in a binary search tree, at a node, both branches may need to be traversed. If the query is for all points greater than a value, then the search degenerates to traversing all the branches and nodes of the tree, thereby suffering a performance worse than that of linear scan.

RANGE TREES have been designed to answer such queries efficiently [Bentley, 1979, Leuker, 1978, Willard, 1979]. A one-dimensional range tree is similar to a balanced binary search tree where all the data is stored in the leaves, with two important modifications:

1. The leaves of the tree are maintained in a *sorted* order.

2. The leaves are *linked* to the next and previous ones.

The combined effect is that the data points form a sorted doubly linked list. Figure 3.6 shows an example.

3.5.1   Range Searching

Suppose a search is issued for the range $[p : q]$, i.e., find all points that are $\geq p$ and $\leq q$. The query proceeds by first searching for the leaf that has the largest value just less than or equal to p. It then traverses all the leaves using the forward pointers till a leaf that is just greater than q is reached.

Example 3.1 [Range Tree Searching]. Search the range $[33 : 63]$ in the range tree shown in Figure 3.6.

First, the node having a value just less than or equal to $p = 33$ is searched. The search starts from the root and proceeds in the following manner:

- Since $p < 60$ (value at root), the left branch is searched.

- Since $p < 35$ (value at next level), again the left branch is followed.

- Since $p > 20$, the right branch is searched.

- The value at the leaf is 30.

This leaf forms the node whose value is just less than p. The forward pointers are then followed to find the answer set, till the value exceeds the right range $q = 63$. □

If the range search is of the form $[p : \infty]$, i.e., all values greater than or equal to p are queried, then the search proceeds by returning all leaves that can be traversed using the forward pointers from p. Similarly, the backward pointers from q are used if the search is of the form $[-\infty : q]$, i.e., when all values less than or equal to q are queried.

The correctness of the search procedure is guaranteed by the fact that the leaves are sorted. The time taken for the range search for a tree having n objects is $O(\log_2 n + |A|)$ where A is the answer set.

3.5.2 Multi-Dimensional Range Tree

A multi-dimensional range tree is a balanced binary search tree, but for multiple dimensions [Lee and Wong, 1980]. The objects in this tree, however, are not points, but the balanced binary search trees built from those points themselves but in other dimensions. In other words, a d-dimensional range tree can be viewed as a one-dimensional range tree of $(d - 1)$-dimensional range trees.

Each node in a multi-dimensional range tree is another range tree, but of one less dimensionality. The dimensions are first ordered as $x_0, x_1, \ldots, x_{d-1}$. The main range tree or the "base" tree is built on dimension x_0. For each node T_{x_0} of this base tree, there is a range tree R_{x_1} of dimensionality $(d - 1)$ associated with the node. The range tree R_{x_1} contains all the points contained in the subtree T_{x_0}, but the points are now organized according to dimension x_1.

Key Concept 3.4 [Range Tree]. A one-dimensional range tree is a balanced binary search tree. A multi-dimensional range tree is a balanced binary search tree where each node corresponds to another range tree.

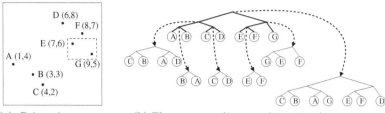

(a) Points in a two-dimensional space.

(b) The corresponding two-dimensional range tree.

Figure 3.7: Two-dimensional range tree.

This range tree is built on the same points that are under the subtree of the node, but uses one less dimension.

Figure 3.7b shows an example of a two-dimensional range tree for the points shown in Figure 3.7a. The base tree (shown in bold) is built on the x dimension. Each node in the tree shows a link to another range tree, which is built on the y dimension. Note that the points under the subtree of a node and the range tree linked from it are the same, although their order may vary due to the difference of sorted values. For example, consider the subtree for E, F, and G. The linked tree built on y dimension becomes G, E, and F as that is the sorted order in that dimension.

3.5.3   Multi-Dimensional Range Searching

To query for points within a multi-dimensional range, the search is first issued on the base tree built on dimension x_0. The leftmost and rightmost leaves L and R that cover the entire range of x_0 are first identified. Then, the least common ancestor Q of L and R is determined. Since it is guaranteed that all results will lie in the subset associated with Q, range search for dimensions x_1 to x_{d-1} is issued on the range tree linked from Q.

Example 3.2 [Multi-Dimensional Range Tree Searching]. Consider the window query $([6.5, 9.5], [4.5, 6.5]$ for the tree in Figure 3.7. The query is shown in dotted lines in Figure 3.7a.

The base tree is searched only for the range in x dimension, i.e., $[6.5, 9.5]$. The points E, F, and G are returned. The least common ancestor of all these points is then found. The subtree under this node contains all points that have the x range satisfied.

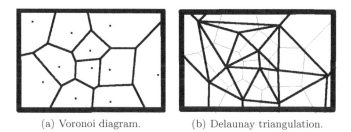

(a) Voronoi diagram. (b) Delaunay triangulation.

Figure 3.8: Voronoi diagram and its corresponding Delaunay triangulation.

Next, to satisfy the y range, the range tree linked from this node which is built on the y dimension is searched. This corresponds to the tree of G, E, and F from which G and E are returned. □

The searching time, thus, involves searching through multiple range trees for all the d dimensions. The total time spent for n points, thus, is $O(\log^d n + |A|)$ where A is the answer set. The total space requirement is $O(n \log^{d-1} n)$.

3.6 Voronoi Diagram

All the structures discussed so far are hierarchical in nature since they divide the space recursively. Moreover, the divisions are along the axes.

One of the most elegant structures for organizing space containing n points is the VORONOI DIAGRAM [Aurenhammer, 1991, de Berg et al., 2008]. The entire space is divided into *convex polygons* where each polygon corresponds to a single point (called *site*). The polygons maintain the following two properties:

1. Each polygon contains one and only one site.

2. Every point in a polygon is closest to the site that corresponds to this polygon than any other site. (The closest point is defined as the one having the least Euclidean distance.)

Key Concept 3.5 [Voronoi Diagram]. Corresponding to n sites (i.e., points), the space is divided into n polygons such that all points in the polygon are closer to the site in the polygon than to any other site.

Figure 3.8a shows an example of a Voronoi diagram. Voronoi diagrams are also called *Voronoi tessellation* or *Thiessen tessellation*. The polygons are known in different names: *Voronoi regions*, *Voronoi cells*, *Thiessen polygons*, etc. In metric spaces where only distances are available but not the coordinates of the points, the structure is called DIRICHLET TESSELLATION and the corresponding regions are called *Dirichlet domains*.

Voronoi diagrams can immediately return the result for a 1-NN query for any point in the space. The site corresponding to the polygon where the query point belongs to is the answer.

The dual of a Voronoi diagram is called the DELAUNAY TRIANGULATION [de Berg et al., 2008]. The Delaunay triangles are constructed by joining the sites in a manner such that the circumcircles of every triangle is empty, i.e., it does not contain any other site. The resulting structure resembles a graph with the sites forming the vertices (called *Voronoi vertices*) and the sides of the triangles forming the edges (called *Voronoi edges*). The graph is called the DELAUNAY GRAPH. Figure 3.8b shows the Delaunay triangulation corresponding to the Voronoi diagram in Figure 3.8a.

3.6.1   Construction

A straightforward construction of a Voronoi diagram involves finding the bisectors of every pair of sites and then joining them to construct the polygons. This simple algorithm requires a time of $O(n^2)$ for n sites.

However, there exists a better algorithm that runs in $O(n \log_2 n)$ time, known as the *Fortune's algorithm* [Fortune, 1986, de Berg et al., 2008]. It is optimal in the sense that it is not possible to design any other algorithm that has a better running time.

Fortune's algorithm falls in the paradigm of *plane sweep* algorithms. A horizontal line, called the *sweep line*, is swept from top to bottom over the space. The information about the Voronoi diagram needs to be maintained at every sweep position. This information changes only at certain special points, called *event points*.

At a particular position of the sweep line, every site that is above it computes the *beach line*. The beach line indicates the locus of points that are closer to some site above the sweep line than the sweep line itself.

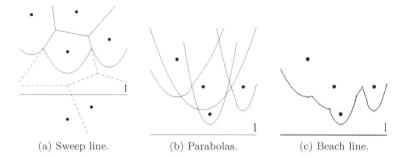

(a) Sweep line.   (b) Parabolas.   (c) Beach line.

Figure 3.9: Fortune's algorithm.

Since any site below the sweep line cannot be closer to this point than the sweep line itself, hence, for points above this line, the computation of the Voronoi diagram is complete as it has already found its nearest site.

The beach line consists of a set of parabolic arcs. Each arc of a parabola denotes the points that are equidistant from the sweep line and the site corresponding to that parabola. Figure 3.9 shows the sweep line and the beach line formed by the different parabolas at a particular sweep position.

The beach line is important as the Voronoi diagram constructed above it does not change when the sweep line proceeds downwards. Fortune's algorithm, therefore, only needs to maintain the beach line. The beach line changes when an arc of a parabola gets added or when it gets deleted.

A parabolic arc is added to the beach line only when the sweep line hits a site. This event is called a *site event*. Figure 3.10a depicts the site event. Once the sweep line passes a site, a new parabolic arc is added. This arc corresponds to every point that now has this site as the closest one.

An arc only gets deleted from a beach line when it reduces to a point and then disappears. Figure 3.10b depicts such an event, called a *circle event*. When the arc b reduces to a point, the point q is equidistant from all the three sites i, j, and k. Thus, a circumcircle can be defined that passes through all i, j, and k. The circumcircle also touches the sweep line, i.e., it is tangent to it. As soon as the sweep line moves downward a little, the arc b disappears.

There are at most $O(n)$ circle events and site events. Processing each event requires $O(\log_2 n)$ time (since the sites are sorted). Therefore, the total running time is $O(n \log_2 n)$. The space requirement is $O(n)$. Details

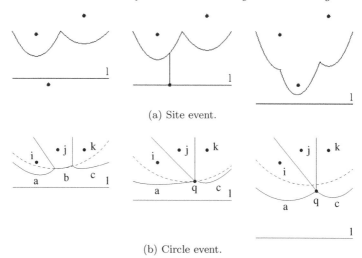

(a) Site event.

(b) Circle event.

Figure 3.10: Addition and deletion of a parabolic arc to the beach line.

of the Fortune's algorithm and its analysis can be found in [de Berg et al., 2008].

3.6.2   Extensions and Variants

The usual Voronoi diagram is employed in a two-dimensional space with the distance between points measured using the Euclidean distance. Different variants of the basic Voronoi diagram have been developed that are found to be useful in specific contexts. The most useful is the one that uses a weighted version of the Euclidean distance (see Section 5.2 for the definition). This amounts to stretching the dimensions at different rates. Consequently, the algorithm to construct the Voronoi diagram remains the same. Similarly, a more sophisticated distance such as the Mahalanobis distance (see Section 5.3.1) can also be used, since it only amounts to stretching and rotation of axes. As a result, the basic construction procedure remains the same and such a diagram is guaranteed to exist.

Voronoi diagrams can also use weights on the sites where the Euclidean distance from a site is modified according to its weights [Aurenhammer and Edelsbrunner, 1984, Fortune, 1986].

A particularly interesting variant uses the L_1 distance or the Manhattan distance (see Section 5.2). Such a structure is, however, not guaranteed to exist. In other words, there may not be a partition of the space into convex polygons such that points inside the polygon are closer to the site corresponding to it, where the distance is measured using the L_1 norm.

Similarly, given only the distances, it is not always possible to construct the Dirichlet tessellation. Even in cases where it is possible, there may be multiple such structures that respect the properties.

Attempts have been made to extend the Voronoi diagram into higher dimensional spaces (using the Euclidean distance) [Klee, 1980]. In a d-dimensional space with n sites, it requires $O(n^{\lceil d/2 \rceil})$ time to construct a Voronoi diagram [Edelsbrunner, 1987]. Due to the exponential factor on the number of dimensions, higher dimensional Voronoi diagrams are rarely used in practical applications.

The ordinary Voronoi diagram is also called a Voronoi diagram of *order 1* as the partition depends on only one nearest site. In a Voronoi diagram of *order k*, the partition is done based on k nearest sites, i.e., each polygon contains k sites such that every point in the polygon has the corresponding k sites as the nearest k points [Agarwal et al., 1998]. Such a diagram is very useful for k-nearest-neighbor searches as the information is readily available. A particular variant of the above structure is the *farthest point Voronoi diagram* where the construction is done based on the farthest sites [Aggarwal et al., 1987]. It is equivalent to a Voronoi diagram of order $(n-1)$ as the complement of the nearest $(n-1)$ sites is the farthest site. In two dimensions, construction of a Voronoi diagram of order k requires $O(n \log_2 n + k^2(n-k))$ time and $O(k(n-k))$ space [Agarwal et al., 1998].

3.7 Tries

We next describe string indexing. While strings can be treated as regular 1-dimensional objects since two strings can be always compared, the special property of a string being a sequence of characters is then not utilized. The TRIE family of structures [Fredkin, 1960, Aoe et al., 1992] use this sequence property to index strings in a radically different way. The word "trie" comes from re*trie*val.

The structure of a *basic trie* is that of a tree [Fredkin, 1960]. The root represents the empty string. Each edge defines the next character of a string. The last character ends in a leaf node. Every path from a root to a leaf, therefore, encodes a string, with each internal node representing a prefix of a string. The common prefixes of multiple strings share the path. This is the reason why the structure is also called a PREFIX TREE.

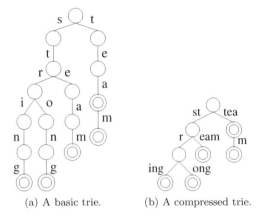

(a) A basic trie.   (b) A compressed trie.

Figure 3.11: Examples of trie structures.

Key Concept 3.6 [Trie]. A trie is a tree structure where every path from the root to a leaf defines a string. Two or more strings that have the same prefix share the path from the root up to the end of the common prefix.

Example 3.3 [Basic Trie]. Construct a basic trie for the strings "steam", "string", "strong", "tea", and "team".

The basic trie is shown in Figure 3.11a. Strings with the same prefix such as "steam" and "string" share the same path up to the common prefix "st-". The end of a string is denoted by a double circle, as in the case of "tea". If it is a proper prefix of another string, such as "team", then there is an edge from it again.   □

Tries reduce the redundancy in storing all the strings. However, if two strings are very similar but differ in even one character, they are stored along different paths of a trie. The strings "steam" and "team" exemplify an extreme case where they are stored completely separately even though one is a proper suffix of the other.

3.7.1 Searching

The biggest use of tries is in *exact* string retrieval. When a string is queried, the path from the root is traversed by looking up the characters in the query successively. If any character is absent, the query returns no answer; otherwise, if it ends in an ordinary node (denoted by a single circle in the figure), it is still not returned. Only when the search ends in a final node (denoted by a double circle in the figure), the corresponding string is returned. For a query string of length l, the search finishes in $O(l)$ time.

For a database of n strings, a binary search tree requires $O(\log_2 n)$ time to search a string. For large databases, l is much smaller than $\log_2 n$ and, therefore, a trie searches more efficiently.

3.7.2 Variants

The basic trie structure has different variants. A space-saving version of trie, appropriately called a COMPRESSED TRIE (sometimes also called a COMPACT TRIE), compresses all the unary nodes of a trie on a path into a single node [Maly, 1976]. The edges are then labeled by substrings, and not necessarily single characters.

Example 3.4 [Compressed Trie]. Construct a compressed trie for the strings "steam", "string", "strong", "tea" and "team".

Figure 3.11b shows the compressed trie version. The substring "team" is broken into "tea" that ends in a node having a single outgoing edge as it is a complete string by itself. If this was not done, a query for "tea" would have failed. □

3.7.3 Discussion

An important problem in the domain of string matching is that of *substring search* where given a database of strings $\{S\}$ and a query string Q of length l, the problem is to find the strings of which Q is a *substring*, i.e., it occurs anywhere in the string. For a single database string, most structures require $O(m)$ time for the above query to either return a matching occurrence of Q in S or the fact that Q is not a substring, where the total length S is m and Q is of length l. Generally, $m \gg l$.

One of the most efficient structures for solving this problem and many other related queries is the *suffix tree*, which returns the answer in $O(l)$ time by spending a pre-processing time of $O(m)$ on the database strings.

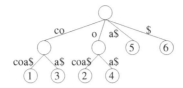

Figure 3.12: Suffix tree for "cocoa$".

3.8 Suffix Tree

A SUFFIX TREE [Weiner, 1973, Gusfield, 1997] for a string encodes all the suffixes of the string in a tree setup. The root of the tree represents the empty string. Every edge represents the next character(s) from a suffix and every leaf represents a suffix of the string. A suffix tree for the string S can, thus, be viewed as a compressed trie of all suffixes of S.

An important assumption for constructing a suffix tree is that no suffix is a prefix of another suffix. Since this can be violated in strings such as "banana" (where "ana" is a prefix of "anana"), a simple trick is used to ensure this. The original alphabet is augmented with a special end-of-string symbol, which is generally denoted by $. The above string now becomes "banana$" (and, thus, "ana$" does not remain a prefix of "anana$" any more).

Key Concept 3.7 [Suffix Tree]. A suffix tree for a string builds a compressed trie of all its suffixes. Every path from the root to a leaf, thus, encodes a suffix of the string.

Example 3.5 [Suffix Tree]. Build a suffix tree for the string "cocoa$".

Figure 3.12 shows the suffix tree for "cocoa$". Each leaf is additionally marked with the starting position of the suffix it encodes.   □

When a suffix tree is built for a dataset of strings instead of a single one, the resulting structure is called a GENERALIZED SUFFIX TREE. It incorporates all the substrings of the two strings.

Example 3.6 [Generalized Suffix Tree]. Build a generalized suffix tree for the strings "cocoa$" and "choco#".

Figure 3.13 shows the generalized suffix tree. For ease of identifying the original string, every string is provided with a separate end-of-symbol

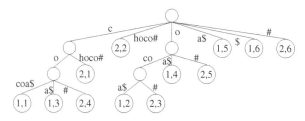

Figure 3.13: Generalized suffix tree for "cocoa$" and "choco#".

marker and each suffix (leaf) is marked with the string identifier as well in addition to the starting position. □

3.8.1 Searching

The generalized suffix tree can be used to search (all) occurrences of a query substring. As an example, suppose the substring "co" is queried to the tree shown in Figure 3.13. Searching from the root, the leftmost pointers are traversed for the first two levels. Every leaf under this sub-tree ("cocoa$", "coa$", "co#") returns an answer to the occurrence of "co". An unsuccessful search (e.g., for "cha") will end without reaching a node.

Finding one occurrence of a substring of length l, therefore, requires only $O(l)$ time while finding all the $|A|$ occurrences require $O(l + |A|)$ time due to the additional subtree traversal overhead.

3.8.2 Construction

A simple algorithm to construct a suffix tree for a string of length m requires $O(m^2)$ time. The suffixes, starting from the largest one, are inserted one by one into the tree.

However, it is possible to construct a suffix tree for a string S of length m in $O(m)$ time [Weiner, 1973, McCreight, 1976, Ukkonen, 1995]. For a detailed description of all the algorithms and the corresponding proofs, etc., the reader is referred to [Gusfield, 1997].

Ukkonen's algorithm [Ukkonen, 1995] is the most preferred one since it is the fastest in practice and is the easiest to comprehend. The algorithm considers each substring from the *beginning* of the string. At any point, it has seen up to k symbols, and has built a suffix tree that is correct for that k-length prefix. The suffix trees built in the interim are known as *implicit suffix trees*. The algorithm is "online" since once it has processed a symbol, it never needs to re-visit it and is, therefore, very attractive to streaming applications.

The algorithm runs in *phases*. The total number of phases for a m-length string S is $m - 1$. Each phase, in turn, has several *extensions*. The number of extensions for phase i runs from 1 to $i + 1$. Before phase i and extension j starts, it is assumed that the substring $S[j \ldots i]$ is in the implicit suffix tree. It is then extended by the symbol $S[i + 1]$ such that the substring $S[j \ldots (i + 1)]$ is now in the tree.

The extension is done in three ways:

1. The path for the substring $S[j \ldots i]$ ends in a leaf: $S[i+1]$ is added to the path.

2. The path for the substring $S[j \ldots i]$ ends in an internal node and there is no path from that node starting with $S[i + 1]$: $S[i + 1]$ is added as a new path from the node.

3. The path for the substring $S[j \ldots i]$ ends in an internal node and there is a path from that node starting with $S[i + 1]$: Nothing is done.

Figure 3.14 shows the different phases in the construction of the suffix tree for "cocoa$". Consider the addition of 'o' to "c" (left branch in Figure 3.14b). In the second phase, 'o' is added to both "c" and "". The path "c" ended in a leaf. The symbol 'o' is added to the path to obtain "co". This is, thus, an example of the first kind of extension. On the other hand, adding 'o' to the empty string "" (right branch in Figure 3.14b) is an example of the second kind of extension where a new path (from the root) is constructed. Finally, consider the addition of the second 'c' (Figure 3.14c). Since the suffix "coc" has already been added, there exists an internal node (root) starting with 'c'. Therefore, according to the third rule, nothing needs to be done.

It can be verified that once the entire string is processed, the suffix tree is correctly constructed. The naïve way of implementing the above steps results in an $O(m^3)$ algorithm. The running time is improved by using some implementation tricks such as suffix links. For details, the reader is referred to the book by [Gusfield, 1997].

3.9   Bitmap Index

BITMAP INDEXING [Silberschatz et al., 2010] is a very simple form of indexing, but it can help answer some specific kinds of queries quite

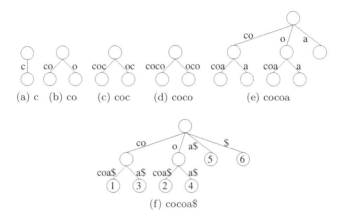

(a) c (b) co (c) coc (d) coco (e) cocoa

(f) cocoa$

Figure 3.14: Online construction of suffix tree for "cocoa$".

efficiently. It is applicable when the attribute domain consists of only a small number of distinct values. *Bit vectors* (also called *bitmaps* and *bit arrays*) are maintained for each such distinct value. The length of the vector is equal to the size of the database.

Each bit corresponds to a particular object in the database. Suppose the number of objects is n and the number of distinct values is m (the values being $v_1, v_2, \ldots, v_m$). If the value of the attribute for the ith object is v_j, then the ith bit of the jth bit vector is 1. The ith bits of all the other vectors is 0. The total size of this representation is $m \times n$ *bits* and can be simply stored as a regular two-dimensional array.

Key Concept 3.8 [Bitmap Indexing]. Corresponding to each value of a categorical attribute, a bit vector is maintained. The bits in the bit vector indicate the object in the database that have the particular value for the attribute (and, therefore, as a result, also indicate the objects that do not have that particular value).

Example 3.7 [Bitmap Indexing]. Construct the bitmap index for the dataset shown in Table 3.1.

There will be two sets of bit vectors, corresponding to each type of attribute. The distinct attributes for "gender" are {male, female} and that for "grade" are {A, B, C, D}. Correspondingly, the bit vectors constructed are:

Table 3.1: Example of bitmap indexing.

Object	Gender	Grade
O_1	male	C
O_2	female	A
O_3	female	C
O_4	male	D
O_5	male	A

- male = (10011), female = (01100)

- A = (01001), B = (00000), C = (10100), D = (00010)

The bit vector for *male* shows that the first person is a male, the next two persons are not (although it cannot specify what they are), and the last two are male again.   □

Simple queries can be answered using these vectors and bitmap operations. Since operating systems allow very fast bitmap operations when these vectors are packed in word sizes, the bitmap operations are extremely fast.

Example 3.8 [Bitmap Index Searching]. Find "male" students who got "C" for the example in Example 3.7.

The bitmaps of *male* and C are bit-wise AND-ed. The answer is 10011 AND 10100 = 10000, i.e., the first person.   □

A slight problem arises in relational databases when certain values are set to "null" to denote unknown, erroneous or not applicable values. A special bitmap is used to denote the "null" value. When the bit-wise operations are performed, the bitmap corresponding to the null values are taken special care of. They are not returned as answers.

Part III

Disk-Based Index Structures

Chapter 4

Hierarchical Structures

The bulk of the index structures are hierarchical disk-based structures. They pay special attention to the organization of data at the disk level. Since fetching data from a random location on disk, i.e., the random I/O operation, is much more costly than fetching data from consecutive locations, i.e., the sequential I/O operation, the structures focus mostly on saving the random I/O costs. (See Appendix A for details on this comparison.) The CPU costs on processing the data once they are brought to memory is negligible as compared to these costs.

In this chapter, we study the hierarchical disk-based index structures. We start with the single-dimensional structures: the B-tree and the B+-tree. The B+-tree is still the most widely employed index structure in commercial databases. We then describe another low-dimensional structure, the K-d-B-tree, before explaining the basic framework for hierarchical object-based index structures. We next describe the different bounding box geometries based on which various structures, including the R-tree, have been designed. Finally, we finish the chapter with a discussion on how to build better index structures when the entire dataset is made available before the construction.

4.1 B-Tree and B+-Tree

The B-TREE is a balanced hierarchical data structure for organizing keys residing on secondary storage, i.e., disk [Comer, 1979]. It is an optimization of the balanced binary search tree structure by making the index node size correspond to the disk access unit, i.e., a disk page or a block.

A B-tree of order Θ has the following properties:

- The tree is balanced, i.e, all the leaf nodes are in the same level

- The root node has at least 1 key

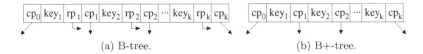

(a) B-tree.   (b) B+-tree.

Figure 4.1: Structure of an internal node of B-tree and B+-tree.

- All other nodes have between Θ and 2Θ keys

- A node having k keys has $k + 1$ child pointers

The *branching factor* or *fanout* of a B-tree of order Θ is at least $\Theta+1$ and at most $2\Theta + 1$. The child pointers in the leaf node are null. The structure does not allow storage of keys multiple times and, hence, the pointer to the record corresponding to a key is stored along with it.

Key Concept 4.1 [B-Tree]. A B-tree is a generalization of a perfectly balanced binary search tree where instead of two children, an internal node can have many children based on multiple keys. The multiple keys divide the entire range into multiple disjoint divisions, each of which is handled by a child node.

The most important variant of B-tree that is used extensively for disk-resident data is the B+-TREE [Comer, 1979]. In a B+-tree, the internal nodes store *only* the keys (and not the pointers to records). The leaf nodes store the pointers to the record corresponding to the key. Often, the leaf nodes are connected in a doubly linked list fashion to facilitate their traversal without accessing the parents. The rest of the structure remains exactly the same.

Key Concept 4.2 [B+-Tree]. A B+-tree is a variant of B-tree where all the data is stored at the leaves, and the internal nodes contain only the keys.

Figure 4.1 shows the structure of the internal nodes of the two trees. A B-tree internal node, in addition to $k + 1$ child pointers (denoted by $cp_0, \ldots, cp_k$) corresponding to the $k + 1$ divisions inflicted by k keys ($key_1, \ldots, key_k$), hold k record pointers (shown as $rp_1, \ldots, rp_k$ in the figure). A B+-tree internal node does not store the record pointers.

Since less information is stored in an internal node of B+-tree, more keys can fit. This increases the fanout of the tree, thereby decreasing its height. Thus, although it is possible to reach a search key faster in a B-tree by not requiring to traverse up to the leaf level, because of the large number of keys stored at the leaf level, on an average, searching is faster in a B+-tree, as the number of levels is lower. Also, the insertion, deletion, and update routines for a B-tree are more complicated than those for a B+-tree.

The order of a B+-tree is calculated using the disk page size, the size of the key, and the size of the pointers. For a disk page having a capacity of C bytes, the order Θ is the largest number such that 2Θ keys and $2\Theta + 1$ pointers fit within C. If a key consumes γ bytes and a pointer consumes η bytes, then

$$C \geq 2.\Theta.\gamma + (2.\Theta + 1).\eta \tag{4.1}$$

$$\Rightarrow \Theta_{\text{B+-tree}} = \left\lfloor \frac{C - \eta}{2(\gamma + \eta)} \right\rfloor \tag{4.2}$$

For a B-tree, in addition to 2Θ keys, there are 2Θ pointers to records residing on disk. Since these are data pointers, they consume η bytes each. Thus,

$$C \geq 2.\Theta.\gamma + 2.\Theta.\eta + (2.\Theta + 1).\eta \tag{4.3}$$

$$\Rightarrow \Theta_{\text{B-tree}} = \left\lfloor \frac{C - \eta}{2(\gamma + 2\eta)} \right\rfloor \tag{4.4}$$

Example 4.1 [B+-Tree and B-Tree Order]. What is the order of a B+-tree and a B-tree with a page size of 4 KB indexing keys of 8 bytes each, and having pointers of size 4 bytes?

Using the formulae given in Eq. (4.2) and Eq. (4.4) respectively, the order for a B+-tree is $\Theta_{\text{B+-tree}} = \left\lfloor \frac{4 \times 1024 - 4}{2(8+4)} \right\rfloor = 170$ while that for a B-tree is $\Theta_{\text{B-tree}} = \left\lfloor \frac{4 \times 1024 - 4}{2(8+2 \times 4)} \right\rfloor = 127$. □

Example 4.2 [B+-Tree and B-Tree Height]. What is the height of the B+-tree and the B-tree with the parameters in Example 4.1 for 3×10^7 keys?

Since a B-tree can contain at most $2 \times 127 = 254$ keys per node, the height is at least $\lceil \log_{254}(3 \times 10^7) \rceil = 4$. A B+-tree, on the other hand, may contain as many as $2 \times 170 = 340$ keys per internal node and, thus, may fit into a height of $\lceil \log_{340}(3 \times 10^7) \rceil = 3$. □

4.2   K-D-B-Tree

While B-trees and B+-trees handle the disk-based design for accessing keys quite well, they are meant for single-dimensional keys only. For keys having multiple dimensions, K-D-B-TREES [Robinson, 1981], which are disk-based versions of *K-d-trees*, have been proposed. It attempts to combine the multi-dimensional search efficiency of K-d-trees with the disk I/O efficiency of B+-trees.

4.2.1   Structure

K-d-B-tree is a *balanced* structure that partitions the entire space into buckets or disk pages. All the data reside in the leaf nodes, which are called *point pages*. The internal nodes, called the *region pages*, contain only the region keys. The hyperplanes along which the space is partitioned are axis-oriented. The regions in a region page are *disjoint*, and they together constitute the entire region. The children pages in a region, therefore, resemble those in K-d-trees.

The one serious relaxation that K-d-B trees offer is that the region pages can underflow, i.e., the restriction of having the internal pages at least half-filled is relaxed. This, however, can lead to extremely low space utilization.

Key Concept 4.3 [K-D-B-Tree]. A node is split into disjoint children which together constitute the entire space. A split is done on the basis of a single dimension and it extends the entire range of the other dimensions.

4.2.2   Splitting

During insertion, a region page may overflow and may, therefore, need to split. The split is always made using an axis-oriented hyperplane that extends all the way along the entire range for the other dimension. In other words, if a split is made along a particular dimension dim_i at a particular value v, all the children nodes through which the hyper-surface $dim_i = v$ passes gets split as well. This goes on recursively till the leaf pages. Hence, a single region split may generate a lot of cascading node splits.

Figure 4.2 shows an example. Suppose the region A needs to be split

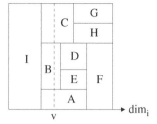

Figure 4.2: Splitting in a K-d-B-tree.

at the value v. The split axis is extended all the way along the other dimension. As a result, the regions B and C get split as well.

There are two main variants of choosing the split dimension. In the first, the dimension with the largest range is chosen. In the second, the split dimensions are cycled in a round-robin fashion in a manner similar to a K-d-tree. The value where the split occurs is generally chosen in the middle of the range or at the median.

4.2.3 Deletion

The deletion of a region page cannot always be done blindly. Since the entire space needs to be reclaimed, the bounding box corresponding to the deleted region must be incorporated in the parent region. Thus, it must be *merged* with one or more of its sibling neighbor nodes. Due to the axis-oriented nature of the pages, it may happen that the merge does not create a convex hyper-rectangle.

Thus, a subset of the sibling nodes is found that together maintain the property. These nodes are called *joinable*. New children pages are created out of these, and all the contents of these nodes are then re-inserted into these new pages. In the worst case, if no such subset is found, the contents of the entire region page are re-inserted.

The region B in Figure 4.2 exemplifies such a situation. When it is deleted, it cannot merge with any of its neighbors, A, E, D, C, or I. The set of joinable nodes for B consist of D and E together. When I is deleted, the only set of joinable nodes is the entire collection A to H together. On the other hand, when G is deleted, it can simply merge with H.

Although there is no concept of an underflow parameter, to maintain space utilization, this re-organization can be done for nodes having very few entries. An additional constraint that then gets imposed is that the joinable sibling nodes together must not overflow.

The authors [Robinson, 1981] did not specify any algorithm for finding the joinable nodes. However, it can be observed that the joinable nodes can be determined by maintaining a *split history*. The node B, for example, was created by splitting the region consisting currently of B, D, and E. Hence, this set will always be joinable.

4.2.4   Searching

The details of different searching procedures follow that of a general hierarchical structure, as elaborated in the next section.

4.2.5   Discussion

The space utilization of K-d-B-trees is generally low. Also, due to the space-partitioning and disjointedness properties of the children nodes, the structure is not suitable for more than 2 or 3 dimensions.

4.3   General Framework

Before we discuss any other particular index structure in detail, we first explain the general framework of a hierarchical object-based index structure. There are n objects in a d-dimensional vector space that need to be organized. The objects (or sets of objects) are represented by a hyper-dimensional bounding geometric convex "box" (either a rectangle or a sphere or a convex polygon). These bounding boxes are organized in a hierarchy.

The original objects are at level 0. At every level i of the hierarchy, m boxes fit into a bigger bounding box at the next level, i.e., level $(i + 1)$. The smaller boxes lie in the subtree of the larger box. The invariant that a bounding box must maintain is that a larger box B_i at level i must *completely encompass* all smaller boxes B_{i-1} that lie in its subtree. Note that a smaller box may lie in the subtree of two or more larger boxes, thus indicating that two boxes at the same level need not be disjoint. However, they must be exhaustive, i.e., all boxes at level $i - 1$ must be in the subtree of some box at level i. The structure may not be balanced, although a balanced structure guarantees better average search performance.

This whole hierarchy is called an *object pyramid*. The object pyramid provides a *multi-resolution representation* of the entire database of objects.

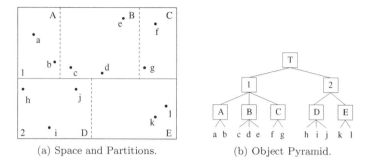

(a) Space and Partitions. (b) Object Pyramid.

Figure 4.3: Hierarchical structure.

The root contains only one box corresponding to the entire space. The number of leaves are $\lceil (n/m) \rceil$. If there is a total of n objects and m boxes fit in a larger box, then the total number of bounding boxes is $\lceil (n/m) \rceil + \lceil (n/m^2) \rceil + \cdots = O(n/m)$. Taking m to be a constant, the size overhead of the index, therefore, is *linear* in the number of objects.

The height of this object pyramid is $h = \lceil \log_m n \rceil$. Thus, to access any particular object, it requires h steps of traversal through the index, i.e., h disk accesses.

Figure 4.3a shows an example of a two-dimensional space with 12 objects a through l. The corresponding object pyramid is shown in Figure 4.3b. The entire space is represented by node T which is partitioned into two boxes 1 and 2 and so on. In this particular example, all the boxes are disjoint. Also, the boxes at any level cover the entire space. We next consider how queries are solved over such an index structure.

4.3.1 Point Queries

Consider a point query for the object j. The search starts at the topmost level, i.e., with node T. Of its two children, it is found that object j belongs to the bounding box corresponding to node 2. This is due to the geometric properties of inclusion of a point within a rectangle. Therefore, the entire subtree rooted at node 1 can be pruned. This pruning behavior is the advantage of using the index structure as it avoids searching many of the database objects.

Similarly, at the second level, among the children of node 2, only the path corresponding to node D needs to be traversed, thereby again eliminating the need to search through the space represented by node E. Finally, within node D, object j is located and returned.

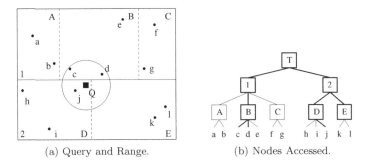

(a) Query and Range.   (b) Nodes Accessed.

Figure 4.4: Range query.

4.3.2 Range Queries

Next, consider a similarity search in the form of a range query for the query object Q with a particular radius as shown in Figure 4.4a. Since the query region (i.e., the circle) intersects both nodes 1 and 2, *both* the corresponding boxes need to be searched. Thus, unlike a point query, a similarity search query may need to be solved by traversing multiple children of a node.

Finding the intersection of the query circle with a bounding box is done by finding the minimum and maximum possible distance of any point within the box from the query (see Appendix B for how to calculate such distances). If the minimum distance of a point within the box is greater than the query radius, then no object inside the box can be an answer to the range query, and hence, the box can be completely pruned. On the other hand, if the maximum distance is less than the query radius, then it is guaranteed that all objects inside the box are part of the answer. They can be simply returned without further checking.

Thus, within node 1, only node B needs to be searched. Hence, the index structure offers benefit over the naïve method of searching through all the database objects by pruning the spaces corresponding to nodes A and C. Within node B, objects c and d are returned as answers.

Next node 2 is traversed. There is no pruning at this level and both the nodes D and E need to be searched. Note that although node E does not produce any answer finally, it needs to be considered as it intersects the query region. From node D, object j is returned. Figure 4.4b shows in bold the nodes accessed.

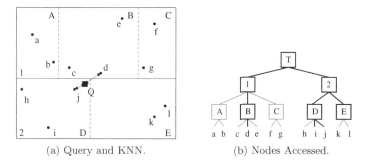

(a) Query and KNN. (b) Nodes Accessed.

Figure 4.5: KNN query.

4.3.3 Nearest Neighbor Queries

Consider the same query object Q and $k = 2$ for a kNN query (Figure 4.5a). Since the kNN query does not have any pre-defined range, it first tries to get k answers. The distance to the kth object from the query, d_k, then defines the range which is used to guide the subsequent search. As and when new objects (or boxes) are found which can be part of the kNN answer set, the range is modified. Note that, in this manner, the range keeps decreasing.

The current k nearest objects, along with their distances, are maintained in a max-heap structure [Cormen et al., 2009]. Every time a new data object is encountered, its distance to the query is computed. If the distance is better than the object at the top of the heap (which is d_k), the worst object (which is at the top) is extracted and the new object is inserted. In this way, the heap always maintains the size k.

As an example, suppose the query first descends to node 2 and then node D, and chooses objects j and i as the current best estimates of the two nearest neighbors. The current nearest neighbor set is, therefore, $\{j, i\}$. The distance $d_{k=2}$ is the distance from Q to object i.

While this step can arbitrarily pick up k neighbors, the search performs better when the nearest nodes (in terms of minimum distance) are first accessed. Thus, out of nodes 1 and 2, it is better to access node 2 first, and among the children of node 2, it is better to access node D.

Using the current d_k, suppose node E is next checked. This follows the *depth-first search* procedure of exploring the tree. The other alternative is the *breadth-first search* procedure. In depth-first searches, all nodes in a single path from the root to a leaf are first examined before selecting another path, while in breadth-first searches, the nodes are examined in a level-by-level order.

Since the minimum distance of node E to the query is less than d_k, node E needs to be accessed. Within that, however, no better candidate is found, and therefore, the range remains unchanged. Next, node 1 is accessed. Of its three children, since node B has the least minimum distance to Q, it is accessed. Within node B, object d is closer to Q than object i. Consequently, the nearest neighbor set is updated to $\{j, d\}$ and the range is reduced to the distance of Q to object d. Nodes A and C do not need to be accessed as their minimum distances are more than the current range, and are pruned. The algorithm terminates and $\{j, d\}$ is returned as the answer set. Figure 4.5b shows the nodes of the tree that are accessed during the query.

Unlike the range query, the order in which the nodes are accessed during the kNN query has an effect on the performance. For example, instead of accessing nodes 2 and D first, if nodes 1 and C were accessed, then the initial range estimate would have been quite bad, and all the nodes of the tree would have been accessed. Thus, among a set of children, it is better to access the one with the least minimum distance first. This generally produces a more efficient search.

4.3.3.1   Best-First Search

A particularly efficient way of solving nearest neighbors queries is by employing the *best-first search* mechanism [Hjaltason and Samet, 1999]. At every iteration, the best-first algorithm examines the next most likely candidate (an internal node or a leaf) as the nearest neighbor. In this way, it differs significantly from both depth-first and breadth-first searches.

The algorithm maintains a priority queue (as a min-heap [Cormen et al., 2009]) of the candidates ordered by their minimum distances to the query. If the candidate is a leaf, its actual distance to the query is stored. If, on the other hand, the candidate is an internal node, the minimum distance to its representative bounding box is stored.

At all times, the distance to the current k^{th} nearest neighbor, d_k, is maintained. At every iteration, the best candidate from the head of the priority queue is extracted. If it is a leaf and is a k nearest neighbor, i.e., if its distance to the query is less than d_k, it is included in the answer set, and d_k is updated. When an internal node is extracted, if the minimum distance is less than d_k, there is a potential of finding better neighbors. Consequently, its children are inserted into the priority queue; the node itself is purged. If the minimum distance is more than d_k, the node can be pruned right away.

The algorithm starts by inserting the root as the sole candidate in an empty queue. The process continues as long as the minimum distance of the candidate at the head of the queue is less than d_k. As soon as it is

Table 4.1: Best-first search.

Extract	Insert	Priority queue	Answer	$d_{k=2}$
-	T	$(T, 0)$	Φ	∞
T	1, 2	$(2, 0), (1, 4)$	Φ	∞
2	D, E	$(D, 0), (E, 2), (1, 4)$	Φ	∞
D	h, i, j	$(E, 2), (1, 4), (j, 6),$ $(h, 27), (i, 30)$	Φ	∞
E	k, l	$(1, 4), (j, 6), (h, 27),$ $(i, 30), (k, 36), (l, 38)$	Φ	∞
1	A, B, C	$(B, 4), (j, 6), (A, 12), (C, 22),$ $(h, 27), (i, 30), (k, 36), (l, 38)$	Φ	∞
B	c, d, e	$(j, 6), (d, 8), (c, 11), (A, 12),$ $(C, 22), (h, 27), (i, 30), (e, 32),$ $(k, 36), (l, 38)$	Φ	∞
j	-	$(d, 8), (c, 11), (A, 12), (C, 22),$ $(h, 27), (i, 30), (e, 32),$ $(k, 36), (l, 38)$	$\{j\}$	∞
d	-	$(c, 11), (A, 12), (C, 22), (h, 27),$ $(i, 30), (e, 32), (k, 36), (l, 38)$	$\{j, d\}$	8

more than d_k, none of the objects in the queue including the head can be part of the answer set. Thus, the objects in the queue can be safely pruned and the algorithm can terminate.

Example 4.3 [Best-First Search]. Using the example from Figure 4.5a, solve the 2-NN query for Q using best-first search.

Table 4.1 shows how the best-first search proceeds for Q.

Since the distance of the element at the beginning of the queue, 11, is greater than the current estimate of d_k, the algorithm stops. The objects j and d are returned as answers. □

4.3.3.2 Incremental Nearest Neighbor Queries

In many applications, the nearest neighbors are not always needed at once, but may be queried one by one. For example, a user may first obtain the nearest 10 objects, and if not satisfied with the results, may then request 5 more nearest objects. While the above can be solved by first issuing a 10-NN query and then a 15-NN query, the procedure is

Table 4.2: Incremental nearest neighbor query.

Extract	Insert	Priority queue	Answer	$d_{k=4}$
...	...	...	...	...
d	-	$(c, 11)$, $(A, 12)$, $(C, 22)$, $(h, 27)$, $(i, 30)$, $(e, 32)$, $(k, 36)$, $(l, 38)$	$\{j, d\}$	∞
c	-	$(A, 12)$, $(C, 22)$, $(h, 27)$, $(i, 30)$, $(e, 32)$, $(k, 36)$, $(l, 38)$	$\{j, d, c\}$	∞
A	a, b	$(b, 15)$, $(C, 22)$, $(a, 26)$, $(h, 27)$, $(i, 30)$, $(e, 32)$, $(k, 36)$, $(l, 38)$	$\{j, d, c\}$	∞
b	-	$(C, 22)$, $(a, 26)$, $(h, 27)$, $(i, 30)$, $(e, 32)$, $(k, 36)$, $(l, 38)$	$\{j, d, c, b\}$	15

not efficient. This is due to the fact that the answer to the later 15-NN query contains results from the earlier 10-NN query.

It is more effective if the information gathered during the earlier search can be used without solving the query afresh. This paradigm is called the *incremental nearest neighbor search* [Hjaltason and Samet, 1999].

These queries are best solved by the best-first search discussed in the previous section. The state of the priority queue is retained and whenever a new nearest neighbor is requested, the algorithm starts processing from the queue.

Example 4.4 [Incremental Nearest Neighbor Search]. Show how the 4-NN query for Q in Figure 4.5a is answered incrementally assuming that the first 2 neighbors have already been found using the best-first search in Example 4.3.

Table 4.2 shows how the query proceeds. Note that the incremental work done for the 3rd and 4th neighbors are quite less (only 3 more steps) due to the work done previously. $\square$

4.3.4   Window Queries

Window queries are similar to range queries except for the fact that the query region is a hyper-rectangle instead of a hyper-sphere. Section B.5 in Appendix B shows how the minimum distance from a hyper-rectangle to another hyper-rectangle is computed.

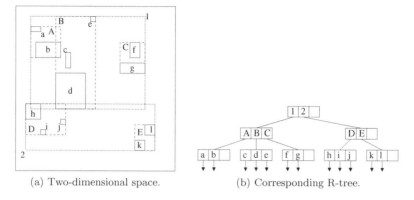

(a) Two-dimensional space. (b) Corresponding R-tree.

Figure 4.6: An example of an R-tree.

4.3.5 Minimum Bounding Geometries

Based upon the bounding box idea as discussed in the last section, several important index structures have been designed. The geometry of the bounding box can vary as long as it remains *convex* and *covers* the entire children set of objects. The most important shape is that of hyper-rectangles. The R-tree family of structures (Section 4.4 to Section 4.7) follow the hyper-rectangle geometry. However, there are some important structures that use hyper-spheres as the bounding box. This is motivated by the observation that the range and kNN queries are spherical in shape. The SS-tree (Section 4.8) and the SR-tree (Section 4.9) fall in this category. Finally, there is one structure, the P-tree (Section 4.10), that conceptually uses any arbitrary convex polygon as the bounding geometry. We next discuss all these structures in detail.

4.4 R-Tree

After B+-tree, R-TREE [Guttman, 1984] is the most successful index structure that has ever been designed for database applications. It is a landmark in the area of database indexing, and is heavily responsible for the development of this field. Even after the passage of three decades since its inception, it is still used for many modern indexing tasks and is a good competitor to even specialized structures. Over the years it has inspired a whole family of index structures [Manolopoulos et al., 2006].

The R-tree has a similar structure to a B+-tree (Section 4.1), although it is meant for multiple dimensions. It is versatile as it can store not just point objects, but also any other shape including lines, etc. The objects are enclosed in a minimum bounding rectangle (MBR) for ease of treatment. A point object is also represented as a MBR with zero volume where the lower coordinates in each dimension are the same as the higher ones.

4.4.1   Structure

An R-tree is a balanced structure. The internal nodes contain *index entries* which are hyper-rectangles that most tightly fit the entries of the children. For a d-dimensional space, the hyper-rectangle is specified by $2d$ parameters, two in each dimension to indicate the minimum and maximum values along that dimension. In addition, they also contain the child pointers. The leaf nodes contain the data pointers and the index entries (i.e., the MBR) for the actual data object. Thus, only the leaves contain the data.

Key Concept 4.4 [R-Tree]. An R-tree node indexes the space using minimum bounding hyper-rectangles in multiple dimensions. The space corresponding to a hyper-rectangle is delegated to a child node. The actual data objects are indexed only at the leaf nodes.

Figure 4.6 shows an example. The entire space has two MBRs corresponding to nodes 1 and 2 which overlap. They do not index the dead space (such as towards the right end of the space) where there is no data. The node 1 has, in turn, three internal nodes A, B, and C. Following recursively in this manner, the leaf levels are reached. Note that, in this example, the leaf MBRs are also bounding boxes. They contain pointers to the actual data objects with their detailed geometries and other attributes.

Figure 4.7 shows an example of an R-tree node with m keys in a d-dimensional space. Note that each dimension in a key has two values, l and h corresponding respectively to the lower and higher end-points of the hyper-rectangle in that dimension.

Each node corresponds to a disk page or a block. An (α, β) R-tree has the underflow and overflow restrictions of having at least α entries and at most β entries for every internal node ($\alpha = 2$ for the root node). The overflow parameter β is computed the same way as in a B+-tree, i.e., it is the largest number of entries that just fits in a disk page. The underflow restriction α guarantees space utilization.

The largest number of entries of an R-tree (i.e., β) is calculated using

Figure 4.7: An R-tree node.

the disk page size, the number of dimensions for each key, and the size of the pointers. For a disk page having a capacity of C bytes, the parameter β is the largest number such that β keys (each having 2 values per d dimensions) and β pointers fit within C. If a dimension consumes γ bytes and a pointer requires η bytes of storage, then

$$C \geq 2.d.\beta.\gamma + \beta.\eta \qquad (4.5)$$

$$\Rightarrow \beta_{\text{R-tree}} = \left\lfloor \frac{C}{2.d.\gamma + \eta} \right\rfloor \qquad (4.6)$$

The underflow parameter has the restriction of being at most half the overflow parameter, i.e.,

$$\alpha \leq \left\lceil \frac{\beta}{2} \right\rceil \qquad (4.7)$$

This condition is necessary so that when two underflowing nodes merge, the resulting node does not overflow.

Figure 4.6b shows an R-tree for the objects shown in Figure 4.6a. Here, $\alpha = 2$ and $\beta = 3$.

An important point to note is that the child nodes need not be disjoint and may overlap considerably. Consequently, it is not clear which node contains a particular data object and multiple paths may need to be searched for even a point query.

For example, to search for a point in the intersection region of nodes B and D (refer to Figure 4.6a), both nodes 1 and 2 need to be searched. The search proceeds to nodes B and D and then to d and h.

The non-disjointedness property of the children nodes, although helps in organizing the structure better, makes the structure not so useful in higher dimensions. We elaborate on this "curse of dimensionality" phenomenon in Chapter 7.

4.4.2 Searching

The searching procedure follows the same method as discussed in Section 4.3 for general hierarchical structures.

4.4.3   Insertion

Data is inserted only at the leaves. However, since the leaves can overlap, a particular data object may have a choice to be inserted in multiple leaves. The way it is resolved is the following.

The insertion procedure starts at the root. If there is only one child where the insertion can happen, it delegates the insertion to that node. Otherwise, out of multiple candidates, the child having the *least volume enlargement* due to this insertion is chosen. This is to ensure that the amount of "dead space" introduced, i.e., the space which is indexed although it contains no data, is the least. In case of a tie, the child with the least volume, and then the one with the least number of children are chosen.

In this way, a particular leaf is reached. If there is no overflow in the leaf, it is simply inserted and the index entry of the parent node is adjusted. If there is an overflow, the leaf is split and the $\beta + 1$ entries are distributed between the two leaves. We discuss the splitting procedure in detail in Section 4.4.6. The overflows may continue to the root level, at which point the root splits, and the height of the R-tree gets incremented by one.

4.4.4   Deletion

To delete an entry, it is first searched, and then deleted. If underflow occurs, the leaf node is deleted and all its entries are put in a temporary set. The index entries of all the nodes from the leaf to the root are next adjusted. All the entries from other underflowing nodes in this path are also collected in the temporary set. Finally, the entries from this set are *re-inserted* into the R-tree. The height of the tree decreases only if the underflow proceeds to the root.

In many cases, however, in order to avoid the costly operation of re-inserting all the $\alpha - 1$ entries of the leaf, the deleted data is simply marked as "deleted". It retains its entry, but is not returned when searched. When another object is inserted into this particular leaf, it is actually deleted and replaced by this new entry.

4.4.5   Update

An update operation is performed by first deleting the entry and then re-inserting the modified data. So, it uses the deletion and insertion algorithms.

4.4.6 Splitting

The problem of splitting a node is essentially how to distribute $\beta + 1$ entries to two leaves such that each has at least α entries. To distinguish between two splits, they must be evaluated according to some measure. While there can be many such measures, since the search efficiency is the most important goal of an index structure, the objective should be to minimize the probability that *both* the new nodes are accessed during a search.

Minimizing the probability, however, requires the knowledge of the query distribution. Assuming the query regions to be uniformly distributed across the space, the probability of accessing a node is directly proportional to the volume of its corresponding MBR. Hence, the objective is to choose a split that minimizes the *overall* volume of the nodes, i.e., the *sum* of volumes of their MBRs.

Based on this, there are three different strategies to choose a good split:

1. Exhaustive

2. Quadratic

3. Linear

These are explained next.

4.4.6.1 Exhaustive Split

The exhaustive split approach examines all possible splits and chooses the best one. Even though this produces the optimal answer, due to an exponential number of possibilities, the approach is too slow and impractical.

4.4.6.2 Quadratic Split

The quadratic split approach starts by choosing a pair of entries that is the *most wasteful*. The amount of waste w for two entries a and b is defined as $w = vol(U) - vol(a) - vol(b)$, where U is the *covering* hyperrectangle of a and b. The waste signifies the volume that is indexed extra by accommodating a and b in the same node. Once this pair is chosen, they become the *seeds* for the two new nodes, because surely they should *not* be in the same node. Choosing this pair of entries requires a quadratic number of operations.

For each non-assigned entry c, the waste of combining c with the groups corresponding to node a and node b are computed; c is assigned to the one with lesser waste. If it is a tie, the group with the smaller volume and then the lesser number of entries is chosen. Note that this choice may depend on the order in which the entries are chosen. The procedure continues till one of the groups has $\beta + 1 - \alpha$ entries, in which case, all the rest are assigned to the other group to satisfy the underflow condition.

4.4.6.3   Linear Split

The linear split approach differs from the quadratic split in only the way the two initial seeds are chosen. The assignment of other entries to the groups remain the same. For each dimension, the entries with the highest minimum and the lowest maximum are chosen. The difference between these two values are normalized by dividing by the total range of the dimension. The entries that exhibit the largest normalized difference become the seeds. Since choosing the minimum and maximum in each range is a linear procedure, this approach makes the overall split mechanism faster.

4.4.7   Discussion

Experiments on R-trees have revealed that the split time increases with the page size. This happens as the number of entries (i.e., $\beta + 1$) increases. The overall insertion time, however, decreases with increasing β as fewer nodes overflow, thereby decreasing the number of splits. However, with increasing α, the deletion time suffers badly since more re-inserts take place.

The searching time is relatively insensitive to the splitting algorithms, thereby justifying the faster linear approach. With large page sizes, the number of random disk I/Os decrease although the CPU cost increases as more entries need to be handled. The overall size of the index decreases with increasing α as more entries are packed in a single node.

A detailed discussion on various aspects of the R-tree and its variants can be found in [Manolopoulos et al., 2006].

4.5   R*-Tree

The success of the concept of R-trees led to many different variants of it. One of the most successful successors is the R*-TREE [Beckmann et al., 1990]. It performs three engineering optimizations over R-tree in the algorithms for

1. Insertion

2. Splitting

3. Forced re-insertion while overflowing

4.5.1   Insertion

While inserting in a node, if the child pointers are internal nodes, then the subtree with the least volume increase is chosen. This is the same as the R-tree. However, if the child pointers are leaf nodes, i.e., the level is one up from the leaves, then the *overlap* measure is used. If the child entries in a node are $E_1, \ldots, E_k$, then the *overlap* of E_i is defined as $\sum_{j=1, j \neq i}^{k} volume(E_i \cap E_j)$. The child for which the overlap is increased by the least amount is chosen as the entry to insert. This method is not very efficient, though, as it requires a quadratic amount of computations in the number of child entries.

4.5.2   Splitting

The splitting procedure considers three parameters:

1. Sum of the *volumes* of the two groups created by the split.

2. Sum of their *margins*, i.e., the lengths of the sides of the hyper-rectangles.

3. *Overlap*, i.e., the common space (in other words, the intersection of the volumes) of the two groups.

The split axis is chosen in the following way. For each axis, the MBRs are first sorted by their lower values and then their upper values. All the possible $(\beta - 2\alpha + 2)$ distributions of the $\beta + 1$ MBRs are then considered. The kth distribution has the first $(\alpha - 1 + k)$ MBRs in the first group and the rest $(\beta - \alpha + 2 - k)$ MBRs in the second group (k runs from 1 to $\beta - 2\alpha + 2$). For each such distribution, the three splitting parameters are then considered to compute the *goodness value.*

Experiments show that the best results are obtained when the split axis is chosen using the margin goodness value. However, for that split axis, the groups are partitioned best based on the overlap goodness value (to break ties, volume goodness value is used). The running time is of the order of $O(d.\beta \log \beta)$ where d is the number of dimensions.

4.5.3   Forced Re-Insertion

Due to the rather high costs of splitting, the R*-tree employs a forced re-insertion mechanism where instead of splitting a node immediately upon overflowing, p entries of it are re-inserted into the tree. To determine which p entries are to be re-inserted, the entries are sorted by the distances of their centers to the center of the overflowing MBR (with $\beta + 1$ entries). The time requirement is, thus, $O(\beta \log \beta)$.

The sorted list in *descending* order can start with the maximum distance (called *far reinsert*) or the minimum distance (called *close reinsert*) from the center. The first p entries from this list are removed, the MBR of the overflowing node is re-adjusted, and the p entries are re-inserted in the tree. The re-insertion is done only once to avoid an infinite loop. In other words, if all the p entries are again inserted back into the same node, it is then split.

While the increase in volume after the insertion is likely to be less for far reinsert, close reinsert makes it more probable that the new entry will be re-inserted in some other node as the volume of the original node reduces. Empirically, the best results are obtained for close reinsert with $p = 30\%$.

Key Concept 4.5 [R*-Tree]. R*-tree provides optimizations over the R-tree by using the criteria of overlap and margin of two nodes for insertion and splitting and by applying forced re-insertion of certain entries from an overflowing node.

4.6   R+-Tree

The R+-TREE [Sellis et al., 1987] was conceived as a balance between the space partitioning strategy of K-d-B-trees and the data partitioning strategy of R-trees. It aims to reduce the dead space problem of K-d-B trees by using indexing rectangles similar to R-trees. However, unlike an R-tree, siblings, i.e., children of a same parent are *disjoint*. This reduces the node overlap and ensures that a point query needs to follow only one path. Data objects that have an extent, i.e., non-point data objects, may be split into disjoint hyper-rectangles such that the union of them returns the original object. Each such part may be indexed by a separate child. Thus, a single data object may be stored in multiple leaves.

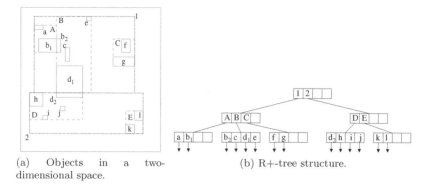

(a) Objects in a two-dimensional space.

(b) R+-tree structure.

Figure 4.8: An example of an R+-tree structure.

Additionally, an R+-tree relaxes the underflow restriction in a node, and therefore, may suffer from low space utilization.

Key Concept 4.6 [R+-Tree]. The R+-tree is an R-tree-like structure that constrains the child nodes to be disjoint. The constraint is enforced, if necessary, by even breaking the data objects into multiple parts. This guarantees a single path for a point query.

4.6.1   Structure

Figure 4.8 shows an example of a two-dimensional space with some data objects and how it is partitioned for an R+-tree. The figure can be compared against the corresponding R-tree in Figure 4.6. While node A in the R-tree contains the data object b completely, thereby overlapping with node B, the R+-tree avoids this overlap by breaking b into two separate data objects b_1 and b_2. While b_1 is indexed by node A, node B indexes b_2. As a result, nodes A and B now become disjoint. Similarly, the data object d is broken into two parts d_1 and d_2 which are indexed by completely different subtrees.

4.6.2   Discussion

Consider a query Q marked by a circle in Figure 4.9. While in the R-tree, both nodes 1 and 2 need to be searched since the query region overlaps with both of them, it is sufficient to search only node 2 in the R+-tree. In general, thus, there is a trade-off between searching overlapping nodes in an R-tree versus searching through an increased

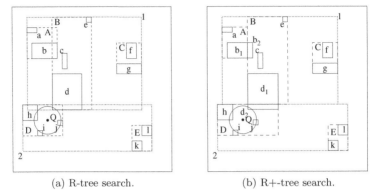

(a) R-tree search.   (b) R+-tree search.

Figure 4.9: Example of searching in an R-tree and its corresponding R+-tree.

height in an R+-tree. Results show that for most cases, R*-tree, if not the basic R-tree, outperforms R+-tree. Further, the maintenance operations (i.e., insertion and deletion) are much more complicated in an R+-tree, thereby making it not so popular.

4.7 Hilbert R-Tree

The HILBERT R-TREE [Kamel and Faloutsos, 1994] was proposed as a mix of B+-tree and R-tree. The main idea is to impart an ordering on data rectangles that guides how splits are handled. As argued in Section 2.5.3, since the Hilbert curve provides the best ordering for indexing purposes [Faloutsos and Roseman, 1989] (for a review of the properties of different space-filling curves, see Section 2.5), the Hilbert key is used.

The Hilbert R-tree has a similar structure to other R-trees. Every internal node stores its corresponding MBR. Additionally, it maintains its own Hilbert key value which is the *largest* Hilbert key value of all the data rectangles under its subtree. The Hilbert key value of a data object is taken to be the Hilbert key value of its center.

4.7.1 Splitting

The main difference of the Hilbert R-tree lies in the splitting algorithm. Instead of a 1-to-2 split in an R-tree where as soon as a node overflows, it is split into two new nodes, the Hilbert R-tree proposes an s-to-$(s + 1)$ split. In an s-to-$(s + 1)$ split, each node designates $s - 1$ sibling nodes as *co-operating sibling nodes*. When a node overflows, its contents are pushed into these co-operating sibling nodes. Only when all such s co-operating sibling nodes overflow, the entries in them are re-assigned to $s + 1$ new nodes.

Since every node has a Hilbert key value, all the siblings are ordered according to that, and the sibling nodes for a node are immediately identified. This split strategy also helps in increasing the average space utilization in a node.

Key Concept 4.7 [Hilbert R-Tree]. The largest Hilbert key of the contents of each MBR is recorded. When a node splits, its contents are inserted into certain sibling nodes that have close Hilbert key values. When all such sibling nodes overflow, an extra node is allocated and the contents are re-assigned.

The choice of s for the split strategy depends on two factors. Increasing s increases space utilization, but simultaneously increases the insertion cost as well. Overall, $s = 2$, i.e., a 2-to-3 split, is determined to be the best empirically.

During insertion, the node to insert is chosen as the one having the minimum largest Hilbert key value greater than the Hilbert key of the entry. This ensures that the entry gets inserted in a node where the increase in volume is low.

4.7.2   Discussion

Hilbert R-trees perform better than R*-trees, especially when the data is skewed, i.e., non-uniform. However, the performance deteriorates rapidly for higher dimensions as the property of nearby objects in space enjoying proximity in the Hilbert key ordering, gets less respected.

4.8   SS-Tree

The SS-TREE [White and Jain, 1996] index structure uses *minimum bounding spheres* (MBSs) to cover the children nodes. The center of the sphere is the centroid of the spheres representing the children nodes (weighted by the number of data objects in the children) and the radius

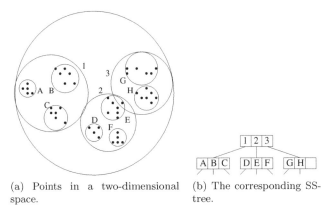

(a) Points in a two-dimensional space.

(b) The corresponding SS-tree.

Figure 4.10: An example of an SS-tree.

is the most tight one that covers all the underlying data objects. Each node also maintains an additional information: the number of objects in its subtree.

Due to lesser storage requirements, the fanout of an SS-tree is higher than that of an R-tree. Consider a d-dimensional setting. The storage of a hyper-rectangle requires $2d$ parameters, the lowest and highest along each dimension, while that of a hyper-sphere requires only $d + 1$ parameters, d for the coordinates of the center and 1 for the radius. Thus, the fanout is roughly twice in an SS-tree as almost two times the number of spheres can be packed in the same amount of storage. When the number of data objects is large, this allows the tree to have a smaller height, thereby saving random disc accesses per query.

Key Concept 4.8 [SS-Tree]. An SS-tree uses minimum bounding hyper-spheres. Since specifying a hyper-sphere requires lesser amount of data than a hyper-rectangle, the fanout of an SS-tree is larger than an R-tree and, therefore, the height is potentially lesser.

Figure 4.10 shows an example of an SS-tree. Note how the children of an SS-tree node can have considerable volume overlap. This is due to the property of spheres (see the discussion in the next section on SR-trees). However, SS-tree nodes generally have shorter diameters. Thus, while SS-trees have regions with shorter diameters, R*-trees have regions with smaller volumes.

The algorithms of insertion, splitting and searching are similar to

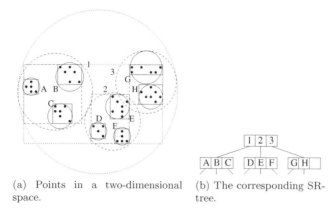

(a) Points in a two-dimensional space.

(b) The corresponding SR-tree.

Figure 4.11: An example of an SR-tree.

that of an R*-tree except that the split axis is chosen based on the one having the largest variance.

4.9   SR-Tree

The analysis of the two most regular high-dimensional geometric shapes, namely, rectangles and spheres, reveals certain interesting facts. Assuming a data space of $[0, 1]^d$, the diameter of both the shapes can be at most $\sqrt{d}$. While with this diameter, the volume of the hyper-rectangle remains 1, that of the hyper-sphere can be very large (for a diameter of $\sqrt{d}$, the volume is $\frac{(\sqrt{d}/2)^d \pi^{d/2}}{\Gamma(d/2+1)} \gg 1$). For a particular subset of data, hyper-spheres generally have shorter diameters, though. Ideally, therefore, an index node should have shorter diameter regions of spheres and smaller volume regions of rectangles.

The SR-TREE [Katayama and Satoh, 1997] realizes this idea by using *both* bounding spheres and bounding rectangles in the index node. Figure 4.11b shows an example of an SR-tree for the two-dimensional space of Figure 4.11a. The actual index region is the *intersection* of the two shapes although it is not maintained explicitly; rather, whenever a computation is required, it is checked against *both* the bounding sphere and the bounding rectangle. This results in a much tighter index as shown in Figure 4.12. The savings in space are larger for the internal nodes that

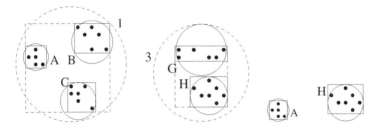

Figure 4.12: Internal nodes in an SR-tree.

are higher up in the tree. For example, in Figure 4.12, the intersections in nodes 1 and 3 are tighter in comparison to nodes A and H.

4.9.1   Structure

Each internal node of an SR-tree maintains the MBR, the MBS, and the number of data objects per child entry. The centroid of the MBS is the weighted average of the centroids of the children. The radius is maintained as the *minimum* of maximum distances to bounding spheres of child nodes and bounding rectangles of child nodes. This results in a tighter radius than an SS-tree. The MBR is computed the same way as in an R-tree.

Since both spheres and rectangles are explicitly maintained, the storage per child requires $3d+1$ parameters for a d-dimensional setting. The storage cost is, thus, roughly 1.5 times that of an R-tree and 3 times that of an SS-tree. Consequently, the fanout is much lower, thereby potentially resulting in a tree with a greater height.

Example 4.5 [R-Tree, SS-Tree and SR-Tree Fanouts]. What is the maximum fanout of an internal node for an R-tree, an SS-tree and an SR-tree indexing 5-dimensional values of 8 bytes each with child pointers of size 4 bytes for a page size of 4 KB? Assume that integers require 4 bytes of storage.

Table 4.3 shows the calculations.

For example, consider an index entry in the SR-tree. The corresponding child pointer requires 4 bytes. The specification of the lower and higher values of the 5 dimensions of the MBR requires 80 bytes while that for the radius and the 5 dimensions of the center of the MBS requires 48 bytes. In addition, storing an integer for the number of objects takes up 4 more bytes of storage. In total, this requires 136 bytes. The fanout, therefore, can be at most 30.   □

Table 4.3: Fanouts of R-tree, SS-tree, and SR-tree (all sizes are in bytes).

Tree	R-tree	SS-tree	SR-tree
Child pointer	4	4	4
Bounding rectangle	$2 \times 5 \times 8 = 80$	-	$2 \times 5 \times 8 = 80$
Bounding sphere	-	$5 \times 8 + 8 = 48$	$5 \times 8 + 8 = 48$
Number of objects	-	4	4
Total size	84	56	136
Fanout	$\lfloor 4096/84 \rfloor = 48$	$\lfloor 4096/56 \rfloor = 73$	$\lfloor 4096/136 \rfloor = 30$

Key Concept 4.9 [SR-Tree]. An SR-tree contains both minimum bounding hyper-rectangles and minimum bounding hyper-spheres. The probability of searching through a node is lesser than an R-tree and an SS-tree as it is accessed only if the query region intersects both the geometries.

4.9.2 Searching

The volume of an index node, by definition, is less than that of a minimum bounding sphere or a minimum bounding rectangle as it is the intersection of the two. Thus, during a query, the chances of overlapping between the sibling nodes, i.e., the probability of a search proceeding to two or more siblings is less.

During searching, the minimum distance from a query object to an index node is the *maximum* of the minimum distances of the query object to the bounding sphere and the bounding rectangle. Similarly, the maximum distance from a query object is the *minimum* of the maximum distances to the bounding sphere and the bounding rectangle. By design, these estimates provide better lower and upper bounds of the actual distance to the query object.

Due to a higher fanout, the number of internal node accesses are typically more than that in an R-tree or an SS-tree. However, the tighter index nodes results in fewer number of leaf node accesses, thereby ultimately leading to a more efficient overall search performance.

4.9.3   Discussion

The SR-tree has more complicated routines for insertion, deletion, updating, etc., since both the geometries need to be handled. In higher dimensions, the hyper-spheres tend to be less effective than the hyper-rectangles due to larger volumes. In other words, the volumes of hyper-spheres become so large due to their exponential behavior with the dimensionality that almost all the query regions intersect. Consequently, their utility in pruning becomes extremely low.

4.10   P-Tree

The P-TREE [Jagadish, 1990] is a generalized hierarchical index structure where the index geometry is an arbitrary *bounding polyhedron* defined by several hyperplanes. However, in order to make it tractable, the hyperplanes are constrained to be normal to only certain orientation vectors. The number of such orientation vectors defines the size of each index entry.

A P-tree is a generic concept. For example, an R-tree in a d-dimensional space can be considered as a P-tree where the orientation vectors are the d axes.

A particularly useful version of P-tree that saves a lot of overlaps uses $2d$ orientation vectors by choosing the d diagonals in addition to the d axes.

Although the overlap is less, determining whether the query hyper-rectangle intersects with an index polyhedron requires complex computations. To avoid that, the index polyhedron in the d-dimensional *attribute space* is mapped to a hyper-rectangle in an m-dimensional *orientation space* where m is generally the number of orientation vectors used. The mapping is such that two convex polyhedra intersect in the attribute space if and only if the corresponding hyper-rectangles intersect in the orientation space. In essence, it becomes an m-dimensional space.

Key Concept 4.10 [P-Tree]. The P-tree uses convex polygons defined by the axes and the diagonals as index bounding boxes. The intersection tests are done by mapping the space to a new space where the orientation vectors of the original space (i.e., the diagonals and the axes) become the basis vectors.

A useful feature of P-tree is that orientation vectors may be added or deleted with no change in the index hierarchy. However, when the orientation vectors change, it is better to re-organize the data.

4.11 Bulk-Loading

Almost all the disk-based index structures discussed in this chapter are dynamic in nature in the sense that they allow insertion operations fairly efficiently. Thus, the naïve way of constructing an index structure given a large collection of objects is to insert them one by one. While this builds a valid structure that helps in efficient searching, the potential of the index structure is rarely fully realized using such a method.

The reasons are two-fold. First, the space utilization is poor. Second and more importantly, the organization of the objects is not done well and has many overlaps.

Bulk-loading structures address these deficiencies by considering the whole dataset at once. Most bottom-up construction methods that first decide on the layout of the leaf nodes by clustering the data can be considered as bulk-loading methods.

4.11.1 Generic Framework

The generic setting is as follows. There are a total of n objects that need to be packed. A data page has a capacity of at most c objects. Assuming the tightest packing, the least number of data pages required is, therefore, $p = \lceil n/c \rceil$.

Using some criterion (such as clustering), the n objects are packed into these p pages at the bottom-most level of the index structure. For the next level, the bounding geometries of these p pages act as the basic objects and are recursively packed into $\lceil p/c \rceil$ pages and so on till the root is created.

The packing criteria differs between different methods. A very simple method was used by [Roussopoulos and Leifker, 1985] where the objects were ordered by their first dimensions and sequences of c objects were chosen to fill the pages one by one. While for point objects, the first dimension has no ambiguity, for extended objects such as hyper-rectangles, it was not made clear how the first dimension was chosen (whether it was the lower end or the higher end). Consequently, it was assumed to be the center by the authors of [Leutenegger et al., 1997].

Objects were ordered according to their Hilbert key values by [Kamel and Faloutsos, 1993]. In general, Hilbert keys provide a better ordering

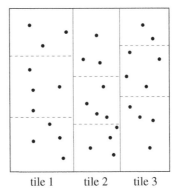

tile 1   tile 2   tile 3

Figure 4.13: Example of STR bulk-loading algorithm.

than using only one dimension. However, when the dimensionality becomes large, a single Hilbert ordering fails to capture the spatial locality of the objects well.

4.11.2   STR Algorithm

The SORT-TILE-RECURSIVE (STR) algorithm provides an alternative way of ordering the objects [Leutenegger et al., 1997]. Each object is represented by its center point.

For the simplest two-dimensional case, the objects are first ordered by the x dimension. The range of the x dimension is sliced into $s = \lceil \sqrt{p} \rceil$ partitions where $p = \lceil n/c \rceil$. The split points, i.e., the vertical split axes are chosen in a manner such that each partition (called *tile*) contains $\lceil n/s \rceil$ objects. The last partition, of course, may contain fewer objects.

Each such partition is then re-partitioned according to the y dimension. Once more, the number of partitions chosen is s. Considering $\lceil n/s \rceil$ objects per tile, this packs at most $\lceil n/s^2 \rceil = \lceil n/p \rceil = c$ objects in each page.

Note that this method keeps the pages disjoint, i.e., they do not have any overlap. Consequently, the search becomes much more efficient.

Moreover, the space utilization is 100% for most of the pages.

Figure 4.13 shows an example with $n = 32$ point objects and a page capacity of $c = 4$. Although the tightest packing is possible in $p = 8$ pages, the packing is done in $s = \lceil \sqrt{8} \rceil = 3$ tiles along the x dimension and 3 tiles along the y dimension, producing a total of 9 pages.

The method for a d-dimensional space is a generalization of the above procedure. The objects are initially sorted according to the first dimension. Then, $s' = \lceil p^{\frac{1}{d}} \rceil$ partitions are created such that each slice contains

$n/s' = c.p^{\frac{d-1}{d}}$ objects. Each such partition is next considered as a $(d-1)$-dimensional dataset with n/s' objects. The process is recursively followed to complete the partitioning in all the d dimensions.

4.11.3 Bulk-Loading in High Dimensions

In high dimensions, it was noticed by [Berchtold et al., 1998a] that the above algorithms do not perform satisfactorily due to the *curse of dimensionality* (see Chapter 7 for a discussion). The situation is more serious when the splits are binary and the data is divided equally between the partitions. This is due to the fact that most high-dimensional data tend to reside towards the borders.

Consequently, [Berchtold et al., 1998a] suggested an interesting split procedure that divides the data into three parts according to a parameter f which is a fraction $\in [0, 1]$. The first f objects and the last f objects form the two extreme partitions while the middle $(1 - 2f)$ objects complete the third one. The above procedure produces better results in higher dimensions by countering the border effect.

Part IV

Distances

Chapter 5

Distance Functions

Most of the similarity search queries studied so far assume that the dissimilarity function between two objects is the standard Euclidean distance. In many specialized applications such as for text, images, videos, etc., this does not work as well. In this chapter, we discuss various distance functions that can be applied to myriad such cases, and their properties. We begin with a definition of metric distances and metric spaces.

5.1 Metric Spaces

A set of elements $\mathcal{M}$ with a distance function $\mathcal{D} : \mathcal{M} \times \mathcal{M} \to \mathcal{R}_+^0$ forms a METRIC SPACE and the function $\mathcal{D}$ is a METRIC DISTANCE if it satisfies the following four properties:

1. *Non-negativity*: $\forall x, y \in \mathcal{M}, \ \mathcal{D}(x, y) \geq 0$

2. *Identity*: $\forall x, y \in \mathcal{M}, \ \mathcal{D}(x, y) = 0 \iff x = y$

3. *Symmetry*: $\forall x, y \in \mathcal{M}, \ \mathcal{D}(x, y) = \mathcal{D}(y, x)$

4. *Triangular Inequality*: $\forall x, y, z \in \mathcal{M}, \ \mathcal{D}(x, y) + \mathcal{D}(y, z) \geq \mathcal{D}(x, z)$

Examples of metric distances are L_p norms that include Euclidean and Manhattan distances. The first condition can be derived from the other three conditions, i.e., a distance that follows identity, symmetry, and triangular inequality, also follows non-negativity.

A distance that does not follow the identity condition but obeys the other two, i.e., symmetry and triangular inequality, is called a *pseudo-metric* distance. If only symmetry is violated, then it is called a *quasi-metric* distance, and if only triangular inequality is violated, it is called a *semimetric* distance.

5.2 L_p Norm

The L_p NORM (also known as the MINKOWSKI NORM or the MINKOWSKI DISTANCE) is one of the most basic distance measures:

$$L_p(x, y) = \left[\sum_{i=1}^{k} (|x_i - y_i|)^p \right]^{1/p} \tag{5.1}$$

The two most common and useful special cases are the L_2 and the L_1 norms better known as the EUCLIDEAN DISTANCE and the MANHATTAN DISTANCE (or CITY-BLOCK DISTANCE) respectively. Two other interesting cases are the L_∞ and the $L_{-\infty}$ norms which become the MAXIMUM and the MINIMUM distances respectively:

$$L_\infty(x, y) = \max_{i=1}^{k} (|x_i - y_i|) \tag{5.2}$$

$$L_{-\infty}(x, y) = \min_{i=1}^{k} (|x_i - y_i|) \tag{5.3}$$

For any $1 \le p < \infty$, the L_p norm is a *metric* distance. Also, as p increases, the L_p norm decreases, i.e., $L_q \le L_p$ for $q \ge p$.

While the L_p norm is the most commonly used measure, it suffers from the fact that if one of the dimensions is more varied and has larger differences, the overall distance gets dominated by this dimension. To counter this, the L_p norm allows each dimension to be weighted as well:

$$WL_p(x, y) = \left[\sum_{i=1}^{k} (w_i |x_i - y_i|)^p \right]^{1/p} \tag{5.4}$$

where w_i is the weight on dimension i. The WEIGHTED L_p NORM is also a *metric* distance.

5.2.1 Normalized Euclidean Distance

Since it is not always easy to "guess" the weights, one particularly useful way of normalizing the distance is by first normalizing the dimensions themselves and then taking the L_p norm of it. For the Euclidean distance, this is known as the NORMALIZED EUCLIDEAN DISTANCE:

$$ED_N(x, y) = \left[\sum_{i=1}^{k} (x_i' - y_i')^2 \right]^{1/2} \tag{5.5}$$

where x' and y' are the normalized object vectors. Each dimension x_i is normalized by using the mean μ_i and standard deviation σ_i (see Section D.3 in the appendix for the definitions) across dimension i of all the objects, i.e.,

$$x'_i = \frac{x_i - \mu_i}{\sigma_i} \tag{5.6}$$

The normalized Euclidean distance is again a *metric*.

5.3 Quadratic Form Distance

The L_p norm measures consider the dimensions of the objects to be independent, and consequently, there is no connection or cross-talk among them. However, for some applications such as image processing, the dimensions can be related. The relationships among the k dimensions can be represented as a $k \times k$ matrix A where A_{ij} denotes the *similarity* of dimension i with dimension j. Using this, the QUADRATIC FORM DISTANCE (QFD) between two object vectors $\vec{x}$ and $\vec{y}$ is defined as

$$Q(\vec{x}, \vec{y}) = \sqrt{(\vec{x} - \vec{y})^T A (\vec{x} - \vec{y})} \tag{5.7}$$

For the distances to make sense, i.e., they are non-negative, the matrix A must be positive semi-definite (see Section C.3 for the definition). If the matrix A is just an identity matrix, then Q is the Euclidean distance; if it is diagonal, then it is the weighted Euclidean distance with the diagonals defining the weights.

QFD is a *metric* distance if A is symmetric and positive definite.

5.3.1 Mahalanobis Distance

If the matrix A in QFD is replaced by the inverse of the covariance matrix (see Section D.3) between all the dimensions, then the resulting distance is the MAHALANOBIS DISTANCE [Mahalanobis, 1936]:

$$M(\vec{x}, \vec{y}) = \sqrt{(\vec{x} - \vec{y})^T \Sigma^{-1} (\vec{x} - \vec{y})} \tag{5.8}$$

where $\vec{x}$ and $\vec{y}$ are two object vectors.

While the locus of points having the same Euclidean distance forms a circle, those having the same weighted Euclidean distance forms an

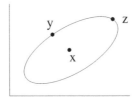

Figure 5.1: Locus of points having the same Mahalanobis distance: $M(x, y) = M(x, z)$.

axis-oriented ellipse, and the locus of points having the same Mahalanobis distance forms an ellipse whose axes are oriented according to the covariance values (Figure 5.1).

When Σ^{-1} is diagonal, i.e., there is no correlation among the dimensions and they are independent, the Mahalanobis distance is equivalent to the normalized Euclidean distance. Since the inverse of the covariance matrix is symmetric and positive definite, the Mahalanobis distance is a *metric* distance.

5.4   Cosine Similarity

The cosine of the angle between two vectors can be measured using their *dot product*. The resulting similarity measure is called the COSINE SIMILARITY [Manning et al., 2008]. Between two vectors $\vec{x}$ and $\vec{y}$ of dimensionality d, it is defined as

$$cos(\vec{x}, \vec{y}) = \frac{\vec{x}.\vec{y}}{\|\vec{x}\|_2.\|\vec{y}\|_2} = \frac{\sum_{i=1}^{d}(x_i.y_i)}{\sqrt{\sum_{i=1}^{d} x_i^2}.\sqrt{\sum_{i=1}^{d} y_i^2}} \qquad (5.9)$$

where $\|\cdot\|_2$ denotes the L_2 norm of a vector (see Section C.1 for the definition). The cosine similarity between two vectors is always constrained to be between -1 and $+1$. A value of -1 indicates that the two vectors are exactly opposite to each other, i.e., they are completely dissimilar, while $+1$ indicates that they are exactly aligned, i.e., completely similar. When the cosine similarity is 0, it indicates that the vectors are perpendicular to each other and can be considered as independent.

Note that since this is just a similarity measure, it is up to the particular application to convert this into a distance function. A simple way is to subtract it from 1 and then scale by $\frac{1}{2}$ to obtain a distance measure between 0 and 1, called the COSINE DISTANCE:

$$\mathcal{D}_{cos}(\vec{x}, \vec{y}) = \frac{1 - cos(\vec{x}, \vec{y})}{2} \tag{5.10}$$

This is *not* a *metric* distance.

The ANGULAR SIMILARITY is obtained from the cosine similarity in the following way:

$$angular(\vec{x}, \vec{y}) = cos^{-1}(cos(\vec{x}, \vec{y})) \tag{5.11}$$

The ANGULAR DISTANCE obtained from it is

$$\mathcal{D}_{angular}(\vec{x}, \vec{y}) = \frac{1 - cos^{-1}(cos(\vec{x}, \vec{y}))}{\pi} \tag{5.12}$$

This is a *metric* distance.

5.5 Statistical Distance Measures

The statistical distance measures are mostly used to measure the dissimilarity between probability distributions (see Section D.2 in the appendix for a brief description of probability distributions). Therefore, a common assumption is that the values of the dimensions in each vector represent probabilities and add up to 1.

5.5.1 Entropy-Based Measures

An important concept in this regard is that of *entropy* of a probability distribution which measures the expected information content in bits. For a probability distribution vector $x = \{x_1, x_2, \ldots, x_d\}$ where $\sum_{i=1}^{d} x_i = 1$, the entropy is defined as

$$Entropy(x) = -\sum_{i=1}^{d}(x_i \log_2 x_i) \tag{5.13}$$

Based on the entropy, there are two important distance measures which are described next.

5.5.1.1 Kullback-Leibler Divergence

The KULLBACK-LEIBLER DIVERGENCE MEASURE, also known as RELATIVE ENTROPY or INFORMATION DIVERGENCE, between two vectors $\vec{x}$ and $\vec{y}$ measures the inefficiency of representing the information content in $\vec{x}$ using $\vec{y}$ in number of bits or, in other words, the change in entropy required to transform $\vec{x}$ to $\vec{y}$ [Kullback, 1959]:

$$KL(\vec{x}, \vec{y}) = \sum_{i=1}^{d} (x_i \log_2(x_i/y_i)) \qquad (5.14)$$

The KL divergence measure is *not* a *metric* distance; it is not even symmetric. For arbitrary distributions, the measure is unbounded.

5.5.1.2   Jensen-Shannon Divergence

The JENSEN-SHANNON DIVERGENCE or the INFORMATION RADIUS makes the KL distance symmetric by considering the average divergence to the average distribution [Schütze and Manning, 1999], i.e.,

$$JS(\vec{x}, \vec{y}) = \frac{KL\left(\vec{x}, \frac{\vec{x}+\vec{y}}{2}\right) + KL\left(\vec{y}, \frac{\vec{x}+\vec{y}}{2}\right)}{2} \qquad (5.15)$$

It still does *not* become a metric distance although it becomes bounded.

The JEFFREY DIVERGENCE is defined as twice that of the JS divergence measure [Endres and Schindelin, 2003]. The JENSEN-SHANNON DISTANCE, defined as the square root of the Jensen-Shannon divergence, is a *metric*. Similarly, the square root of the Jeffrey divergence measure is also a *metric* distance [Österreicher and Vajda, 2003].

5.5.2   Bhattacharyya Coefficient

The BHATTACHARYYA COEFFICIENT [Bhattacharyya, 1943] between two vectors $\vec{x} = \{x_1, x_2, \ldots, x_d\}$ and $\vec{y} = \{y_1, y_2, \ldots, y_d\}$ measures the *cosine* of the angle between the direction cosine vectors $(\sqrt{x_1}, \ldots, \sqrt{x_d})$ and $(\sqrt{y_1}, \ldots, \sqrt{y_d})$ and is, thus, essentially the dot product of the two direction cosine vectors:

$$BC(\vec{x}, \vec{y}) = \cos(\sqrt{x}, \sqrt{y}) = \sum_{i=1}^{d} \sqrt{x_i . y_i} \qquad (5.16)$$

Based on this, two distance measures, HELLINGER DISTANCE and BHATTACHARYYA DISTANCE, are defined:

$$H(x, y) = \sqrt{1 - BC(x, y)} \qquad (5.17)$$
$$B(x, y) = -\ln BC(x, y) \qquad (5.18)$$

While the Hellinger distance is a *metric*, the Bhattacharyya distance is *not*.

5.6 Distances between Sets of Objects

While most of the distances assume that the objects are vectors of a fixed dimensionality, in many applications, it is useful to extend the notion of distance to sets of objects.

5.6.1 Jaccard Coefficient

For two sets of objects A and B, the JACCARD COEFFICIENT or the JACCARD INDEX is the number of common objects normalized by the total number of objects in the two sets [Manning et al., 2008]:

$$JS(A, B) = \frac{|A \cap B|}{|A \cup B|} \qquad (5.19)$$

Using this, the JACCARD DISTANCE is defined:

$$J(A, B) = 1 - JS(A, B) = \frac{|A \cup B| - |A \cap B|}{|A \cup B|} \qquad (5.20)$$

The distance is always between 0 and 1 and is a *metric*.

5.6.2 Pairwise Distances

The pairwise distances, unlike the Jaccard coefficient, utilize the distance between the objects to define distance measures for sets of objects. The two most intuitive ones are AVERAGE PAIRWISE DISTANCE and MINIMUM PAIRWISE DISTANCE [Bhattacharya et al., 2010]:

$$APD(A, B) = \frac{\sum_{\forall a \in A, \forall b \in B} \mathcal{D}(a, b)}{(|A|.|B|)} \qquad (5.21)$$

$$MPD(A, B) = \min_{\forall a \in A, \forall b \in B} \{\mathcal{D}(a, b)\} \qquad (5.22)$$

Although the average pairwise distance follows the symmetry and the triangular inequality, it is *not* a metric in the strictest sense as the self-distance can be greater than zero, i.e., $APD(A, A) > 0$. It is, thus, a *pseudometric*. The minimum pairwise distance, on the other hand, follows symmetry and identity, but does not obey the triangular inequality and is, hence, only a *semimetric* and *not* a metric distance.

5.6.2.1   Hausdorff Distance

A particularly interesting pairwise distance is the HAUSDORFF DIS-TANCE [Munkres, 1999]:

$$DH(A, B) = \max_{\forall a \in A} \left\{ \min_{\forall b \in B} \mathcal{D}(a, b) \right\} \qquad (5.23)$$

The basic definition of this distance (also called the *directed* Hausdorff distance) is not symmetric and, hence *not* a *metric*.

The Hausdorff distance is made symmetric by extending it in the following way:

$$H(A, B) = \max \left\{ DH(A, B), DH(B, A) \right\} \qquad (5.24)$$

$$= \max \left\{ \max_{\forall a \in A} \left\{ \min_{\forall b \in B} \mathcal{D}(a, b) \right\} \right\} \qquad (5.25)$$

The *symmetric* Hausdorff distance is still *not* a *metric* distance.

5.7   Earth Mover's Distance

Most distance measures only take into account the feature value and not the feature location. Even the Mahalanobis distance takes into account only the correlations between the feature dimensions, but not whether the dimensions are adjacent or close by. A notable exception is the EARTH MOVER'S DISTANCE (EMD) that not only takes into account the feature value but also which dimension the feature value comes from, i.e., the feature location [Rubner et al., 2000]. As a result, the EMD is particularly useful for retrieving similar images, trees, music, shapes, etc.

EMD considers each feature value as "mass" in the spatial location corresponding to the feature dimension. The distance between spatial locations is called the *ground distance*. The EMD distance between two objects X and Y is the minimum "work" required to *transform* X to Y where one unit of work is equivalent to moving one unit of mass through one unit of ground distance. There are many formulations of EMD that are either equivalent or very close to each other. We use a generic one due to [Ljosa et al., 2006].

Suppose objects X and Y have m and n features respectively. The ground distance matrix $\mathcal{C}$ then is of size $m \times n$ where $\mathcal{C}_{ij}$ denotes the ground distance from the ith feature location of X to the jth feature location of Y. Similarly, there is a "flow" matrix $\mathcal{F}$ of size $m \times n$ between X and Y such that the $\mathcal{F}_{ij}^{\text{th}}$ entry corresponds to the amount of mass moved from spatial region (or location) i of X to spatial region (or location) j of Y.

The flows are not unconstrained, though. The sum of all flows coming out of a region in X must add up to the total amount of mass it started with, i.e., $\sum_{j=1}^{n} \mathcal{F}_{ij} = x_i$ where x_i denotes the mass (or feature value) at the ith region of X. Similarly, the sum of all flows going to a region in Y must add up to the total amount of mass it needs to end up with, i.e., $\sum_{i=1}^{m} \mathcal{F}_{ij} = y_j$ where y_j denotes the mass (or feature value) at the jth region of Y.

The total work done is calculated as the sum of the products of the corresponding $(i,j)^{\text{th}}$ entries of $\mathcal{C}$ and $\mathcal{F}$, i.e., $W = \sum_{i=1}^{m} \sum_{j=1}^{n} (\mathcal{C}_{ij} . \mathcal{F}_{ij})$.

The ground distance matrix is part of the input, i.e., it must be specified by the application or the user. The EMD finds the flow matrix such that the total work done is the *minimum*. The amount of this *minimum* total work is the EMD distance between X and Y:

$$EMD(X,Y) = \min_{\mathcal{F}} \sum_{i=1}^{m} \sum_{j=1}^{n} (\mathcal{C}_{ij} . \mathcal{F}_{ij}) \tag{5.26}$$

$$\text{s.t. } \forall i, j, \mathcal{F}_{ij} \geq 0; \tag{5.27}$$

$$\forall i, \sum_{j=1}^{n} \mathcal{F}_{ij} = x_i; \tag{5.28}$$

$$\forall j, \sum_{i=1}^{m} \mathcal{F}_{ij} = y_j \tag{5.29}$$

Strictly speaking, the EMD is from X to Y, i.e., it is *directed*. However, if it is symmetric, we can say that it is between X and Y.

Example 5.1 [EMD]. Suppose X and Y are two images whose feature values are as shown in Figure 5.2a. The ground distance matrix is encoded as $\mathcal{C}$. Find the flows in F and compute the corresponding EMD.

The solution is shown in Figure 5.2b. The EMD is $1 \times 2 + 1.4 \times 2 + 1 \times 2 = 6.8$. □

The EMD is a *metric* distance provided the ground distance matrix obeys identity and symmetry. Interestingly, the property of triangular inequality is not critical, as the EMD tries to find a *minimum* path from one object to another. The minimum path property ensures that the mass from region i to region j will flow along the minimum ground distance regions, even if it is not a direct flow. This also ensures that the triangular inequality will be obeyed.

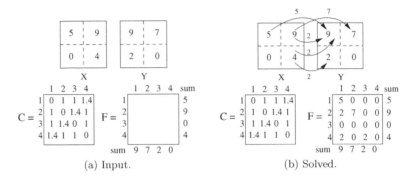

(a) Input.   (b) Solved.

Figure 5.2: Example of EMD calculation.

5.7.1 Generalized Earth Mover's Distance

The EMD formulation of Eq. (5.26) needs to satisfy two assumptions. First, the mass in each region needs to be positive, i.e., the feature values need to be positive. While this is not true for most features, the problem can be easily circumvented by translating the entire range of values by a suitable constant so that the feature values become positive, i.e., for all feature values f, the transformed value will be $f' = f + L \geq 0$ where L is a large positive constant.

The second assumption, that being the total amount of mass in both the source and the target object needing to be the same, is more vital. This arises since the rows and the columns of the flow matrix should add up to the same number. In many applications, a simple normalization (e.g., the feature values adding up to 1) works. However, in certain cases such as for image color histograms, the normalization may render two very different images such as a completely gray and a completely white image to the same object, and the whole notion of dissimilarity fails.

The solution was provided in [Ljosa et al., 2006] by introducing a special region per object, called the "bank". While computing the EMD between X and Y, the "bank" region of X is assumed to have a feature whose value is the *sum* of feature values of all the regions in Y, and vice versa. Denoting these special regions as the $(m + 1)^{\text{th}}$ and $(n + 1)^{\text{th}}$ regions of X and Y respectively, the feature values are $x_{m+1} = \sum_{j=1}^{n} y_j$ and $y_{n+1} = \sum_{i=1}^{m} x_i$. Obviously, the sums of the features in both objects now become equal.

The sizes of the ground distance matrix and flow matrix become $(m+1) \times (n+1)$. The bank-to-bank distance is set to zero, i.e., $\mathcal{C}_{(m+1(n+1)} = 0$ while the distance from the bank to any other region is denoted by the

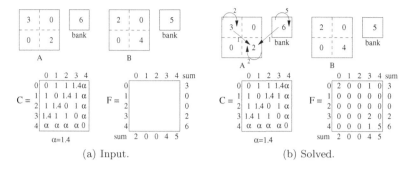

(a) Input. (b) Solved.

Figure 5.3: Example of generalized EMD calculation.

parameter α. The rest of the EMD formulation remains the same:

$$EMD(X,Y,\alpha) = \min_{\mathcal{F}} \sum_{i=1}^{m+1} \sum_{j=1}^{n+1} (\mathcal{C}_{ij}.\mathcal{F}_{ij}) \tag{5.30}$$

$$\text{s.t. } \forall i, j, \mathcal{F}_{ij} \geq 0; \tag{5.31}$$

$$\forall i, \sum_{j=1}^{n+1} \mathcal{F}_{ij} = x_i; \tag{5.32}$$

$$\forall j, \sum_{i=1}^{m+1} \mathcal{F}_{ij} = y_j \tag{5.33}$$

Example 5.2 [Generalized EMD]. Suppose A and B are two images whose feature values are as shown in Figure 5.3a. The ground distance matrix is encoded as $\mathcal{C}$ with the bank distance parameter as α. Find the flows in F and compute the corresponding EMD.

The solution is shown in Figure 5.3b. The EMD is $1 \times 1.4 + \alpha \times 1 = 1.4 + \alpha$. □

The generalized EMD is a *metric* if the ground distance matrix follows identity and symmetry.

5.7.2 Match Distance

The MATCH DISTANCE [Werman et al., 1985, Peleg et al., 1989] is a special type of earth mover's distance for one-dimensional histograms. For two histograms x and y with d bins each, the ground distance between two bins i and j is $\mathcal{C}_{ij} = |i - j|$. The "mass" in the two histograms should add up to the same number. The match distance, consequently, is very useful for defining the distance between discrete probability distributions (see Section D.2) and color histograms.

Although the match distance can be posed as a minimization problem in the form of EMD, it can be shown that it is equivalent to the L_1 distance between the *cumulative* histograms of x and y, i.e.,

$$MD(x, y) = L_1(X, Y) \tag{5.34}$$

where $\forall i = 1 \ldots d, \; X_i = \sum_{j=1}^{i} x_j, \; Y_i = \sum_{j=1}^{i} y_j$. The match distance is a *metric* distance.

Example 5.3 [Match Distance]. Find the match distance between the two histograms x and y:

$$x = \{0.2, 0.3, 0.4, 0.1\} \qquad y = \{0.5, 0.1, 0.0, 0.4\}$$

The cumulative distributions are

$$X = \{0.2, 0.5, 0.9, 1.0\} \qquad Y = \{0.5, 0.6, 0.6, 1.0\}$$

Hence, the match distance is $0.3 + 0.1 + 0.3 + 0.0 = 0.7$.   □

5.8   Edit Distance

Some applications require comparing words or strings of characters. A direct way of computing the dissimilarity between strings is by using the EDIT DISTANCE [Navarro, 2001] (the most common variant of which is the LEVENSHTEIN DISTANCE [Levenshtein, 1965]). The strings are composed of characters from a fixed alphabet set Σ of size m.

The basic version of edit distance is defined as the *minimum* number of "edit" operations needed to transform string x to string y. There are three types of edit operations defined on the characters:

- *Insertion* of character c

- *Deletion* of character c

- *Substitution* of character c by character d

Augmenting the alphabet set Σ by a special "gap" symbol (say #) allows the insertion and deletion to be modeled uniformly as substitution operations: insertion is substituting # by c while deletion is substituting c by #.

The edit distance between two strings x and y is $ED(|x|, |y|)$ where $ED(i, j)$ for substrings $x[1, \ldots, i]$ and $y[1, \ldots, j]$ is defined as

$$ED(i, j) = \begin{cases} 0 & \text{if } i = j = 0 \\ j & \text{if } i = 0 \\ i & \text{if } j = 0 \\ \min \begin{cases} ED(i-1, j) & + & 1, \\ ED(i, j-1) & + & 1, \\ ED(i-1, j-1) & + & I_{x_i \neq y_j} \end{cases} & \text{otherwise} \end{cases}$$

(5.35)

where I_δ is the *indicator* function: I is 1 only when δ is *true*; otherwise $I = 0$.

The first three cases are boundary conditions. In the minimization block, the first term represents insertion, the second deletion, and the third substitution. The formulation is readily solved using dynamic programming.

Example 5.4 [Edit Distance]. Find the edit distance between the strings `idea` and `deem`.

The transformation can be shown as

```
idea#
#deem
```

The 3 substitutions are `i` by `#`, `a` by `e`, and `#` by `m`. Therefore, the edit distance is 3. □

As illustrated by the above example, it is not necessary to align the two strings and insertions and deletions are freely allowed. Further, it is important to note that a different set of edit operations can also lead to the same minimum cost. The basic edit distance is a *metric* distance.

5.8.1 Hamming Distance

The HAMMING DISTANCE is a special type of edit distance defined only between strings having the *same* length [Hamming, 1950]. It is simply defined as the number of mismatches (i.e., substitutions) when the two strings are aligned.

Example 5.5 [Hamming Distance]. Find the Hamming distance between the strings `idea` and `deem`.

The alignment between the strings is

Table 5.1: Cost matrix for generalized edit distance.

	A	T	G	C	#
A	0	1	2	2	3
T	1	0	2	2	3
G	2	2	0	1	3
C	2	2	1	0	3
#	3	3	3	3	∞

```
idea
deem
```

The mismatches, thus, are i against d, d against e, and a against m (the third characters match). Therefore, the Hamming distance is 3. □

5.8.2 Generalized Edit Distance

In the generalized edit distance problem, instead of counting each edit operation as 1, a *cost matrix* $\mathcal{C}$ is supplied that encodes all the possible substitution costs. Modeling insertion and deletion uniformly as substitutions, the size of this matrix becomes $(m + 1) \times (m + 1)$ with $\mathcal{C}_{i,j}$ representing the cost of substituting character i by character j. Generally, $\mathcal{C}_{i,i}$ is 0 except $\mathcal{C}_{\#,\#}$ which is undefined (or ∞ to disallow arbitrarily long alignments). For the basic edit distance, all the costs are considered as 1.

The generalized edit distance is defined as the *minimum* cost needed to transform string x to string y. (Note the similarity with EMD.) The generalized edit distance is very similar to the pairwise sequence alignment problem where the aim is to maximize the score.

Eq. (5.36) can be suitably modified to represent the generalized edit distance formulation by replacing the costs of insertion, deletion, and substitution in the minimization block by the actual costs of $\mathcal{C}_{\#,y_j}$, $\mathcal{C}_{x_i,\#}$, and $\mathcal{C}_{x_i,y_j}$:

$$ED(i,j) = \begin{cases} 0 & \text{if } i = j = 0 \\ \sum_{y_j} \mathcal{C}_{\#,y_j} & \text{if } i = 0 \\ \sum_{x_i} \mathcal{C}_{x_i,\#} & \text{if } j = 0 \\ \min \left\{ \begin{array}{ll} ED(i-1,j) & + & \mathcal{C}_{\#,y_j}, \\ ED(i,j-1) & + & \mathcal{C}_{x_i,\#}, \\ ED(i-1,j-1) & + & \mathcal{C}_{x_i,y_j} \end{array} \right\} & \text{otherwise} \end{cases}$$

$$(5.36)$$

Example 5.6 [Generalized Edit Distance]. Find the generalized edit distance between the strings ACT and GAGA for the cost matrix given in Table 5.1.

The transformation can be shown as

#ACT

GAGA

The generalized edit distance is, therefore, the sum of the costs of replacing # by G, A by A, C by G, and T by A. The total distance, thus, is $3 + 0 + 1 + 1 = 5$. □

The generalized edit distance is a *metric* distance only if the cost matrix $\mathcal{C}$ follows identity and symmetry. Similar to EMD, the triangular inequality is always satisfied as it is a minimization problem.

Chapter 6

Distance-Based Structures

Two important constraints that the index structures discussed in the previous chapters are that the data objects are available as vectors of some fixed dimensionality and the distances between the objects were measured using the L_2 norm. In many applications, however, either the feature vectors are not available explicitly (e.g., text or graphs), or the feature vectors are not of uniform dimensionality (e.g., image keypoints), or the distance between the objects is not a regular L_p distance (e.g., distances in road networks). It is still extremely critical and useful to index such data to allow efficient range and kNN searches. This chapter discusses some of the important index structures that handle such cases where only a distance measure is available between any two data objects.

In many such cases, a single distance computation between two objects can be very expensive, so much so that they become the computation bottlenecks over the random I/O access (e.g., the edit distance or the earth mover's distance, see Section 5.8 and Section 5.7, respectively) and the overall goal then shifts to minimizing the number of distance computations rather than the number of disk accesses.

One of the drawbacks of a distance-based index structure is that once the distance function changes, the whole index needs to be built afresh. In contrast, the hierarchical index structures that depend on the coordinate values of the objects can use multiple distance functions on the same index.

6.1   Triangular Inequality

The most important property of metric distances that is used for indexing is the *triangular inequality*. Suppose the distance from a query Q to an object O is sought. Instead, however, the distance of Q to another object in the dataset P is available (may be computed in some earlier step) and the distance of P to O is pre-computed. Note that since both P and O are dataset objects, the distance between them can always be pre-computed and is independent of the query object Q. Using the triangular inequality, the distance of Q to O can then be bounded from both sides:

$$d(Q,O) \geq |d(Q,P) - d(P,O)| = d_{LB}(Q,O) \qquad (6.1)$$
$$d(Q,O) \leq d(Q,P) + d(P,O) = d_{UB}(Q,O) \qquad (6.2)$$

6.1.1   Indexing Using Triangular Inequality

The general idea of indexing using triangular inequality is as follows. Certain "landmark" objects $\{P_1, P_2, \ldots, P_m\}$ are maintained. Along with each such object P_i, a number of objects $\{O_{i_j}\}$ are associated, and their distances $\{d(P_i, O_{i_j})\}$ are pre-computed.

For a range query from Q with range r, the distance of Q to an object O_{i_j} is estimated using triangular inequality. If the lower bound obtained using Eq. (6.1) is greater than r, obviously the actual distance is also greater than r, and the object can be pruned. On the other hand, if the upper bound obtained from Eq. (6.2) is less than r, then the actual distance is also less than r, and the object can be returned as part of the answer set. Only if neither of the two cases happen is the actual distance computation of $d(Q, O_{i_j})$ needed.

The case for nearest-neighbor queries is similar. Suppose k nearest neighbors are sought. At any point in time, assume that k neighbors have been found. The distance to the kth nearest neighbor, d_k, serves as the current best estimate of the range that needs to be searched. Any object whose lower bound distance is more than d_k cannot be part of the k nearest neighbors. Hence, simply replacing r in the range search by d_k works. However, note that the quantity d_k keeps shrinking as nearer neighbors are found.

All the indexing techniques for general metric distances exploit the above bounds. There are two main types of such techniques, the hierarchical index structures and the flat reference-based structures. While the hierarchical ones progressively use the roots of subtrees as the landmark objects, the reference-based indexing methods use a fixed set of such objects which are termed as *pivots* or *reference objects*. The term METRIC TREE stands for the family of hierarchical index structures that use the metric properties of the distance function for efficient similarity searching. It was first coined in [Uhlmann, 1991a]. The main difference of the reference-based techniques from the metric tree structures is that the pivots are maintained in a flat manner and are not organized or arranged in a hierarchy. We first describe the significant members of this family before discussing the important reference-based indexing techniques.

An important point to note is that all these structures also work for regular t-dimensional object vectors with a Euclidean distance since they only require an available metric distance function between a pair of objects.

6.2 VP-Tree

The first important hierarchical distance-based index structure is the VP-TREE [Yianilos, 1993]. The main idea behind it is the *ball decomposition* method that makes use of only the pairwise distances between a set of objects $\mathcal{O}$ [Uhlmann, 1991a].

6.2.1 Structure

An arbitrary object, $P \in \mathcal{O}$, is first selected as the root of the tree. Distances to all other objects from P are computed and the *median* distance d_{med} is found. The rest of the objects are partitioned using d_{med} in the following way.

Every object whose distance to P is less than d_{med} is put in the left subtree and the rest are put in the right subtree, i.e.,

$$O_i \text{ in left subtree } \Longleftrightarrow d(O_i, P) \le d_{med} \qquad (6.3)$$

$$O_i \text{ in right subtree } \Longleftrightarrow d(O_i, P) > d_{med} \qquad (6.4)$$

The partitioning can be viewed as creating a hyper-sphere (or ball) of radius d_{med} around the center P, as shown in Figure 6.1a. Objects inside the hyper-sphere form one group (the left subtree, denoted as $\mathcal{L}$) while those residing outside form the other group (the right subtree, denoted as $\mathcal{R}$). This special object, P, was called *vantage point* by the authors of [Yianilos, 1993], from which the VP-tree derives its name.

The left and right subtrees are then partitioned recursively using the same ball decomposition method. Since the division is based on the median, the above method ensures that the tree is balanced.

Key Concept 6.1 [VP-Tree]. An internal node divides the set of objects into two groups based on the distance from a pivot. The first group has a distance less than or equal to a threshold while the second group has a distance which is more than the threshold. Using this threshold distance, bounds of the distance from the query for the two subtrees can be obtained.

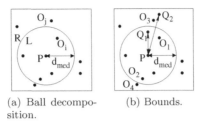

(a) Ball decomposition.   (b) Bounds.

Figure 6.1: VP-tree structure and how bounds work.

6.2.2 Bounds

Consider an object O_1 in the left subtree $\mathcal{L}$, i.e., $d(P, O_1) \leq d_{med}$. If the query Q is within the hyper-sphere representing $\mathcal{L}$, then the minimum distance of Q to O_1 may be 0 since they may coincide. This situation is depicted by Q_1 in Figure 6.1b. If, however, Q is outside the hyper-sphere (Q_2 in the figure) and is, thus, in the space representing $\mathcal{R}$, it cannot be any closer to O_1 than the difference of their distances to the center P, i.e., $d(Q, P) - d(O_1, P)$. Putting the maximum value of $d(O_1, P)$ as d_{med}, the conditions can be summarized as

$$d(Q, O_i \in \mathcal{L}) \geq \max\{d(Q, P) - d_{med}, 0\} = d_{LB}(Q, O_i \in \mathcal{L}) \quad (6.5)$$

The maximum distance of Q to O_i is the sum of Q's distance to P and that of P to O_i. In the figure, O_2 depicts such an example. This does not depend on whether Q is within or outside the separating hyper-sphere. Thus,

$$d(Q, O_i \in \mathcal{L}) \leq d(Q, P) + d_{med} = d_{UB}(Q, O_i \in \mathcal{L}) \quad (6.6)$$

Next, consider an object O_3 in the right subtree $\mathcal{R}$, i.e., $d(P, O_3) \geq d_{med}$. For a query Q_1 within the separating hyper-sphere (see Figure 6.1b), the minimum distance is at least the distance of Q from the separation, i.e., $d_{med} - d(Q, P)$. The object O_3 in the figure exemplifies the situation. If the query is outside (for example, Q_2), the minimum distance bound is 0 since, once more, the query can coincide with an object. Summarizing,

$$d(Q, O_j \in \mathcal{R}) \geq \max\{d_{med} - d(Q, P), 0\} = d_{LB}(Q, O_j \in \mathcal{R}) \quad (6.7)$$

The maximum distance to an object outside is unbounded, since there is no limit to the distance between an object (for example, O_4 in the figure) and the center P. Thus,

$$d(Q, O_j \in \mathcal{R}) \leq d(Q, P) + \infty = d_{UB}(Q, O_j \in \mathcal{R}) \quad (6.8)$$

6.2.3 Searching

Consider a range query Q with radius r. If $d(Q, P) \leq r$, then P is part of the answer set. Using the bounds given by Eq. (6.5) and Eq. (6.7), a subtree can be pruned if the minimum distance of any object within it is more than the range r. For a kNN query, the current best estimate of the distance to the kth object can be maintained which serves as the radius r of the range query.

6.2.4 Choosing Vantage Points

While the pivot or the vantage point at each level can be chosen randomly to produce a valid VP-tree, a more sophisticated algorithm generally produces better results. The authors of [Yianilos, 1993] provide one such heuristic. A random sample of objects is selected. For each such object, the distances to another random subset of the entire dataset is computed and the variance is measured. The object with the largest variance or spread is chosen as the vantage point. This enables the objects in the two subtrees to be well-separated.

6.2.5 Discussion

The most important property of the VP-tree is that only the pairwise distances between the objects are sufficient. However, the structure is a binary tree that makes no attempt to optimize on the disk storage. In other words, the tree is quite deep, and there is no concept of efficiently utilizing the disk pages. The basic version was, thus, assumed to be a memory-based structure. The authors of [Yianilos, 1993] provided two important extensions of the VP-tree that are described next.

6.2.6 VP^{S}-Tree

In the first one, called the VP^{S}-TREE, the distance of a pivot to all its ancestor pivots are stored. Thus, a pivot at level l stores $l-1$ distances to pivots along its path to the root. Similarly, for a leaf object, the distance to all the pivots on the path to the root are stored.

The rationale for this design is the following. If a search has descended up to a level l, the query has already computed the distance to all the $l-1$ ancestor levels. The bounds can be tightened by using these additional distances.

Consider a query Q and an object O_i at the lth level of the tree. Assume that the pivots on the path from the root are P_1, P_2, etc., up to P_l. Using triangular inequality, for any level $j = 1, \ldots, l$,

$$|d(Q, P_j) - d(O_i, P_j)| \leq d(Q, O_i) \leq d(Q, P_j) + d(O_i, P_j) \qquad (6.9)$$

The lower bounds and upper bounds on $d(Q, O_i)$ are chosen as the best ones from these levels, i.e.,

$$d_{LB}(Q, O_i) = \max_{j=1,\ldots,l} \{|d(Q, P_j) - d(O_i, P_j)|\} \qquad (6.10)$$

$$d_{UB}(Q, O_i) = \min_{j=1,\ldots,l} \{d(Q, P_j) + d(O_i, P_j)\} \qquad (6.11)$$

These bounds can be used to filter out subtrees for a similarity search.

The crucial point to note is that the computation of these bounds does not require any new exact distance computation. The distance of an object O_i to all the ancestor pivots, i.e., $d(O_i, P_j)$, are already stored, and the distances of the query to these pivots, i.e., $d(Q, P_j)$ have been computed in the course of the current search.

6.2.7   VP^{SB}-Tree

The VP^S-tree is still a memory-based structure. The second important extension is, thus, to adopt the VP^S-tree for a disk-based design by collapsing the leaves into buckets or disk pages. The resulting structure is called VP^{SB}-TREE. Each individual level is given an identifier and multiple such levels are stored in a single disk page with their identifiers and distances to the ancestor pivots.

6.3   GH-Tree

The GH-TREE is a type of metric tree that uses the *generalized hyperplane decomposition* [Uhlmann, 1991b].

6.3.1   Structure

Instead of dividing the set of all objects using a single center, it uses two objects P_1 and P_2 to perform the division. Every other object O_i is placed in the subtree corresponding to which it is closest.

$$O_i \text{ in left subtree} \iff d(O_i, P_1) \leq d(O_i, P_2) \qquad (6.12)$$

$$O_i \text{ in right subtree} \iff d(O_i, P_1) > d(O_i, P_2) \qquad (6.13)$$

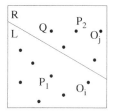

Figure 6.2: Generalized hyperplane decomposition.

The effect is that of creating a dividing hyperplane mid-way between P_1 and P_2.

The left and right subtrees are then partitioned by conducting the generalized hyperplane decomposition in the same manner by picking two such objects in each of them. The balance of the resulting tree is not guaranteed at all for two arbitrary dividing objects.

Key Concept 6.2 [GH-Tree]. An internal node divides the set of objects into two groups based on two pivots, each group being closer to one particular pivot than the other. Using this division, bounds of the distance from the query for the two subtrees can be obtained.

Figure 6.2 shows an example of generalized hyperplane decomposition. All objects on the left subtree $\mathcal{L}$ are on the left side of the separating hyperplane and are closer to P_1 than P_2. The situation is reversed for the objects in the right subtree $\mathcal{R}$.

6.3.2 Bounds

Consider an object O_i in the left subtree $\mathcal{L}$. The distance of a query object Q to it can be bounded by triangular inequalities using the objects P_1 and P_2.

$$d(Q, O_i) \geq d(Q, P_1) - d(O_i, P_1) \qquad (6.14)$$
$$d(Q, O_i) \geq d(O_i, P_2) - d(Q, P_2) \qquad (6.15)$$

Adding the two equations and using the fact that $d(O_i, P_2) > d(O_i, P_1)$ (since $O_i \in \mathcal{L}$),

$$2.d(Q, O_i) \geq d(Q, P_1) - d(Q, P_2) + d(O_i, P_2) - d(O_i, P_1)$$
$$\geq d(Q, P_1) - d(Q, P_2)$$
$$\Rightarrow d(Q, O_i) \geq \frac{d(Q, P_1) - d(Q, P_2)}{2} \qquad (6.16)$$

If the right side in Eq. (6.16) is negative, the lower bound on $d(Q, O_i)$ is 0 as the distance must be non-negative.

6.3.3 Searching

Consider a range query from query Q with a radius r. Using Eq. (6.16), the left subtree $\mathcal{L}$ needs to be accessed if and only if $(d(Q, P_1) - d(Q, P_2)) \leq 2r$. Otherwise, it is guaranteed that no object in $\mathcal{L}$ can be closer to Q by r.

Since the left and right subtrees are symmetric, it can be concluded that the right subtree $\mathcal{R}$ needs to be accessed if and only if $(d(Q, P_2) - d(Q, P_1)) \leq 2r$.

No upper bounds on the distances can be computed since an object in a subtree can be arbitrarily away from the root.

6.3.4 Discussion

The generalized hyperplane decomposition generally produces partitions that intersect less with the query hyper-sphere than the ball decomposition. Similar to the basic VP-tree, however, the GH-tree ignores the disk design completely. It simply acts as a binary tree. Further, due to the inherent unbalanced nature of the decomposition, the performance may suffer significantly for certain queries.

6.4 GNAT

A more generalized version of the hyperplane partitioning was proposed by [Brin, 1995]. The structure was called GEOMETRIC NEAR-NEIGHBOR ACCESS TREE (GNAT).

6.4.1 Structure

Instead of using two pivots, k pivots (called *split points*) are used in each level to partition the objects. Each non-pivot object is associated with the closest split point. The space, thus, is broken into *Dirichlet domains*, the vector space equivalent of which is the *Voronoi diagram* (see Section 3.6). The partitioning is carried on recursively to yield a tree with fanout k.

The important enhancement that GNAT provides over GH-trees is the information kept in a branch about the other branches. More specifically, for the set of objects S_j under a split point P_j, the minimum and maximum distance to *other* split points P_i are also retained:

$$d_{LB}(S_j, P_i) = \min_{\forall O_j \in S_j \cup \{P_j\}} \{d(O_j, P_i)\} \tag{6.17}$$

$$d_{UB}(S_j, P_i) = \max_{\forall O_j \in S_j \cup \{P_j\}} \{d(O_j, P_i)\} \tag{6.18}$$

This additional information substantially increases the search efficiency as explained next.

Key Concept 6.3 [GNAT]. An internal node utilizes k pivots to divide the objects under it into k groups based on the closest pivot. In addition, lower and upper bound distances to other pivots are maintained. This helps in significantly tightening the distance bounds to a query.

6.4.2 Similarity Searching

Assume a range query from Q with radius r. At the root, among the k split points, one of them (say, P_i) is chosen arbitrarily. If $d(Q, P_i) \le r$, then P_i is added to the answer set. Consider another split point P_j.

The distance $d(Q, O_j)$ of Q from any object $O_j \in S_j \cup \{P_j\}$ can be lower bounded as follows:

$$d(O_j, P_i) \le d(Q, O_j) + d(Q, P_i)$$
$$\Rightarrow d_{LB}(S_j, P_i) \le d(O_j, P_i) \le d(Q, O_j) + d(Q, P_i) \text{ [using Eq. (6.17)]}$$
$$\Rightarrow d(Q, O_j) \ge d_{LB}(S_j, P_i) - d(Q, P_i) \tag{6.19}$$

Similarly,

$$d(Q, P_i) \le d(Q, O_j) + d(O_j, P_i)$$
$$\Rightarrow d(Q, P_i) - d(Q, O_j) \le d(O_j, P_i) \le d_{UB}(S_j, P_i) \text{ [using Eq. (6.18)]}$$
$$\Rightarrow d(Q, O_j) \ge d(Q, P_i) - d_{UB}(S_j, P_i) \tag{6.20}$$

Since both these bounds can be negative, the lower bound is the maximum of these two and the quantity 0:

$$d(Q, O_j) \ge d_{LB}(Q, O_j) = \max \left\{ \begin{array}{c} d_{LB}(S_j, P_i) - d(Q, P_i), \\ d(Q, P_i) - d_{UB}(S_j, P_i), \\ 0 \end{array} \right\} \tag{6.21}$$

Thus, the subtree under P_j can be completely pruned if the lower bound $d_{LB}(Q, O_j) > r$. Using Eq. (6.21), the condition reduces to

$$d_{LB}(S_j, P_i) - d(Q, P_i) > r \quad \text{or} \quad d(Q, P_i) - d_{UB}(S_j, P_i) > r \quad (6.22)$$

The upper bound on $d(Q, O_j)$ can be also obtained by similar applications of the triangular inequality:

$$\begin{aligned} d(Q, O_j) &\leq d(Q, P_i) + d(O_j, P_i) \\ &\leq d(Q, P_i) + d_{UB}(S_j, P_i) \text{ [using Eq. (6.18)]} \end{aligned} \quad (6.23)$$

These bounds are tighter than the ones that use only a single pivot.

6.4.3   Choosing Split Points

The k split points are chosen from those assigned to a node in the following way. First, a random sample of $3k$ candidate objects is drawn. Then, an object is selected randomly from this subset and designated as the first split point. For each of the subsequent choices, the object that is farthest from *all* the previous pivots is selected as the next split point. The distance of an object from a set of previously chosen pivots is taken to be the minimum of the distances to the pivots. This is continued till k split points are selected.

6.5   M-Tree

M-TREE [Ciaccia et al., 1997] is perhaps the most well-known member of the metric tree family. It is a dynamic balanced hierarchical disk-based data structure that works with metric distances.

6.5.1   Structure

Each entry of an internal node of an M-tree indicates a subtree of objects called a *covering tree*. Corresponding to each such entry for a covering subtree T, a node stores the following four fields of information:

1. The *routing object* O which is the root of T

2. The *pointer Ptr* to O

3. The *covering radius* ρ which is the distance from O within which all objects in T reside, i.e.,

$$\rho = \max_{O_i \in T}\{d(O, O_i)\} \tag{6.24}$$

4. The distance to *parent* P of O, i.e., $d(O, P)$

For the leaf nodes, the covering radius $\rho = 0$ while the pointer *Ptr* points to the actual data object.

6.5.2 Bounds

Consider any query object Q. Applying the triangular inequality, the minimum distance from Q to *any* object O_i in the covering tree T of O can be computed as follows:

$$d(Q, O_i) \geq d(Q, O) - d(O, O_i)$$
$$\Rightarrow d(Q, O_i) \geq d(Q, O) - \rho = d_{min}(Q, O_i) \tag{6.25}$$

The minimum distance, $d_{min}(Q, O_i)$, can be 0 if the query Q falls within the covering radius of O since, then, it can coincide with any of the objects.

Similarly, the maximum distance can be also computed:

$$d(Q, O_i) \leq d(Q, O) + d(O, O_i)$$
$$\Rightarrow d(Q, O_i) \leq d(O, Q) + \rho = d_{max}(Q, O_i) \tag{6.26}$$

6.5.3 Similarity Search

Consider a range search from Q with query radius r. The search proceeds in a top-down manner from the root and tries to prune subtrees that are guaranteed not to provide any answer.

A subtree T rooted at O can be pruned if the minimum distance of Q to any $O_i \in T$ is greater than r, i.e., if

$$d_{min}(Q, O_i) > r$$
$$\Rightarrow d(Q, O) - \rho > r$$
$$\Rightarrow d(Q, O) > r + \rho \tag{6.27}$$
$$\Rightarrow |d(Q, P) - d(O, P)| > r + \rho \tag{6.28}$$

Eq. (6.27) provides a direct bound on the query distance. However, it involves computing an actual distance, that of Q to O. The fact that the subtree rooted at O is investigated implies that its parent P has been looked at already. Thus, the distance of Q from P should already be available. Consequently, Eq. (6.28) can be used. More importantly, this is cheaper to evaluate as none of the distances need to be computed afresh ($d(O, P)$ is stored). However, it has less pruning power than Eq. (6.27) as it only provides a bound on $d(Q, O)$. Thus, although both the pruning conditions are used in an M-tree, Eq. (6.28) is used *before* Eq. (6.27).

Key Concept 6.4 [M-Tree]. The root of an internal node maintains a covering radius within which all objects in the subtree reside. It also maintains the distance to its parent. Using the distance to the parent, the distance to a query from any object in the subtree is bounded without requiring any actual distance computation. If needed, the bound is further refined by computing the actual distance from the query to the root of the subtree.

The kNN search for a query Q and the number of nearest neighbors k proceeds similarly in a top-down manner from the root. At any point in the algorithm, a heap of k *current best* objects are maintained. The distance to the kth object in the heap, d_k, is used as the range to search. This estimate gets more and more refined as the search proceeds.

Among the children of a node that cannot be pruned, while it does not matter in a range search in what order they are traversed, it can matter in a kNN search as a subtree with nearer objects refines the value of d_k better. Thus, the one that is the most promising is searched first, and so on. This is determined by the *minimum* distance estimate of an object $O_i \in T$ from Q, i.e., $d_{min}(Q, O_i)$ as obtained from Eq. (6.25). This order of search is akin to the *best-first* search order (see the details in Section 4.3.3.1).

6.5.4   Insertion

The M-tree is a dynamic structure, i.e., it supports insertion and deletion of data objects. The data objects are always stored at leaves. When an object needs to be inserted in a node, among all possible children candidates, the one that suffers the *least* covering radius enlargement is chosen. If there are ties, the child whose routing object is the *closest*, is chosen. When there is an overflow, splitting is done, which is discussed next.

6.5.5 Splitting

When a node splits, two objects from its set are chosen and inserted into its parent node as routing objects for the two new nodes. The entries are then divided between these two new nodes according to a split policy as discussed in the next section.

The covering radius ρ' of a new node is set to be the sum of the old covering radius ρ and the distance from the old routing object O to the new routing object O', i.e.,

$$\rho' = d(O, O') + \rho \tag{6.29}$$

Ideally, the new covering radius should be computed as the maximum distance of an object within the subtree from the new root. However, this may involve many new distance computations. Instead, Eq. (6.29) is used as it provides a bound. The correctness is ensured by the triangular inequality property of the distance function.

The two steps of routing object selection (called *promotion*) and distribution of objects to nodes (called *partition*) together constitute a particular *split policy*. The M-tree offers several split policies that can be chosen according to the specific needs.

6.5.6 Split Policies

The partition of objects into two groups is based on two parameters:

1. *Covering radius:* Subtrees with smaller covering radii are better as pruning improves due to tighter clusters and less dead space indexing.

2. *Overlap:* Two sibling routing objects that are far apart are better as it reduces the probability of a search entering both the subtrees.

6.5.6.1 Choosing Routing Objects

The routing objects can be chosen according to two ways:

1. *Confirmed*, where the old routing object is maintained as one of the new ones.

2. *Non-confirmed*, where no such constraint is imposed.

Confirmed promotions are simpler, although non-confirmed promotions have a larger number of possibilities and, thus, have a bigger chance of choosing a better organization of the groups. Consequently, it shows better performance.

The different alternatives for choosing the routing objects are:

- The pair that minimizes the sum of covering radii

- The pair that minimizes the maximum covering radius

- The pair that minimizes the maximum covering radius from among a sample of objects

- The pair that maximizes the distance between the two routing objects; the non-confirmed version uses only the pre-computed distances while the confirmed one chooses the new routing object as the farthest from the old one

- A random pair

According to the authors of [Ciaccia et al., 1997], minimizing the maximum covering radius using a non-confirmed policy shows the best performance.

6.5.6.2   Distribution of Non-Routing Objects

Once the two routing objects are chosen, the M-tree follows two strategies for distributing the rest of the objects between them:

1. Each object chooses the nearest routing object.

2. The routing objects incorporate their nearest objects in a round-robin fashion. At the start, the first routing object incorporates its nearest object; then the second routing object incorporates the one closest to it among those that are left, and so on.

Although the first strategy can produce fairly unbalanced splits while the second one is guaranteed to balance the distribution, it is the first one that results in better splits.

6.5.7   Deletion

The original proposal of M-trees [Ciaccia et al., 1997] did not contain any algorithm for deletion. Although there have been attempts to modify an M-tree to allow deletions, the process can be quite cumbersome and inefficient. The best way is to mark the object as "deleted" so that even if a subsequent query locates it, the object is not returned as an answer. Periodically, of course, a batch operation of inserting all the non-deleted entries in a fresh M-tree can be performed.

6.6 SA-Tree

The SPATIAL APPROXIMATION TREE (SA-TREE) [Navarro, 2002] proposes a significantly different approach to searching for an object where only the distances are available and the goal is to minimize the number of distance computations. Instead of following a divide-and-conquer mechanism where in each step of the search, a part of the database is pruned away after establishing that it is irrelevant to the query at hand, the SA-tree approaches the desired object *spatially* by getting closer and closer to it in every step. The spatial closeness is approximated by modeling the set of data objects as a graph where the objects form the nodes and the edges capture the neighborhood.

To understand the process better, consider a 1-NN query. Suppose, at any point in the search, the query is in a particular node. It is allowed to move to another node in the next step provided it is a neighbor, i.e., there is an edge from the current node to it. The query evaluates all the neighbors and moves to the one that is the closest. This process goes on until the query cannot move to any other neighbor, i.e., the current node is the best, which is then returned as the answer.

The above "object" graph should satisfy certain properties. It should be connected, and there should be enough edges so that the query can proceed to the answer. The *complete* graph having all possible edges, of course, satisfies the conditions. However, for an n-sized database, evaluating all the neighbors then requires n computations, and the indexing does not gain any advantage over the naïve brute-force linear search. Thus, the goal is to find a graph having the *least* number of edges that still allows answering all the queries *correctly*. The correctness property must ensure that if a query cannot proceed to any neighbor from a node, then the node must be the answer.

6.6.1 Optimal Graph

It is relatively simpler to imagine the situation in a two-dimensional vector space with L_2 being the distance function. Here, the optimal graph is the Delaunay graph obtained through Delaunay triangulation (see Section 3.6 and Figure 3.8b). In this graph, two nodes are neighbors if and only if they share a Voronoi edge. The Delaunay graph is optimal in the sense that if an edge is deleted from it, the properties are violated while at the same time, no additional edge is required to satisfy those.

If a query is in the Voronoi cell of a node, it is closer to that node than any other. Thus, when the traversal of the graph stops, it is guaranteed that the query is in the Voronoi region of the current node, which is then returned as the correct answer.

In a general metric space, the Delaunay graph corresponds to the *Dirichlet domain*. Given just a set of distances between n objects, it is *not* always possible to compute the Dirichlet domain. Thus, to ensure correctness, the only feasible graph is the complete graph, which, unfortunately, is useless for indexing purposes. A flavor of *approximation* is, hence, necessary for the construction. The search results, however, are *not* approximate and are always correct.

6.6.2   Structure and Construction

A heuristic to build a reasonable graph for 1-NN queries where the query is one of the data objects itself is outlined below. The structure obtained is actually a tree that approximates the spatial properties of the Delaunay graph. The structure is, thus, named *spatial approximation tree*.

A random object is selected as the root. A set of children is chosen for the root such that any child is closer to the root than to any of its siblings, i.e., any other child, and all the non-children are closer to one of the children than the root itself. Each of the rest of the non-children objects are then assigned to the child of the root that it is closest to. The process is next repeated for each child of the root to complete the construction of the tree.

Since the above definition of choosing the children is circular and depends on the order of examining the objects, a way to make the process deterministic is to first sort all the objects according to their increasing distances to the root, and then consider them in order.

Key Concept 6.5 [SA-Tree]. A tree of the dataset objects is maintained. For every node, its children are closer to it than any of the siblings. The query proceeds to the closest child. Using the distance to the closest child, the distances from other children are bounded.

Example 6.1 [SA-Tree]. For the set of objects shown in Table 6.1, build an SA-tree. (Ignore the distances from the queries Q_1 and Q_2 for the time being.)

Figure 6.3a shows how the points are laid out in a two-dimensional space. Note that this is shown purely for illustration purposes. Only the distances between the objects are used for the construction, and not their coordinates.

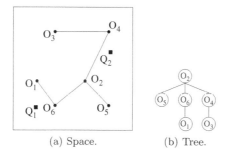

(a) Space.   (b) Tree.

Figure 6.3: Example of an SA-tree.

Table 6.1: Distance matrix for building SA-tree.

	O_1	O_2	O_3	O_4	O_5	O_6
O_1	-	10	11	18	16	6
O_2	10	-	12	11	7	8
O_3	11	12	-	11	19	15
O_4	18	11	11	-	15	19
O_5	16	7	19	15	-	11
O_6	6	8	15	19	11	-
Q_1	5	8	15	21	15	3
Q_2	16	8	12	4	11	15

Assume that O_2 is chosen as the root. The rest of the objects are ranked in ascending order of their distances to O_2. The sorted list is O_5, O_6, O_1, O_4, O_3. Thus, first, O_5 is added as a child. Next, O_6 is considered. Since O_6 is closer to the root O_2 than the other child O_5, i.e., $d(O_6, O_2) < d(O_6, O_5)$, it is assigned as a child. The next candidate O_1, however, is not added, since its distance to a child O_6 is lesser than that to the root, i.e., $d(O_1, O_2) > d(O_1, O_6)$. The other two objects are processed in the same manner: O_4 becomes a child but O_3 does not.

The non-children objects that remain after this step are O_1 and O_3. O_1 falls in the subtree of O_6 since that is the child of the root closest to it, and in turn, becomes its child. Similarly, O_3 becomes a child of O_4.

The tree structure is shown in Figure 6.3b. The solid lines in Figure 6.3a show the layout of the tree in the underlying two-dimensional space.   □

6.6.3 Exact Searching

Searching for a database object directly follows the exact same procedure as in a Delaunay graph. First, the distance to the root and its children are considered. If the root is the closest, it is returned as the answer. Otherwise, the subtree of the nearest child is then searched recursively. This results in a *single* search path.

For example, consider searching for O_1. The algorithm first computes the distance to O_2 and all its children and traverses the best option O_6. From there, it again computes the distance to all the children of O_6 and returns O_1 as the answer.

The reason this search terminates correctly is that it essentially mimics the way the tree was built. For every non-assigned object, it was put in the subtree of the child it was *closest* to. Hence, accessing that subtree guarantees proceeding towards that object and finally reaching it.

Of course, it is of little importance to search for a database object directly. A much more useful case is a similarity search for an arbitrary query with a range or number of nearest neighbors. Although the procedure is a little more elaborate, it uses the same philosophy as described next.

6.6.4 Similarity Searching

In addition to the children, each root of a subtree maintains a *covering radius* which is the maximum distance from it to any object in the subtree.

Consider a range search from a query Q for a distance r. For an answer to be present in a subtree rooted at P_t, it must follow the same pruning rules as in an M-tree (for details, see Eq. (6.27) and Eq. (6.28) and the surrounding discussion).

The query first examines the closest object among the root and its children. Suppose this is P_1. In addition to P_1, it must also traverse all the other children that potentially contains an answer. Consider such a possible answer O_i in another subtree rooted at P_2. Since O_i is inserted in the subtree of P_2 and not P_1, it must be that $d(O_i, P_2) \leq d(O_i, P_1)$. Applying triangular inequality on the objects O_i, Q and the two subtree roots P_1 and P_2,

$$
\begin{aligned}
d(Q, P_2) - d(Q, O_i) &\leq d(O_i, P_2) \\
&\leq d(O_i, P_1) \\
&\leq d(Q, P_1) + d(Q, O_i) \\
\Rightarrow d(Q, O_i) &\geq \frac{d(Q, P_2) - d(Q, P_1)}{2} = d_{LB}(Q, O_i)
\end{aligned}
\qquad (6.30)
$$

The choice of P_1 as the closest object from Q is justified as it tightens the bound in Eq. (6.30) the most.

If this lower bound is greater than the range of the search r, then no object O_i in the subtree rooted at P_2 can be the answer. The condition translates to

$$d_{LB}(Q, O_i) > r$$
$$\Rightarrow d(Q, P_2) - d(Q, P_1) > 2.r$$
$$\Rightarrow d(Q, P_2) > d(Q, P_1) + 2.r \qquad (6.31)$$

In other words, all other subtrees P_2 satisfying $d(Q, P_2) \le d(Q, P_1) + 2.r$ must be searched as potential answers may reside in them.

As an example, consider the query from Q_1 with a range 5 (Figure 6.3 and Table 6.1). The closest among the root and the children is O_6 with a distance of 3. The subtree rooted at O_4 can be pruned since $21 > 3 + 2 \times 5$. Similarly, O_5 can also be pruned and only O_6 needs to be searched from which O_1 and O_6 are returned as answers.

For the second query Q_2 with radius 5, O_4 is the closest. Although the subtree rooted at O_6 can be pruned since $15 > 4 + 2 \times 5$, the one rooted at O_5 cannot be pruned since $11 \not> 4 + 2 \times 5$.

The range search can, thus, degrade to multiple search paths instead of the original idea of approximating the spatial distance and approaching the answer(s) using a single path. This is the price paid due to the heuristic nature of the spatial relationships maintained using the SA-tree.

The kNN search follows the same procedure. The distance to the kth object found so far is maintained as the radius. Initially, this radius is set to ∞ and it is gradually refined.

6.7 AESA

We next discuss some of the important reference-based structures. APPROXIMATING AND ELIMINATING SEARCH ALGORITHM (AESA) is one of the earliest reference-based algorithms [Ruiz, 1986, Vidal, 1994]. It treats all the objects as potential pivots and, therefore, computes and stores the pairwise distances between all pairs of objects as a pre-processing step before any query arrives. When the distance computation between two objects is more time-consuming, the algorithm is more effective.

6.7.1 Querying

Assume a range query Q with the parameter of the query being the range r. First, its distance $d(Q, O_i)$ to an arbitrary object O_i is computed. If this distance is less than the range r, O_i is added to the answer set.

The object O_i is then used to (lower) bound the distances of Q to other objects. Thus, in essence, O_i acts as a pivot (called a *prototype*). For any other object O_j, the distance from Q is at least

$$d(Q, O_j) \geq |d(Q, O_i) - d(O_i, O_j)| = d_{LB}(Q, O_j) \qquad (6.32)$$

Note that computing the lower bound does not require any actual distance computation and should, therefore, be quite beneficial as against the (costly) true distance computation of O_j from Q.

All the objects O_j whose lower bound is greater than the range r, i.e., $d_{LB}(Q, O_j) > r$, are then pruned, as the actual distance $d(Q, O_l) \geq d_{LB}(Q, O_j) > r$ will be also outside the range. This is the *eliminating* step in the name of AESA.

From among the objects that are not pruned, the next "best" pivot O_l is then chosen. The selection is based on the lower bounds of the new object to all the old pivots chosen $\{O_p\}$. The criteria is either the sum of the lower bounds [Ruiz, 1986]

$$O_l = \operatorname{argmin} \left\{ \sum_{\forall O_p \in P} |d(Q, O_p) - d(O_p, O_l)| \right\} \qquad (6.33)$$

or the maximum [Vidal, 1994]

$$O_l = \operatorname{argmin} \left\{ \max_{\forall O_p \in P} |d(Q, O_p) - d(O_p, O_l)| \right\} \qquad (6.34)$$

This corresponds to the *approximating* step.

Once O_l is chosen, the lower bounds of all the non-pruned objects are updated by taking the maximum of the lower bound computed using O_l and the old lower bound:

$$d_{LB}(Q, O_j) = \max \left\{ d_{LB}(Q, O_j), |d(Q, O_l) - d(O_l, O_j)| \right\} \qquad (6.35)$$

Intuitively, this new pivot O_l is the one that helps the most in pruning.

The algorithm can be easily extended to kNN search by maintaining the kth best nearest-neighbor distance estimate so far, and using that as the range in the pruning.

Table 6.2: Example of AESA.

	O_1	O_2	O_3	O_4	O_5	O_6
O_1	-	10	11	18	16	6
O_2	10	-	12	11	7	8
O_3	11	12	-	11	19	15
O_4	18	11	11	-	15	19
O_5	16	7	19	15	-	11
O_6	6	8	15	19	11	-
Q_1	5	8	15	21	15	3
Q_2	16	8	12	4	11	15

Key Concept 6.6 [AESA]. All the pairwise distances between the objects are stored. Once an object is examined, it is treated as a pivot. Distances of other objects to the query are lower bounded by using their distances to this pivot.

Example 6.2 [AESA]. Table 6.2 shows an example of 6 objects with their pairwise distances. It also shows the distances of the objects from two queries Q_1 and Q_2. Note that these will not be available and are noted here only for understanding the example. Find the 1-NN answers for these two queries using AESA.

When a 1-NN query is issued for Q_1, assume it arbitrarily picks up O_1 as the first object. The exact distance to O_1 is computed. It is 5 (shown in italicized fonts) in the first row of Table 6.3.

Using this, the lower bounds to other objects are computed next. For example, the bound for O_6 is $d_{LB}(Q_1, O_6) = |d(Q_1, O_1) - d(O_1, O_6)| = |5 - 6| = 1$.

Now, since one object (O_1) has already been found with an actual distance 5, the objects O_3, O_4, and O_5 whose lower bound distances are more than 5 are pruned.

Of the remaining, O_6 is picked up for the next round since it has the lowest lower bound. Since its actual distance, 3, is lesser than the bounds of all other objects, they can be pruned. Consequently, O_6 is correctly returned as the answer.

When 1-NN is queried for Q_2, suppose it again chooses O_1 arbitrarily as the first object. Note that this distance (16) is very large and, therefore, does not allow pruning any other object.

In the next round, since O_5 has the best lower bound, it is chosen next. The actual distance of O_5 is computed, and the lower bounds

Table 6.3: Query processing of AESA (actual distances are shown in italicized fonts).

Query	Pivot	$d_{LB}(Q., O.)$					
		O_1	O_2	O_3	O_4	O_5	O_6
Q_1	O_1	*5*	5	6	13	11	1
	O_6	5	-	×	×	×	*3*
Q_2	O_1	*16*	6	5	2	0	10
	O_5	16	6	8	4	*11*	10
	O_4	16	-	-	*4*	11	-

of O_3 and O_4 are improved using this. For example, the lower bound of O_3 earlier using O_1 as the pivot was $d_{LB}(Q_2, O_3) = |d(Q_2, O_1) - d(O_1, O_3)| = |16 - 11| = 5$. Using O_5, the bound is now $d_{LB}(Q_2, O_3) = |d(Q_2, O_5) - d(O_5, O_3)| = |11 - 19| = 8$.

Still, no object can be pruned and O_4 is chosen for the next step. The exact distance of O_4 (which is 4) is small enough to allow AESA to stop right away by pruning all the other objects. The object O_4 is returned as the answer.   □

6.7.2   Discussion

The number of pivots used in AESA is at most all the objects, i.e., n. AESA requires quadratic storage and preprocessing times (to be precise, it is $O(n(n - 1)/2)$) and at most linear *actual* distance computations. Note that the other query overheads are necessarily linear since it involves computing the lower bounds of all the objects, etc. AESA is still considered efficient since the distance computation is assumed to be so expensive that the overheads are negligible in comparison.

A particular search, however, may not show any benefit (since a linear search also requires linear time). In practice, though, the authors of [Vidal, 1994] reported an asymptotically small number of pivot distance computations. Nevertheless, the quadratic overhead of storage and preprocessing severely limits the applicability for large datasets.

6.8   Linear AESA (LAESA)

To solve the problem of quadratic costs of storage and preprocessing of AESA, a *linear* version, appropriately named LINEAR AESA (LAESA), was proposed by [Micó et al., 1994].

The basic improvement is that LAESA treats only a small number of objects as pivots (called *base prototypes*). Consequently, it stores the distances of all the objects from this small set only. Assuming that the number of such pivots, p, is small, the cost $O(n.p)$ for n objects is essentially linear.

6.8.1   Pivots

When a similarity search is issued, LAESA follows almost the same technique as in AESA, i.e., (a) choosing an object, (b) finding its actual distance, (c) updating the nearest-neighbor distance (if applicable), (d) updating the lower bounds of other objects, and (e) pruning other objects (if possible). However, since not all pairwise object distances are available, some minor modifications are necessary.

LAESA differs from AESA in the following two decisions:

1. How is the next object chosen?

2. Should be a pivot be pruned?

The authors of [Micó et al., 1994] suggested two simple heuristics for these decisions. For the first one, the next object to examine is always chosen from the set of pivots. The reason is that this allows updating the lower bounds of all the remaining objects. Choosing an arbitrary object will not let the updating possible since the distances to the other objects are not available.

For the second one, note that pruning a pivot (when its lower bound distance is greater than the range or the actual nearest-neighbor distance) affects tightening the lower bounds of other objects. Thus, a pivot is not pruned blindly. Instead, it is pruned only if the number of pivots already chosen is greater than a fraction f of the original number of pivots p. This ensures that the lower bound for an object is computed using at least $f.p$ pivots. The fraction f can vary and can be even 1 in which case no pivot is ever pruned.

In sum, LAESA acknowledges that pivots are special objects and are, hence, chosen earlier and not pruned so easily.

Table 6.4: Example of LAESA.

	O_1	O_2	O_3	O_4	O_5	O_6
O_1	-	10	11	18	16	6
O_6	6	8	15	19	11	-
Q_1	5	8	15	21	15	3
Q_2	16	8	12	4	11	15

Key Concept 6.7 [LAESA]. LAESA stores the distances of all objects from a small number of pivots. Using these, the distance from the query to other objects is lower bounded using the same strategy as in AESA. In every iteration, LAESA prefers choosing pivots for inspection earlier than non-pivots. Also, it always maintains a threshold fraction of pivots.

Example 6.3 [LAESA]. Table 6.4 shows an example of 6 objects with their distances from two objects O_1 and O_6 that are designated as pivots. It also shows the distances of the objects from two queries Q_1 and Q_2. Note that these will not be available and are noted here only for understanding the example. Find the 1-NN answers for these two queries.

When a 1-NN query is issued for Q_1, assume that it arbitrarily picks up O_1 as the first object. The query processing then follows the exact same steps as in AESA (see Example 6.2). This happens as it picks up O_6 next which is a pivot. Table 6.5 shows the steps.

When 1-NN is queried for Q_2, suppose it again chooses O_1 arbitrarily as the first object. Note that this distance (16) is very large and, therefore, does not allow pruning any other object. Thus, the first step remains the same as in AESA.

In the second iteration, while AESA could pick up O_5, LAESA cannot do so since O_5 is not a pivot. As a result, it picks up the pivot O_6. The actual distance of O_6 is computed, and the lower bounds of the other objects are improved.

Still, no object can be pruned. Now that all the pivots have been chosen, LAESA has to resort to choosing non-pivot objects. Therefore, it chooses O_5 as the one having the best lower bound. In this step, it can only update the actual distance of O_5 (to 11 as shown in the third row for Q_2). The lower bounds of none of the objects can be updated as their distance to the non-pivot object O_5 is not available. (The object O_5 is shown in brackets to distinguish it as a non-pivot object.)

Finally, O_4 is chosen. Its actual distance (4) is small enough to allow LAESA stop processing and to return O_4 as the answer. □

Table 6.5: Query processing of LAESA (actual distances are shown in italicized fonts).

Query	Pivot (Object)	$d_{LB}(Q., O.)$					
		O_1	O_2	O_3	O_4	O_5	O_6
Q_1	O_1	*5*	5	6	13	11	1
	O_6	*5*	-	×	×	×	*3*
Q_2	O_1	*16*	6	5	2	0	10
	O_6	*16*	7	5	4	4	*15*
	(O_5)	*16*	7	5	4	*11*	*15*
	(O_4)	*16*	-	-	*4*	*11*	*15*

6.8.2 Choosing Pivots

The choice of pivots affects the search efficiency. If there is a pivot that is close to the query, then the distances from the query to the other objects are better approximated and the pruning becomes more effective [Burkhard and Keller, 1973]. Hence, it is desired that the pivots be *maximally separated* so that for any query, not all the pivots are far off.

However, optimally choosing p maximally separated objects from a set of n objects is a computationally challenging problem. Hence, the authors of [Micó et al., 1994] resort to a heuristic that shows good practical results. The first pivot is chosen arbitrarily. For the next $p - 1$ steps, the ith pivot is chosen such that its sum of distances to the previous $i-1$ pivots is the largest. The total number of distance computations for choosing pivots is $O(n.p)$.

6.8.3 Discussion

Simulations done by [Micó et al., 1994] show that there is generally an optimal number of pivots for any dataset when some pivots are pruned (i.e., the fraction $f < 1$). With small number of pivots, the lower bounds of the distances from the query are not tight enough and, hence, the objects are not pruned early. Consequently, more steps are required for LAESA to finish. When there are more pivots, the preprocessing time increases and there is an increased number of distance computations overall. In the limiting case, when $p = n$, LAESA becomes AESA.

6.9 AESA for Vector Spaces

An efficient version of AESA for vector spaces was proposed by [Ramasubramanian and Paliwal, 1992] where only $k + 1$ pivots are needed when the dimensionality of the space is k and the distance function used is Euclidean.

The algorithm uses the fact that a point in a k-dimensional vector space can be uniquely identified by $k+1$ distances from $k+1$ fixed pivots (called *anchor points*). Using one of the anchor points as the base, the k *difference anchor vectors* produce k simultaneous linear equations. Assuming the equations to be linearly independent, the solution leads to an unique point.

This idea was used to design the FIXED ANCHOR POINT AESA (FAP-AESA) algorithm. An object is located by *simultaneously* using its distances to the $k + 1$ pre-fixed anchor points. An incremental version, named INCREMENTAL FIXED ANCHOR POINT AESA (IFAP-AESA), that mimics the traditional AESA in the sense that the distance of an object to an anchor point is used incrementally was also proposed by [Ramasubramanian and Paliwal, 1992].

Key Concept 6.8 [AESA for Vector Spaces]. A k-dimensional point can be uniquely identified by its distances to $k + 1$ fixed points. Hence, $k + 1$ pivots are used to obtain the distance estimate for an object.

6.9.1 Choosing Anchor Points

The authors of [Ramasubramanian and Paliwal, 1992] suggested an interesting way of choosing the $k + 1$ anchor points. The base pivot is chosen as the origin (the data space is assumed to be mean-centered). The rest k pivots are chosen at equal distances from the base pivot along the k principal vectors obtained by using PCA (see Section 9.5) on the dataset.

6.9.2 Discussion

The space and preprocessing overhead of FAP-AESA is $O(n.k)$ which can be considered linear since, in general, the dimensionality $k \ll n$.

Thus, IFAP-AESA is similar to LAESA except for two differences. First, LAESA uses the pairwise distances directly and do not need the coordinates of the points. Second, the number of pivots needed for LAESA is a parameter, while for IFAP-AESA it is fixed to one plus the dimensionality of the space.

Part V

High-Dimensional Spaces

Chapter 7

Curse of Dimensionality

Although the hierarchical structures show marked benefits in searching at lower dimensions, as the dimensionality increases, the performance suffers. For high dimensions (roughly, greater than 8), almost all the nodes are accessed and the overhead of searching becomes so high that a linear scan of the database performs better. In this chapter, we analyze the search in high dimensions and understand this phenomenon called the "curse of dimensionality".

7.1 Analysis of Search for High-Dimensional Data

We assume a d-dimensional space with uniformly distributed data within a unit hyper-cube $[0, 1]^d$. We also assume that the distance function is Euclidean and the dimensions are independent. We note three crucial observations.

7.1.1 Volume at the Boundary

The first observation is that most of the data lies on the boundary. Assume a small width of ϵ from the outer boundary. The volume inside is $(1 - 2\epsilon)^d$. When d is large, this is quite small. Table 7.1 shows how the volume decreases rapidly with increasing dimensionality. As an example, for $\epsilon = 0.1$ and $d = 20$, the inside volume is only $0.8^{20} = 0.0115$, i.e., only 1% of the data lies inside and 99% of the data resides on the boundary of the space.

7.1.2 Range of a Query

The second observation is on the range of a query. Suppose the selectivity of a query is α, i.e., α fraction of points is returned as the answer to the query. Thus, the volume of the query hyper-rectangle is α.

Table 7.1: Inside volume in high dimensions.

Dimension	Width ϵ			
	1e-2	5e-2	1e-1	2e-1
1	9.80e-01	9.00e-01	8.00e-01	6.00e-01
2	9.60e-01	8.10e-01	6.40e-01	3.60e-01
5	9.04e-01	5.90e-01	3.28e-01	7.78e-02
10	8.17e-01	3.49e-01	1.07e-01	6.05e-03
20	6.68e-01	1.22e-01	1.15e-02	3.66e-05
50	3.64e-01	5.15e-03	1.43e-05	8.08e-12
100	1.33e-01	2.66e-05	2.04e-10	6.53e-23

Table 7.2: Query range.

Dimension	Selectivity α				
	1e-4	5e-4	1e-3	5e-3	1e-2
1	1.00e-04	5.00e-04	1.00e-03	5.00e-03	1.00e-02
2	1.00e-02	2.24e-02	3.16e-02	7.07e-02	1.00e-01
5	1.58e-01	2.19e-01	2.51e-01	3.47e-01	3.98e-01
10	3.98e-01	4.68e-01	5.01e-01	5.89e-01	6.31e-01
20	6.31e-01	6.84e-01	7.08e-01	7.67e-01	7.94e-01
50	8.32e-01	8.59e-01	8.71e-01	8.99e-01	9.12e-01
100	9.12e-01	9.27e-01	9.33e-01	9.48e-01	9.55e-01

Consequently, the query range on each dimension should be $\sqrt[d]{\alpha}$. Again, when d is large, this query range is quite long, even for very small selectivity. For example, when $\alpha = 0.0001$ and $d = 20$, the query range becomes $\sqrt[20]{0.0001} = 0.63$. Table 7.2 shows that at high dimensions, the range approaches 1.

7.1.3   Number of Data Points

The third observation is that the database must contain many points for even a large query to be effective. If a hyper-spherical query region has to be completely inside the space, the radius can be at most 0.5. The volume of such a hyper-sphere with radius $r = 0.5$ is $V = \left(\pi^{\frac{d}{2}}(0.5)^d \right) / \left(\Gamma(\frac{d}{2} + 1) \right)$. Since the volume of the entire space is normalized to 1, this forms the probability that there is at least 1 point within this hyper-sphere. Hence, for the query to return at least 1 answer, the database should contain $1/V$ number of points. The volume falls exponentially with increasing dimensionality (Table 7.3). As a result, the

Table 7.3: Volume of hyper-sphere having radius 0.5.

Dimension	Volume	Number of points
2	7.85e-01	1.27e+00
5	1.64e-01	6.10e+00
10	2.49c-03	4.02e+02
20	2.46e-08	4.07e+07
50	1.54e-28	6.49e+27
100	1.87e-70	5.35e+69

number of points increases in an exponential fashion and it soon becomes infeasible to have so many points in a dataset. For example, when $d = 20$, $V = 2.46 \times 10^{-8}$ and, therefore, $1/V = 4.07 \times 10^7$. However, when $d = 50$, the number of points jumps to $1/V = 6.49 \times 10^{27}$.

7.2 Expected Nearest Neighbor Distance

In this section, we analyze the expected distance of the nearest neighbor (NN) of a query point. Assume a query Q with a range r. The probability that a particular database point is not within a distance of r from Q is the same as the point not lying within the hyper-sphere of radius r with Q as the query center. This volume is

$$V(r) = \frac{\pi^{\frac{d}{2}} . r^d}{\Gamma(\frac{d}{2} + 1)} \tag{7.1}$$

Hence, the probability that the point is not within this volume is $1 - V(r)$.

If the database contains n points, the probability that none of them is within this hyper-sphere, therefore, is

$$P(r, n) = (1 - V(r))^n \tag{7.2}$$

If the nearest neighbor (NN) of Q has to reside within the range r, then at least one point should be within this volume. This event is the complement of the event that none of the n points is within $V(r)$. The probability, therefore, is

$$P_{NN}(r, n) = 1 - (1 - V(r))^n \tag{7.3}$$

The *expected* distance of the query Q to its nearest neighbor can then

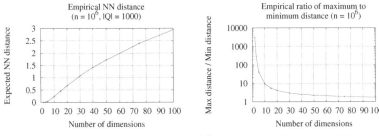

(a) Expected nearest neighbor distance. (b) Ratio of maximum to minimum distance.

Figure 7.1: Distances in high dimensions.

be computed by varying the range r over all ranges:

$$E_Q[\text{NN-dist}] = \int_0^\infty r.\frac{\partial P_{NN}(r, n)}{\partial r} \, dr \qquad (7.4)$$

The *expected nearest-neighbor distance* over all queries is

$$E[\text{NN-dist}] = \int_Q E_Q[\text{NN-dist}] \, dQ \qquad (7.5)$$

Figure 7.1a shows the result of a simulation. A set of 10^6 points were generated uniformly and randomly within a unit cube of $[0, 1]^d$. Then, $|Q| = 10^3$ query points were also generated uniformly and randomly within the same hyper-cube. For each of these queries, the nearest neighbor point in the dataset was located and its distance was noted. The average nearest neighbor distance is plotted in the graph.

The expected nearest neighbor distance increases rapidly with dimensionality. Even for a large database of 10^6 points, the average distance to the nearest neighbor for 1000 queries in a 20-dimensional space is more than 0.67 in a unit cube, i.e., it covers more than $(2/3)^{\text{rd}}$ the range in every dimension. For dimensions more than 30, the nearest neighbor is more than a distance of 1.0 away (this happens because the largest distance is $\sqrt{30}$).

7.2.1 Effectiveness of Distance

As the dimensionality increases, the data space becomes extremely sparse. Consequently, the difference between the minimum and maximum pairwise distances between two objects diminishes. Using the same simulation framework as described earlier, the minimum and maximum distance from each query point to all the points in the dataset are noted. The ratio of the maximum to the minimum is computed. The average ratio over all $|Q| = 10^3$ query points is depicted in Figure 7.1b.

The ratio of maximum to minimum distance rapidly approaches 1 (note the logarithmic scale of the y-axis). In other words, in high dimensions, there exists little difference in distances to two random objects from the query. This implies that the notion of a nearest neighbor becomes almost meaningless and the distance function loses its effectiveness.

7.3 Expected Number of Page Accesses

We next analyze the expected number of page accesses for a query. Assume a query range of r. The query needs to access a particular page if the MBR corresponding to the page intersects with the query hypersphere. In order to analyze whether such an event occurs, the *Minkowski sum (MS)* technique is used [Berchtold et al., 1997].

This technique transforms a range query to an equivalent point query by enlarging all MBRs by the query range r. An alternative way to think of the enlargement is to consider the volume traced by the center of the query when it is rolled on the surface of the MBR. An example in two dimensions is shown in Figure 7.2. The dotted lines show the Minkowski sum of the MBR R with respect to query Q with range r.

The test of whether a query hyper-sphere intersects with the MBR or not then becomes equivalent to the test of whether the query point is contained within the Minkowski sum of the MBR or not. Thus, a range query of Q with range r is equivalent to the point query of Q when the MBRs are replaced by their Minkowski sums.

A query needs to access a page if it intersects the MBR corresponding to the node. With the MBRs replaced by their Minkowski sums, a page is accessed only if the query point falls inside it. Therefore, in a unit volume, the probability of accessing a page is simply its Minkowski sum volume.

Consider a 1-NN query. It is equivalent to a range query with r being equal to the expected nearest-neighbor distance. Thus, the probability of accessing the ith page is

$$P_{visit}(i) = \text{Volume}(MS(MBR_i, E[\text{NN-dist}])) \qquad (7.6)$$

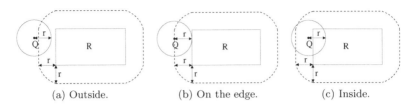

(a) Outside.   (b) On the edge.   (c) Inside.

Figure 7.2: Minkowski sum of an MBR R with respect to query Q with range r.

where $MS(M, r)$ denotes the Minkowski sum of a structure M enhanced by the radius r.

If there is a total of n objects and each page can accommodate at most β objects, the total number of leaf pages is at least $\lceil n/\beta \rceil$. Hence, the expected number of total page visits, T_{visit}, is at least

$$T_{visit} = \sum_{i=1}^{\lceil n/\beta \rceil} P_{visit}(i) \qquad (7.7)$$

We next explain why the probability of visiting a page becomes 1. We analyze different types of hierarchical index structures separately.

7.3.1   Space-Partitioning Structures

Assume a space-partitioning structure residing in a d-dimensional space. If d is very large, splitting all the dimensions at least once would result in 2^d partitions. If there are n objects and at most β objects fit in a page, then there are at least $\delta = \lceil n/\beta \rceil$ pages. If $2^d > \delta$, then these partitions are useless and unnecessary. Hence, assume a smaller number of dimensions $d' < d$ such that $2^{d'}$ is just greater than δ. Thus, only these d' dimensions will be split.

Assuming an equal split, an MBR, thus, contains d' sides of length 0.5 and $d - d'$ sides of length 1.0. The *maximum* distance of any point within the space from this MBR is, therefore,

$$l_{max} = \frac{1}{2}\sqrt{d'} = \frac{1}{2}\sqrt{\left\lceil \log_2\left(\frac{n}{\beta}\right) \right\rceil} \qquad (7.8)$$

The important point to note about l_{max} is that it does not depend on the full dimensionality d; it saturates with the effective number of partitioning dimensions d'. On the other hand, as we saw earlier, the expected NN distance $E[\text{NN-dist}]$ keeps increasing monotonically with

d. Hence, at some dimensionality $d_{critical}$, $E[\text{NN-dist}] > l_{max}$. Therefore, the minimum distance at which a query finds at least one neighbor from the dataset is larger than the maximum distance of any point from an MBR. Since the MBRs are enlarged by this expected distance, the enlarged volumes extends the entire space, i.e., they become larger than 1. As a result, the probability of visiting an MBR, $P_{visit}(i)$, reaches 1.

7.3.2 Data-Partitioning Structures: Hyper-Rectangles

The analysis with respect to data-partitioning structures that use hyper-rectangles for indexing is similar. Again, it can be argued that the maximum possible distance from any query point to an MBR does not grow beyond a point. The argument follows the similar lines of an MBR not possible of being split across all the dimensions. Since the expected NN distance keeps increasing, at some dimensionality, it again exceeds the maximum distance and the Minkowski sum volume of the MBR exceeds the volume of the space.

7.3.3 Data-Partitioning Structures: Hyper-Spheres

We next consider data-partitioning structures that index using hyper-spheres. If there are β objects in a hyper-sphere corresponding to a page, one of the objects forms the center while the rest $\beta - 1$ objects complete the sphere. Hence, the radius of the sphere, rad, is at least $(\beta - 1)^{\text{th}}$ NN distance from the center.

Denoting a hyper-sphere in d dimensions with radius rad by $S^{(d)}(rad)$, the probability of visiting a page is the Minkowski sum volume of the hyper-sphere corresponding to the page. Since the Minkowski sum of a sphere simply increases its radius, the probability is

$$
\begin{aligned}
P_{visit} &= \text{Volume}(MS(S^{(d)}(rad))) \\
&= \text{Volume}(S^{(d)}(rad + E[\text{NN-dist}])) \\
&= \text{Volume}(S^{(d)}(E[(\beta - 1)^{\text{th}} \text{ NN-dist}] + E[\text{NN-dist}])) \\
&\geq \text{Volume}(S^{(d)}(E[\text{NN-dist}] + E[\text{NN-dist}])) \\
&= \text{Volume}(S^{(d)}(2.E[\text{NN-dist}])) \qquad (7.9)
\end{aligned}
$$

The volume as computed by Eq. (7.9) increases with dimensionality d and exceeds 1 after some critical dimensionality $d_{critical}$. Consequently, P_{visit} becomes 1 and all the hyper-sphere pages are accessed.

7.3.4   Arbitrary Structures

We finally consider an arbitrary hierarchical index structure. The only requirement is that every parent structure must completely encompass the children structures. Even in such a structure, the parent must consist of at least two children. Since the geometry of such a structure must be convex, the limiting case for a structure is when it just covers the line joining two points. Such a structure has zero volume.

The Minkowski sum volume generated by augmenting this line by the expected NN distance is, however, non-zero. With an increase in dimensionality, this volume steadily increases. (The rigorous analysis can be understood from [Weber et al., 1998].) Hence, even for this structure, the Minkowski sum volume must exceed 1 after some critical dimensionality $d_{critical}$. Thus, beyond this dimensionality, the probability of visiting any such structure becomes 1.

7.4   Curse of Dimensionality

From the analyses done in the previous section, we can see that after some critical dimensionality, the probability of accessing a page, $P_{visit}(i)$, approaches 1 for almost every page. Thus, the total number of page accesses becomes the same as the total number of pages and the index structures accrue no benefit over a linear scan. In fact, since the linear scan goes over the data objects systematically, it only pays sequential I/O costs. This relies on the quite reasonable assumption that the data is stored in contiguous blocks on the disk. In contrast, an index scan accesses the pages randomly. Hence, the linear scan is actually faster. (Appendix A discusses the comparison of sequential I/O versus random I/O costs.) This effect for indexing structures is the infamous "curse of dimensionality".

Chapter 8

High-Dimensionality Structures

As discussed in the previous chapter, at high dimensions the idea of hierarchical indexing fails. Nevertheless, there are many applications, most notably the image databases, that need to deal with objects of very high dimensionality. A routine task in many image applications is to search for similar images.

In this chapter, several index structures that attempt to solve the searching problem without getting affected by the curse of dimensionality are discussed. We start with a hierarchical structure, X-tree. We then discuss the pyramid technique and the iMinMax technique that focuses on the border effect that is prominent in high dimensional spaces. The VA-file, which is simply an unordered list of quantized data points, is next discussed. We finally end the chapter by discussing two structures that use the idea of quantization for handling high dimensional spaces.

8.1 X-Tree

The X-TREE [Berchtold et al., 1996] is a hierarchical index structure belonging to the R-tree family. It tries to nullify the curse of dimensionality by behaving more like a *linear array* as the dimensions increase.

For that, it introduces the concept of *supernodes*. Essentially, a supernode is a concatenation of two or more disk blocks with the crucial property that they are stored *contiguously*. This allows accessing the contents of the supernode with only one random I/O. This random I/O is needed only for the first disk page; the rest are accessed using sequential I/O operations. The difference in the access speeds, as discussed in Appendix A, highlights the importance of such a design. The basic idea behind the X-tree is that when a split creates too much overlap between two new nodes, any query is likely to visit both the nodes and, therefore, creating a supernode is better.

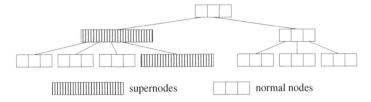

Figure 8.1: An X-tree.

Key Concept 8.1 [X-Tree]. When two sibling nodes overlap a lot, a query is likely to visit both of them. Thus, storing them contiguously as a supernode allows accessing the two nodes using one random disk access and one sequential disk access operation. This is much faster than two random disk accesses that are spent with a normal design.

8.1.1   Overlap

Thus, to analyze the search performance of a hierarchical structure, the amount of *overlap* among the multiple children nodes needs to be estimated. The overlap among multiple sibling nodes represented by their MBRs R_i, R_j, etc., is measured by the ratio of the volume of their pairwise intersections to their union:

$$\text{Overlap } O = \frac{vol(\cup_{i,j,i \neq j}(R_i \cap R_j))}{vol(\cup_i R_i)} \tag{8.1}$$

The above definition assumes that the query is distributed uniformly over the space. However, queries or the data are rarely distributed in such a fashion, and a better way of measuring the overlap to estimate the search performance is to use the distribution of the data, i.e., the number of data objects in the intersection regions. Consequently, the *weighted overlap* measure is used:

$$\text{Weighted Overlap } W = \frac{|\cup_{i,j,i \neq j}(R_i \cap R_j)|}{|\cup_i R_i|} \tag{8.2}$$

where the volume is replaced by the number of objects in the intersections or unions.

An even better estimate is *multiple overlap* that counts the actual number of regions overlapping with a certain volume. However, multiple overlap is hard to estimate and is, therefore, not used in practice.

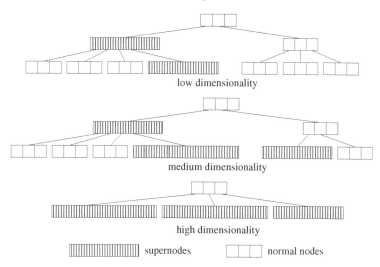

low dimensionality

medium dimensionality

high dimensionality

⫿⫿⫿⫿ supernodes   ▢▢▢ normal nodes

Figure 8.2: Change in X-tree structure with dimensionality.

Experiments by the authors of [Berchtold et al., 1996] reveal that overlap for uniform data or weighted overlap for real data reaches 90% even for medium dimensionality (6-10). Accordingly, a linear search through an array-like structure produces better results than accessing through multiple nodes and multiple levels of a hierarchical index structure. For low dimensions, however, the situation is just the reverse.

The X-tree attempts to balance both these designs by *dynamically* and *automatically* adjusting itself. At higher dimensions, the number and size of supernodes increase and, therefore, the X-tree behaves similar to a linear array, while in lower dimensions, there are very few supernodes, and the structure resembles an R-tree.

8.1.2 Structure

The structure of a typical X-tree is shown in Figure 8.1. The shape changes with different dimensionalities as shown in Figure 8.2. The X-tree, thus, varies between the following two extremes:

1. When there is no supernode, all the nodes are arranged hierarchically, and the tree is an R-tree.

2. When all the data is collected in a single supernode (which is the root), the tree is a linear array of the entire dataset.

With increasing dimensions and increasing supernodes, the height of the tree reduces. Intuitively, this can be understood from the fact that since supernodes are created only during splitting, on average they will be more full than normal nodes as they will be packed tighter. Thus, overall the tree exhibits a larger fanout thereby resulting in a shorter height.

8.1.3 Splitting

Splitting in an X-tree is handled very sensitively as it is the only method that can create supernodes. The X-tree follows two policies for splitting: *topological* and *overlap-minimal*. The topological split is based on the geometric properties of the node such as margin, volume, etc., and is similar to that followed in an R*-tree.

If the overlap of the split nodes suggested by the topological split is too high (i.e., over a threshold as discussed in Section 8.1.3.1 next), then the overlap-minimal split algorithm is invoked. For point data, the overlap-minimal split algorithm can return an *overlap-free split*, which may not be balanced, though. For objects, however, no such guarantee about an overlap-free split can be given.

An overlap-free split for point data can happen only for a dimension along which all the children nodes have been split at least once earlier. If no such dimension exists, then obviously, the data in one of the children nodes spans across the entire range of that dimension. The group to which this child is assigned, hence, stretches all the way along this dimension. The other group, therefore, must have a zero range along this dimension. This, then, contradicts the property of this group being an MBR.

To quickly determine such a dimension, the entire split history of all the nodes is maintained as a binary tree, called the *split tree*. The internal nodes of the split tree encode the dimension on which a node is split while the leaves denote the current set of MBRs. When an MBR M splits according to dimension i into L and R, the leaf corresponding to M is replaced by node i with two children L and M. Thus, for any node, the dimensions in the path from the root to this MBR denote the set of dimensions along which at least one split has taken place. Any such dimension can be chosen as the split dimension.

For data objects, there is no easy algorithm to determine an overlap-minimal split, and essentially, only topological splitting policy is observed.

The overlap-minimal split algorithm can, however, result in very unbalanced splits. If the suggested split violates the underflow condition of one of the nodes, the split is deemed invalid, and instead, a supernode is created. This creation is justified as the algorithm has failed to find a way of splitting the data without having a large overlap.

8.1.3.1 Overlap Threshold

The overlap threshold can be estimated nicely using the following heuristic. Assume that when a node splits into two parts, the overlap between them is χ, which is expressed as a ratio of the overall volume. Thus, with probability χ, a search visits both the nodes, while with probability $(1 - \chi)$, it visits only one node. All these accesses are random I/O, however.

When a supernode with these two nodes is formed, the search always visits both the nodes with one random I/O and one sequential I/O access.

Denoting the time to perform a disk seek by r, that of transferring a block from disk to memory by s and the time to process a block in memory by the CPU by c, the total time for a random I/O on a block is $r + s + c$ while that for a sequential I/O on the next consecutive block is $s + c$.

It is, thus, beneficial to have a supernode if

$$r + 2(s + c) < \chi.2(r + s + c) + (1 - \chi).(r + s + c)$$
$$\Rightarrow \chi > \frac{s + c}{r + s + c} \tag{8.3}$$

For typical values of disk seeks and block sizes, this evaluates to around 0.2 [Berchtold et al., 1996].

For larger supernodes the analysis needs to be modified along similar lines. For most practical purposes, the threshold given by Eq. (8.3) provides a fairly decent estimate.

8.1.4 Insertion, Deletion and Searching

The insertion and deletion methods are the same as in an R-tree. If a supernode overflows, the splitting decision, as elaborated in the previous section, decides how to handle the insertion. If the insertion happens in an already existing supernode, its size is increased by one additional disk block. If a supernode with two blocks underflows, it is converted into a normal block. For larger supernodes, its size is reduced by one disk block.

Searching follows the exact same procedure as in an R-tree.

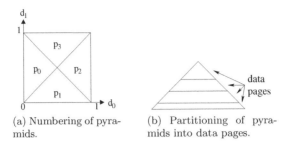

(a) Numbering of pyra-   (b) Partitioning of pyramids.   mids into data pages.

Figure 8.3: The pyramid technique.

8.2   Pyramid Technique

The PYRAMID TECHNIQUE [Berchtold et al., 1998b] was proposed to
handle the "border effect" of high dimensional spaces. It aims to do so
by peeling off hyper-volumes from the border. The peels are shaped as
pyramids with the apex at the center of the high-dimensional space. The
pyramids are sliced into partitions parallel to the base of the pyramid
such that each partition fits into a disk page. Since most of the data
lies near the border, this partitioning method tries to ensure that a
typical range query will not intersect with all the pages. Thus, for higher
dimensions, there are more partitions towards the borders due to higher
data density near the borders.

For every dimension, there are 2 pyramids, one whose base is the lowest value, and one whose base is the highest value. For a d-dimensional
space, the total number of pyramids is, thus, $2d$. Considering the data
space to be $[0, 1]^d$, the base of both the pyramids is a $(d-1)$-dimensional
surface, and the apex is $(0.5, \ldots, 0.5)$. Figure 8.3 shows the general
scheme in 2 dimensions.

Searching in this original space is difficult as it involves the intersection of pyramids with query rectangles or spheres in d dimensions. To al-
leviate this, and to also beat the curse of dimensionality, a transformation
into a 1-dimensional space is specified. Thus, for every d-dimensional
point, a *locational code*, which is simply a single number, can be computed. This has the additional benefit that the data points can be organized in a B+-tree (see Section 4.1). The inverse mapping is not required
as the leaves of the B+-tree point to the actual data objects.

Key Concept 8.2 [Pyramid Technique]. The nodes are shaped as
partitions of pyramids with the apex at the center and the high and

low values of every dimension as the base. This allows mapping a high-dimensional point to a locational code, which is indexed using a B+-tree.

8.2.1 Locational Code

To assign locational codes to points, first the pyramids are numbered in a systematic manner from 0 to $2d - 1$. Consider a $[0, 1]^d$ data space. The pyramid that has its base corresponding to the jth dimension being 0 is numbered as p_j, while the one having the base at the jth dimension as 1 is numbered as p_{j+d}. In other words, pyramid p_i has base as 0 along dimension i if $i < d$ and as 1 along dimension i if $i \geq d$. Figure 8.3a illustrates the numbering scheme for the 2-dimensional case.

All points in a pyramid p_i have the property that the distance along the $(i \bmod d)^{\text{th}}$ dimension from the center is the largest among all other dimensions. If $i < d$, then the value along this dimension is less than 0.5; if $i \geq d$, then this value is more than 0.5. These properties are used to identify the pyramid where a point lies.

Consider a point $v = (v_0, v_1, \ldots, v_{d-1})$. First, the dimension j that maximizes $|v_j - 0.5|$ is identified. Then, if $v_j < 0.5$, the pyramid is $p_i = j$; otherwise, i.e., if $v_j \geq d$, the pyramid is $i = j + d$. Summarizing,

$$p_i(v) = \left\{ \begin{array}{ll} j & \text{if } v_j < 0.5 \\ j + d & \text{if } v_j \geq 0.5 \end{array} \right. \quad \text{where } j = \operatorname*{argmax}_{\forall k = 0, \ldots, d-1} \{|v_k - 0.5|\} \quad (8.4)$$

The second important property for assigning a location code to a point is its relative position inside the pyramid. This is measured by the *height* which is the distance from the apex of the pyramid, i.e.,

$$h(v) = |v_{i \bmod d} - 0.5| \tag{8.5}$$

where i is the pyramid number where v lies according to Eq. (8.4).

The locational code of a point v, called its *pyramid value*, is the sum of its pyramid number and the height:

$$pv(v) = i + h(v) \tag{8.6}$$

Since i is an integer and $0 \leq h(v) \leq 0.5$, pyramid i contains points whose location codes lie between i and $i + 0.5$. Thus, the sets of locational codes corresponding to any two pyramids is disjoint. The mapping is, however, many-to-one, i.e., two points u and v may have the same locational code. In fact, all points in a pyramid along the same height have the same locational code.

However, since these locational codes are only used to organize the points in a B+-tree, reverse mapping is not required. As described in Section 8.2.3, during querying, the query rectangles need to be properly modified, though.

8.2.2 Filter-and-Refine Paradigm

Searching using the pyramid technique follows what is known as the *filter-and-refine* paradigm. It consists of two steps:

1. *Filter*: Candidate objects from the database that are guaranteed to be not part of the answer set are pruned.

2. *Refine*: Candidates that survived the filter step are then thoroughly checked to see if they are really part of the answer set.

8.2.3 Searching

Assume a query hyper-rectangle q where $q_{min} = (l_0, l_1, \ldots, l_{d-1})$ and $q_{max} = (h_0, h_1, \ldots, h_{d-1})$ mark the lower and higher values along all the dimensions. Query hyper-spheres can always be represented by their MBRs. The intersection of this d-dimensional query rectangle is converted into $2d$ 1-dimensional range searches for each pyramid. The ranges are computed in such a way that none of the points within the original query rectangle q are missed; however, some points outside the rectangle may also be flagged as candidates during the 1-dimensional searches. An actual point-in-rectangle test (or a distance test) is finally done to prune all such false candidates.

Ideally, the 1-dimensional ranges should be as tight as possible. However, for ease of operation, all points within the pyramid that fall within the maximum and minimum heights of the query rectangle are searched. This guarantees that none of the actual answers are missed.

Consider a pyramid j having the base at the lower value. The lower value of the query range for the dimension is l_j. When $l_j < 0.5$, all the points whose heights fall between l_j and 0.5 in this pyramid need to be searched. Using Eq. (8.5), the maximum such height is $|l_j - 0.5| = 0.5 - l_j$. The maximum locational code, therefore, is $j + (0.5 - l_j)$. The minimum height is trivially 0. Note that this does not use the higher value of the query range in the dimension. It assumes that the points can be present all the way up to the apex of the pyramid. The minimum locational code is, thus, j. The range of values for the pyramid j, therefore, is $[j, j + (0.5 - l_j)]$. When $l_j > 0.5$, there is no point in the pyramid that is part of the query range. Hence, this pyramid should not be searched at all. This automatically happens as the range becomes invalid since $j + (0.5 - l_j) < j$.

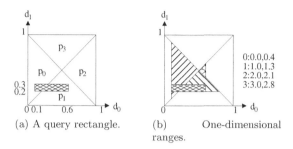

(a) A query rectangle.   (b)   One-dimensional ranges.

Figure 8.4: Example of a query in pyramid technique.

Similarly, consider a pyramid j having the base at the higher value. Considering the higher value, h_{j-d}, of the query range for the dimension, the maximum height of the points in the pyramid is $|h_{j-d} - 0.5| = h_{j-d} - 0.5$. The minimum height, again, is kept trivially at 0. The range, thus, is $[j, \ j + (h_{j-d} - 0.5)]$. Once more, if the higher value is lesser than 0.5, the range becomes invalid, and the pyramid need not be searched.

Summarizing the discussions above, the ranges R_j for every pyramid p_j are:

$$R_j = \begin{cases} [j, \ j + (0.5 - l_j)] & \text{for } j = 0, \ldots, d-1 \\ [j, \ j + (h_{j-d} - 0.5)] & \text{for } j = d, \ldots, 2d-1 \end{cases} \tag{8.7}$$

Example 8.1 [Pyramid Technique]. Find the 1-dimensional ranges for the query rectangle

$$q = \{q_{min}, q_{max}\}; \ q_{min} = (0.1, 0.2), \ q_{max} = (0.6, 0.3)$$

in a 2-dimensional space. Figure 8.4a shows the query rectangle.

Using Eq. (8.7), the ranges for the pyramids are:

- Pyramid p_0: $[0, 0 + (0.5 - 0.1)] = [0.0, 0.4]$

- Pyramid p_1: $[1, 1 + (0.5 - 0.2)] = [1.0, 1.3]$

- Pyramid p_2: $[2, 2 + (0.6 - 0.5)] = [2.0, 2.1]$

- Pyramid p_3: $[3, 3 + (0.3 - 0.5)] = [3.0, 2.8]$

The amount of space searched in the pyramids is shown as shaded in Figure 8.4b.

Note that pyramid p_2 is unnecessarily searched even though the query rectangle does not intersect with it. This happens due to the fact that the

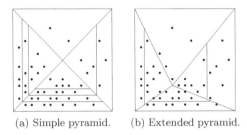

(a) Simple pyramid.   (b) Extended pyramid.

Figure 8.5: The extended pyramid technique.

largest value in dimension 0 stretches to 0.6, which is within the range for
p_2. Without looking at values for dimension 1, it is not possible to prune
this search completely. Pyramid p_3 is, however, completely avoided as
the range from 3.0 to 2.8 is invalid.   □

8.2.4   Discussion

The pyramid technique outperforms other hierarchical structures
that employ *balanced splits* in high dimensions, as in such a case, a query
rectangle with sides more than 0.5 in each dimension will intersect with
all the nodes. In a pyramid technique, however, the same query rectangle
can fully encompass only half the pyramids and at best intersect with
only some part of the rest, thereby saving accesses to all the disk pages.

When the query rectangle is towards the center of the data space, the
"extra" region searched by the pyramid technique is small and, therefore,
the index is efficient. However, when it is near a border or on an edge,
the amount of data searched is much larger than the actual answer set.

Nevertheless, the pyramid technique is generally faster in range
searches than linear scan and other hierarchical structures adapted for
high-dimensional spaces. The comparative advantage over such structures increases with increasing dimensions.

8.2.5   Extended Pyramid Technique

When the data is clustered and not uniformly distributed, the pyramids are not utilized well as some of them contain many data points
while some remain almost empty. The EXTENDED PYRAMID TECHNIQUE
[Berchtold et al., 1998b] proposes a solution where the apex of the pyramids is shifted from $(0.5, \ldots, 0.5)$ to the *median* of the data (the data
space is assumed to be $[0, 1]^d$).

The d-dimensional median is approximated by the combination of the

d 1-dimensional medians along each dimension. Assuming the median thus obtained is $(m_0, m_1, \ldots, m_{d-1})$, the transformations $t_i : [0,1] \rightarrow [0,1]$ for each dimension follow the properties

$$t_i(0) = 0; \quad t_i(1) = 1; \quad t_i(m_i) = 0.5; \quad t_i(x_i \in [0,1]) \rightarrow [0,1] \quad (8.8)$$

The t_i function is chosen to be exponential, i.e., $t_i(x_i) = x_i^r$. In order to satisfy $m_i^r = 0.5$, r works out to be $-1/\log_2(m_i)$; thus, the transformation is

$$t(x_i) = x_i^r = x_i^{-1/\log_2(m_i)} \quad (8.9)$$

Figure 8.5 shows an example of the transformation.

Before insertion, a data point $v = (v_0, v_1, \ldots, v_{d-1})$ is first transformed into $v' = t(v) = (t_0(v_0), t_1(v_1), \ldots, t_{d-1}(v_{d-1}))$. This is used only to determine the pyramid values. The data points themselves are left as they are, and hence, there is no need for an inverse transformation. A query rectangle q specified within q_{min} and q_{max} is similarly transformed into $q' = (t(q_{min}), t(q_{max}))$. These new values are then used to search through the structure.

8.3 IMinMax

The idea of the IMINMAX index [Ooi et al., 2000] is similar to that of the pyramid technique. For every dimension, two hyper-surfaces are used for mapping. These correspond to the minimum and maximum values. Assuming a data space of $[0,1]^d$, the minimum and maximum surfaces correspond to the values 0 and 1, respectively. Thus, for d-dimensional spaces, there are $2d$ hyper-surfaces. A point is associated with the closest surface. Using this association, a point is encoded by a single-dimensional value which is then indexed using a B+-tree. The structure is most suited for hyper-rectangular window queries, which is broken into a series of single-dimensional range queries.

8.3.1 Mapping

For a point $v = (v_0, v_1, \ldots, v_{d-1})$, first the minimum and maximum values along all the dimensions and the corresponding dimensions for which these minimum and maximum values occur are identified:

$$v_{min} = \min_{i=0}^{d-1} v_i \tag{8.10}$$

$$d_{min} = \operatorname*{argmin}_{i=0}^{d-1} v_i \tag{8.11}$$

$$v_{max} = \max_{i=0}^{d-1} v_i \tag{8.12}$$

$$d_{max} = \operatorname*{argmax}_{i=0}^{d-1} v_i \tag{8.13}$$

The closest distance to a minimum surface is

$$\min_{i=0}^{d-1}\{v_i - 0\} = v_{min} - 0 \tag{8.14}$$

Similarly, the closest distance to a maximum surface is

$$\min_{i=0}^{d-1}\{1 - v_i\} = 1 - v_{max} \tag{8.15}$$

The point v is associated to the closest surface, which can be either the minimum surface (Eq. (8.14)) or the maximum surface (Eq. (8.15)). The *mapped value* is a 1-dimensional number $mv(v)$ computed using the sum of the index of the closest surface and the distance of the point from the surface:

$$mv(v) = \begin{cases} d_{min} + v_{min} & \text{if } v_{min} - 0 < 1 - v_{max} \\ d_{max} + v_{max} & \text{otherwise} \end{cases} \tag{8.16}$$

The iMinMax index can use an additional parameter θ to handle the skewness in the data. The parameter θ biases the mapping of points towards the maximum surface more than that towards the minimum:

$$mv_\theta(v) = \begin{cases} d_{min} + v_{min} & \text{if } v_{min} + \theta < 1 - v_{max} \\ d_{max} + v_{max} & \text{otherwise} \end{cases} \tag{8.17}$$

The higher the value of θ, the more handicap the minimum surface has to overcome to win a point. On one extreme, if $\theta \geq +1$, all the points are mapped to the maximum surface as then the minimum surface can never be closer than the maximum one. On the other extreme, if $\theta \leq -1$, the minimum surface is associated with all the points as the maximum surface can never be the closest. The above two indices are called iMAX and iMIN, respectively. The normal index uses $\theta = 0$. The mapped value does not change with θ.

Figure 8.6 shows the iMinMax index with three different θ values. The line separating the points that map to the minimum edges from those mapping to the maximum edges is shifted with change in θ.

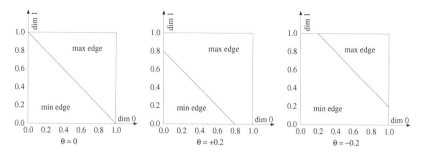

Figure 8.6: IMinMax with different θ values.

Key Concept 8.3 [IMinMax]. Two hyper-surfaces corresponding to the lowest and highest values in every dimension are used. Every point is associated with the closest surface. This allows mapping a point to a unique mapped value using the identity of the closest surface and the distance from it. The mapped values are indexed using a B+-tree.

Example 8.2 [IMinMax]. Find the 1-dimensional mapped values for the point $v = (0.3, 0.6, 0.5)$ when $\theta = 0$, $\theta = +0.2$, and $\theta = -0.2$.

The v_{min} and v_{max} values are 0.3 and 0.6, respectively. The corresponding dimensions are $d_{min} = 0$ and $d_{max} = 1$, respectively.

When $\theta = 0$, the minimum surface is closer since $0.3 < 1 - 0.6$. Therefore, the mapping utilizes the minimum surface and is equal to $mv(v) = 0 + 0.3 = 0.3$.

When $\theta = +0.2$, since $0.3 + 0.2 \nless 1 - 0.6$, the maximum surface becomes closer with the θ augmentation, and the mapping moves to it. The mapped value is $mv(v) = 1 + 0.6 = 1.6$.

When $\theta = -0.2$, since $0.3 - 0.2 < 1 - 0.6$, the minimum surface remains closer with the θ augmentation, and the mapping utilizes it. The mapped value is $mv(v) = 1 + 0.3 = 1.3$. □

8.3.2 Searching

Assume a window query q where $q_{min} = (l_0, l_1, \ldots, l_{d-1})$ and $q_{max} = (h_0, h_1, \ldots, h_{d-1})$ mark the lower and higher values along all the dimensions. The entire query q is converted into d 1-dimensional range searches to the B+-tree that indexes the mapped values. Each range search corresponds to a dimension.

Assume that $l_{min} = \min_{i=0}^{d-1} l_i$ and $l_{max} = \max_{i=0}^{d-1} l_i$ are the minimum and maximum of the lower end values, respectively. Assume

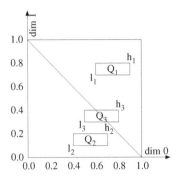

Figure 8.7: IMinMax range searching.

also that the corresponding quantities for the higher end values, $h_{min} = \min_{i=0}^{d-1} h_i$ and $h_{max} = \max_{i=0}^{d-1} h_i$, are defined analogously.

Consider the q_{min} point. If it is on the side of the maximum surfaces, then the entire query hyper-rectangle gets mapped to the maximum surfaces as well. This is exemplified by the query rectangle Q_1 in Figure 8.7. To check whether that is the case, the values l_{min} and $1 - l_{max}$ are compared using Eq. (8.16). In the case that all the points do get mapped to the maximum surfaces (i.e., $l_{min} \geq 1 - l_{max}$), the range of search in each dimension is figured out in the following way. A point x that satisfies the query predicate, i.e., x is inside the query hyper-rectangle q, must be mapped to a maximum surface. In other words, it uses the value $x_{max} = \max_{i=0}^{d-1} x_i$. Now, $x_{max} \geq l_i$, $\forall i = 0, \ldots, d - 1$. This implies that $x_{max} \geq l_{max}$. Thus, the lower range that needs to be checked from the maximum surface is l_{max}. This is true for any dimension j. The higher end of the range for a dimension j remains h_j. Hence, the range for dimension j is $[j + l_{max}, \ j + h_j]$.

Next, consider the q_{max} point. First, it is checked whether this point on the side of the minimum surfaces. If so, i.e., if $h_{min} < 1 - h_{max}$, then the entire query hyper-rectangle is on the side of the minimum surfaces (query rectangle Q_2 in Figure 8.7). Once more, consider a point x that satisfies q. It must be mapped to a minimum surface using the value $x_{min} = \min_{i=0}^{d-1} x_i$. Similar to the first case, it can be shown that $x_{min} \leq h_{min}$. Thus, the higher end of the range is h_{min} for any dimension j. The lower end remains l_j for dimension j. The range, therefore, is $[j + l_j, \ j + h_{min}]$.

When the query hyper-rectangle spans across both the regions, as in query rectangle Q_3 in Figure 8.7, the points inside it can be mapped to either the minimum surfaces or the maximum surfaces. Hence, the range for dimension j remains $[j + l_j, \ j + h_j]$.

Summarizing the entire discussion and adding the parameter θ, the range R_j for every dimension j is

$$R_j = \begin{cases} [j + l_{max}, \; j + h_j] & \text{if } l_{min} + \theta \geq 1 - l_{max} \\ [j + l_j, \; j + h_{min}] & \text{if } h_{min} + \theta < 1 - h_{max} \\ [j + l_j, \; j + h_j] & \text{otherwise} \end{cases} \qquad (8.18)$$

The union of the answers from each of the above range searches constitutes the final answer set. In some case, it may happen that the ranges are invalid (similar to the pyramid technique) and, therefore, those searches can be avoided.

The authors of [Ooi et al., 2000] also showed that the above ranges are "optimal" in the sense that any more shrinking of the ranges may result in missing an answer, and nothing beyond these ranges can contain any answer and is, thus, not required to search.

Example 8.3 [IMinMax Searching]. Find the 1-dimensional ranges for the query rectangles

$$Q_1 = (l_1, h_1); \; l_1 = (0.6, 0.7), \; h_1 = (0.9, 0.8)$$

$$Q_2 = (l_2, h_2); \; l_2 = (0.4, 0.1), \; h_2 = (0.7, 0.2)$$

$$Q_3 = (l_3, h_3); \; l_3 = (0.5, 0.3), \; h_3 = (0.8, 0.4)$$

in a 2-dimensional space as shown in Figure 8.7. Assume $\theta = 0$.

Consider Q_1. The query values are

$$l_{min} = 0.6, \; l_{max} = 0.7, \; h_{min} = 0.8, \; h_{max} = 0.9$$

Since $0.6 \geq 1 - 0.7$, all the points are mapped to a maximum surface. The ranges for each dimension, correspondingly, are:

$$R_0 = [0 + 0.7, 0 + 0.9] = [0.7, 0.9]$$

$$R_1 = [1 + 0.7, 1 + 0.8] = [1.7, 1.8]$$

Consider Q_2. The query values are

$$l_{min} = 0.1, \; l_{max} = 0.4, \; h_{min} = 0.2, \; h_{max} = 0.7$$

Since $0.2 < 1 - 0.7$, all the points are mapped to a minimum surface. The ranges for each dimension, correspondingly, are:

$$R_0 = [0 + 0.4, 0 + 0.2] = [0.4, 0.2]$$

$$R_1 = [1 + 0.1, 1 + 0.2] = [1.1, 1.2]$$

The range R_0 is invalid and, hence, that search is avoided.

Consider Q_3. The query values are

$$l_{min} = 0.3, \ l_{max} = 0.5, \ h_{min} = 0.4, \ h_{max} = 0.8$$

Since neither $0.2 \geq 1 - 0.5$ nor $0.4 < 1 - 0.8$, the points can be mapped to either a minimum or a maximum surface. The ranges for each dimension, therefore, are:

$$R_0 = [0 + 0.5, 0 + 0.8] = [0.5, 0.8]$$
$$R_1 = [1 + 0.3, 1 + 0.4] = [1.3, 1.4]$$

□

8.3.3   Discussion

The iMinMax index performs fewer range searches than the pyramid technique in general and, therefore, can outperform the latter. However, if the data distribution is very skewed, the pyramid technique and more notably the extended pyramid technique can be faster. The two extreme index structures iMin and iMax do not perform as satisfactorily as compared to the iMinMax structure with $\theta = 0$. The parameter θ is related to the skewness of the data, which can be estimated by sampling. Thus, non-zero values of θ can give better results, especially for non-uniform datasets. However, tuning θ optimally remains a challenge.

8.4   VA-File

The VECTOR APPROXIMATION FILE (VA-FILE) [Weber et al., 1998] is, strictly speaking, not an index structure, but rather an unordered list of all the data points in a quantized manner. It is particularly designed for high-dimensional spaces where none of the index structures show any advantage in similarity search queries.

Each dimension of the space is quantized using a certain number of bits. Thus, if 3 bits are used, the total range along that dimension is divided into $2^3 = 8$ equal parts. The value of a data point for that dimension is determined by the partition it falls into and is represented using 3 bits. The overall effect is to impose a high-dimensional grid structure on the space. Representation of any data point requires $b = \sum_{i=1}^{d} b_i$ bits where d is the dimensionality of the space and dimension i is quantized using b_i bits. Thus, each data point is *approximated* using a bit

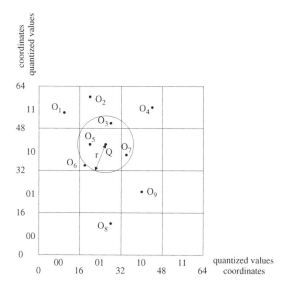

Figure 8.8: An example of a VA-file representation.

string formed by concatenating the bits along the individual dimensions. All such bit strings corresponding to a dataset are then maintained as an *unordered* list.

Key Concept 8.4 [VA-File]. The data is quantized using a fixed number of bits per dimension. The quantized data is stored as a list in an unordered manner. When a query arrives, the entire list is searched and the quantization is used to prune unnecessary points. In very high dimensionality, since almost all the data needs to be searched anyway, examining the quantized list is faster.

Figure 8.8 shows an example with 9 data points and a query point in a 2-dimensional space where each dimension is quantized using 2 bits. The quantization of the objects and the query is given in Table 8.1.

Before describing the technique for searching through a VA-file, it is important and interesting to analyze the structure.

8.4.1 Analysis

Each dimension i has 2^{b_i} slices. The total number of grid cells, therefore, is $\prod_{i=1}^{d} 2^{b_i} = 2^{\sum_{i=1}^{d} b_i} = 2^b$. Assuming uniform distribution, each

Table 8.1: Quantization of points using a VA-file.

Object	Coordinates	Quantization
O_1	10, 54	00 11
O_2	20, 60	01 11
O_3	28, 50	01 11
O_4	44, 56	10 11
O_5	20, 42	01 10
O_6	18, 34	01 10
O_7	34, 38	10 10
O_8	28, 12	01 00
O_9	40, 24	10 01
Q	26, 42	01 10

slice, and each cell, has around the same amount of data. Hence, the probability that there is a point inside a cell is 2^{-b}.

The probability that a grid cell is shared by at least two data points can be calculated in the following way. Assume a total of n data points. Consider a particular cell which is occupied by a data point. The probability that it is shared, denoted by P_{share}, is the complement of the probability that none of the other $n-1$ data points occupy this particular grid cell. The chance of a data point not falling in a particular cell is $1 - 2^{-b}$. Assuming that the data points are generated independently, $P_{share} = 1 - (1 - 2^{-b})^{n-1} \approx n.2^{-b}$.

Consider a billion dataset, i.e., $n = 10^9 \approx 2^{30}$ residing in a modest 10-dimensional data space. If each dimension is quantized using 4 bits, i.e., $b = 10 \times 4 = 40$, then, $P_{share} = 2^{-10}$.

The probability that a cell is populated, denoted by P_{occ}, is also only $n.2^{-b}$. Again, using the previous values, P_{occ} is 2^{-10}.

Thus, for high-dimensional spaces, it is extremely rare that a particular grid cell is occupied.

8.4.2   Searching

Searching follows the filter-and-refine paradigm. The VA-file acts as a good filter in the following way.

Consider a range search with range r from a query object Q. Given the grids, it is easy to determine which cell the query point is in. The *complete* VA-file is then read through in a *linear* fashion.

For every data object, given its bit string (i.e., the grid cell), it can be quickly determined whether it can lie within a distance r from the grid cell corresponding to Q. This can be done by computing the minimum distance between the two rectangular grid cells (as elaborated in Appendix B).

All such data objects that are potential candidates are finally refined by computing their *actual* distances to Q.

Example 8.4 [VA-File Searching]. Perform a similarity search from Q with a range of 11 for the data shown in Table 8.1 using VA-file.

Figure 8.8 shows the query circle from Q.

The filter step is performed by computing the minimum distance of the grid cell that contains an object to the query. For example, consider O_1. The minimum distance of the grid cell $00\,11$ containing O_1 from Q is 11.66 (see Appendix B on how to compute these distance bounds). Thus, O_1 can be filtered out. In the same manner, O_8 and O_9 can also be filtered.

The rest of the objects, however, cannot be filtered. For example, the minimum distance of the grid cell $10\,11$ containing O_4 is 8.49. Since O_4 may be anywhere in the cell, it cannot be pruned.

Hence, their actual distances are computed, after which O_3, O_5, and O_7 are returned as answers. □

8.4.3 Utility of VA-File

The VA-file iterates over *all* the data objects. A natural question to then ask is how is it any better than a linear scan over the database? The answer lies in the quantization which acts as a compression on the database and, therefore, allows reading the entire data contents much faster. Example 8.5 shows a comparison.

Example 8.5 [VA-File Storage]. Assume a dataset of 10^8 objects in a 10-dimensional space. If it is quantized using a VA-file with 4 bits per dimension, what is the gain in reading through the VA-file as opposed to the original database?

Assuming each floating point representation of a real value requires 8 bytes, the raw storage of each object needs $8 \times 10 = 80$ bytes. The total raw storage is, thus, 8×10^9 bytes, i.e., approximately 8 GB.

Each bit string for the VA-file requires $4 \times 10 = 40$ bits, i.e., 5 bytes. The total compressed storage is, therefore, 5×10^8 bytes which is close to 500 MB.

For a standard machine having 4 GB RAM, while the compressed VA-file representation can be loaded in the main memory, thereby allowing very fast filter operations, the raw database must be read from the disk using costly disk I/O operations.

Even if the entire VA-file representation does not fit in the main memory and it must be read from the disk, the compression ratio allows reading the data contents that many times faster as the number of disk blocks required for storage is also fewer in the same ratio. Here, it is 16 times faster. □

8.4.4 Discussion

The comparative performance of VA-file over linear scan improves with increasing dimensionality. The hierarchical indexing structures anyway fail in very high dimensions. VA-file is better as compared to a linear search in higher dimensions since the amount of compression increases, thereby allowing much better read times. Moreover, the probabilities P_{share} and P_{occ} rapidly fall off with increasing dimensions, which indicates that the grid mechanism becomes better. Consequently, the filter step becomes much more accurate. On an average, for high-dimensional data, the filtering step can reduce the number of candidates to as few as 0.1% of the objects.

8.4.5 VA+-File

The VA-file treats the data as being uniformly spread over the entire space. Real data rarely follows such a pattern and is, more often than not, extremely skewed and clustered. Thus, the applicability of VA-file reduces, especially since the quantization of every dimension is done in a uniform manner.

The VA+-FILE [Ferhatosmanoglu et al., 2000] proposes three improvements over the VA-file to handle real data:

1. The axes are transformed using PCA (see Section 9.5) to better represent the data space.

2. The number of bits required in total for all the dimensions are allocated non-uniformly to the different axes so that axes with larger variances get more bits.

3. Assuming the total number of bits for an axis as given, the entire range along the axis is partitioned optimally into non-equal parts such that more partitions fall in denser regions.

In general, the VA+-file produces better lower bounds while filtering and can reduce the number of non-pruned candidates by as much as 10 time in comparison to the VA-file.

8.5   A-Tree

The APPROXIMATION TREE (A-TREE) [Sakurai et al., 2000] was designed to handle high dimensionality by *compressing* the data MBRs. The MBR descriptions of a child node are quantized using *relative approximation*.

For each dimension, instead of using a 32-bit floating point description (or 64-bit as the case may be) of the end-points of a hyper-rectangle, a code length c is chosen. Each end-point, thus, is represented in a compressed format using c bits. The resulting child node is termed as *virtual bounding rectangle* (VBR). The VBR possesses the crucial property that it encompasses the actual MBR. Since $c < 32$, the number of VBRs that can be packed in a node is more than that of MBRs and, hence, the fanout of the tree is increased. This results in lesser disk accesses and a better search performance.

8.5.1   Virtual Bounding Rectangle

The approximation of a child MBR by its corresponding virtual bounding rectangle (VBR) is done *relative* to the parent MBR. First, a code length c is chosen.

Suppose the parent MBR stretches from a_i to b_i in the ith dimension. The range is partitioned into $q = 2^c$ parts. Therefore, the partition marks fall at

$$a_i, \; a_i + \frac{b_i - a_i}{q}, \; a_i + 2.\frac{b_i - a_i}{q}, \; \ldots, \; a_i + (q-1).\frac{b_i - a_i}{q}, \; b_i \quad (8.19)$$

Consider a child MBR in d dimensions whose end-points are $l = (l_0, l_1, \ldots, l_{d-1})$ and $h = (h_0, h_1, \ldots, h_{d-1})$. Every lower end-point l_i of a child MBR is represented by the partition mark that is just *less than or equal* to it. This is called the *subspace code* and is an integer between 0 and $q - 1$. Similarly, every higher end-point h_i of a child MBR is represented by the partition mark that is just *greater than or equal* to it. The subspace code for this case comes out to be between 1 and q which is adjusted to the previous range by subtracting 1.

The subspace code of a child VBR is the concatenation of the subspace codes of the lower and higher end-points of the dimensions.

The above scheme ensures the important property that the VBR completely encompasses the MBR by moving the lower end-points towards smaller values and higher end-points towards larger values.

Thus, each number is an integer of length c. Hence, for d dimensions, the entire child MBR can be encoded in $2.d.c$ bits instead of $2d \times 32$ bits.

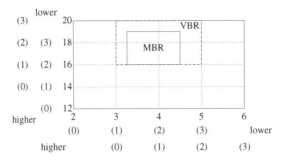

Figure 8.9: Example of a virtual bounding rectangle (VBR).

Example 8.6 [A-Tree Subspace Code]. Consider a parent MBR in two dimensions stretching from $(2, 12)$ to $(6, 20)$ as shown in Figure 8.9. Assuming a value of $c = 2$, find the subspace code of the VBR for the child MBR $(3.25, 16)$ to $(4.5, 19)$.

Figure 8.9 shows the child MBR and the corresponding VBR within the parent MBR. The VBR is marked in dashed lines while the dotted lines mark the partitions. The subspace codes are shown in brackets.

Since $q = 4$, the partition marks in the x and y dimensions are at $\{2, 3, 4, 5, 6\}$ and $\{12, 14, 16, 18, 20\}$ respectively. The lower end-point in the x-dimension, 3.25 is, thus, approximated by 3, the subspace code for which is the integer 1. The higher end-point, 4.5, is approximated by the larger partition mark at 5, whose subspace code is $3 - 1 = 2$. Similarly, the subspace codes for the y-dimension are the integers 2 (for the value 16) and $4 - 1 = 3$ (for the value 19). Consequently, the subspace code for the VBR is 1223.

From the code, the bounding box of the MBR can be deciphered again. Since the x-dimension code is 12, the range is $2 + 1.\frac{6-2}{4}$ to $2 + (2 + 1).\frac{6-2}{4}$, i.e., 3 to 5. Similarly, for the y-dimensional code 23, the range becomes $12 + 2.\frac{20-12}{4} = 16$ to $12 + (3 + 1).\frac{20-12}{4} = 20$. Thus, using the VBR, it is only guaranteed that the child MBR is within $(3, 16)$ to $(5, 20)$.   □

Key Concept 8.5 [A-Tree]. Each MBR is compressed to a virtual bounding rectangle (VBR) using a quantization with a particular code length. The VBR encompasses the MBR and is used for lower bounding the distance from a query. The compressed format requires lesser storage, thereby decreasing the number of node accesses.

8.5.2 Structure

The structure of an A-tree remains hierarchical and is similar to the other height-balanced disk-aware structures. There is one important deviation, though.

Within an internal node, the MBRs of the children are not stored; instead, only their VBRs are maintained. The entire bounding hyper-rectangle of the parent is also stored without any approximation. This, thus, enables computing the approximate coordinates of a child MBR in absolute terms.

The root is treated in a special manner. Since it encompasses the entire search region, storage of the parent MBR is avoided.

Similarly, the leaf nodes are special as well and they store only the approximation (subspace code) of the objects instead of the exact coordinates. Additionally, it stores the data pointers to the objects.

8.5.3 Searching

Similarity search queries follow the same general principle as in hierarchical structures. Given a query region, first the subspace code of a child VBR is tested. If the VBR does not intersect the query region, the child MBR is guaranteed to be not part of the answer and, hence, can be pruned. Otherwise, the child node is accessed.

Since the fanout of the tree is much larger, more child nodes can be tested at each level. If the quantization is good, it enables pruning larger spaces thereby yielding a better search performance.

8.5.4 Discussion

Updating an A-tree node may change the parent MBR and, thus, may require re-computing the subspace codes of all the children VBRs. In addition, although each node can choose its own code length c, no good algorithm has been provided to arrive at a value. When the code length is larger, the approximation is better. In this case, although fewer number of VBRs are packed per node, the number of internal nodes examined is likely to become fewer. The opposite effects are noted when the code length gets smaller.

Although A-tree is projected as a high-dimensionality structure, since it is hierarchical, it becomes unsuitable when the dimensionality becomes very large. The reason is that almost all the VBRs intersect with a query region and, hence, there is no gain through compression.

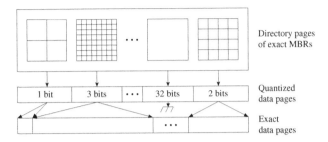

Figure 8.10: Structure of an IQ-tree.

8.6 IQ-Tree

Similar to the A-tree, the INDEPENDENT QUANTIZATION TREE (IQ-TREE) [Berchtold et al., 2000] also aims to combine the concepts of indexing and data compression.

In higher dimensions, a flat-file structure such as linear scan or VA-file shows a better search performance while in lower dimensions or for low selectivity of the query, a branching-based tree structure is better. The IQ-tree uses a mix of both these strategies. In addition, it compresses the data objects to obtain a quantized representation that fits in a smaller number of disk pages.

8.6.1 Structure

The IQ-tree has three levels, as shown in Figure 8.10:

1. A directory of disk pages containing the exact representations of MBRs.

2. A description of data objects compressed using quantization for each MBR.

3. A flat structure of all the actual data objects corresponding to the compressed ones at the second level.

Key Concept 8.6 [IQ-Tree]. Each MBR is quantized using a different bit length. The quantized data pages in an MBR point to exact data objects. The MBRs are themselves maintained as a list.

The size of each MBR is chosen such that the *compressed* description of the data objects in it can be stored in a single disk page. Thus, for each MBR, a separate approximation scheme can be adopted. The number of bits used for quantization of the data objects inside an MBR is *independent* of the quantization in other MBRs. This is how the structure gets its name.

The independent quantization scheme enables the structure to adapt to the object density inside an MBR and, hence, avoids the pitfalls of a single quantization scheme of the VA-file. If an MBR uses g bits to quantize, every dimension is divided into 2^g partitions. A data object inside the MBR, thus, uses a compressed representation of g bits instead of the exact floating-point representation of 32 bits (or 64 bits). If no suitable quantization is found and an MBR is forced to use all 32 bits, then the second level contains the actual data pages and the third level for that MBR is not needed.

8.6.2 Searching

The IQ-tree can be viewed as a hierarchical index structure with the directory serving as a large root node, the compressed data pages as the leaf nodes with the last level being the actual data objects (with no approximation or quantization). Hence, the search procedure remains similar to any general hierarchical structure. We describe it next.

First, the directory is searched and only those MBRs that intersect with the query region are pursued. Within these MBRs, the quantized information is used to further prune away unnecessary data objects. Note that this approximation uses the same philosophy as the A-tree: the quantized representation should be able to provide a lower and upper bound of the distance from the query point. For a query region, the approximate region should, thus, translate to a larger bounding box than the actual object. Finally, for all the approximate data objects that have survived the pruning, the actual data objects in the third level are searched to retrieve the answer.

8.6.3 Construction

The construction of an IQ-tree starts with a partitioning scheme such as bulk-loading (see Section 4.11). The partitioning divides the entire data space into MBRs that fit in a single disk page using only one bit of quantization, i.e., $g = 1$.

Assume that the dimensionality of the space is d. Then, each object has a representation size of $s = g \times d$ bits. If the capacity of a disk page size is C bits, the number of 1-bit quantized objects that can fit in one disk page is $w = \lfloor C/s \rfloor$. Hence, assuming a total of n objects, the initial partition divides the data into roughly $\lceil n/w \rceil$ MBRs, each containing roughly w objects.

Each of these MBRs are then examined in order to determine the optimal number of quantization bits. The effect of doubling the resolution from the initial $g = 1$ bits to $g = 2$ bits is that now all the w objects cannot fit in one disk page but will roughly require two disk pages. The original MBR is accordingly split into two MBRs with each of them having the quantization level $g = 2$. The process goes on with the resolution doubling at each stage till the required level of quantization is achieved. We next discuss how an optimized level of quantization is chosen.

8.6.4   Level of Quantization

The amount of quantization plays a vital role in the search performance. If too much compression is performed, the approximation of the data objects becomes poor and consequently the distance bounds become quite loose and not much can be gained in terms of pruning. On the other hand, if too little compression is done, the approximation is tighter, but the space for storing the objects is larger, thereby incurring more disk accesses for a search even at the quantized level.

The authors of IQ-tree designed an elaborate cost model based on the three important parameters of random I/O cost, sequential I/O cost and probability of a search hitting an MBR. They then optimized the cost function to arrive at a particular level of quantization g for an MBR. The details can be found in [Berchtold et al., 2000].

Part VI

Data Reduction
Techniques

Chapter 9

Dimensionality Reduction Techniques

The general idea of DIMENSIONALITY REDUCTION is to transform vectors from a higher dimensional space to a lower dimensional space. The main objective of this transformation is to preserve the properties of the original space as far as possible, the most important of them being the distance between two objects. A common term that is also used to describe such transformations is EMBEDDING.

Formally, if there are vectors $\vec{u}$ and $\vec{v}$ in a space of dimensionality k with the distance between them measured by the function d, and the transformed feature vectors $\vec{u}'$ and $\vec{v}'$ after the dimensionality reduction technique f are in a space of lower dimensionality k' with the new distance measure d' (which may be the same as d), then

$$k' \ll k \text{ and } d'(\vec{u}', \vec{v}') \approx d(\vec{u}, \vec{v}) \tag{9.1}$$

The biggest motivation for such transformations is that they induce the objects (represented as vectors) onto a lower dimensional space where indexing and searching techniques become more efficient. There are certain dimensionality reduction techniques that do not even require an explicit vector representation of an object. They can work with a distance function or a distance matrix among the objects, and represent the transformed objects as vectors.

In this chapter, we first discuss the properties and quality measures of dimensionality reduction and embedding techniques. We then discuss several common such methods.

9.1 Properties Useful for Similarity Search

We first discuss two properties of dimensionality reduction techniques that are useful in the context of similarity searching.

An important property that is extremely useful for range queries

is when for all possible pairs of vectors, the new distance between the
transformed vectors is less than or equal to the distance between the
original vectors. This is called the *pruning* property:

$$\forall u, v, \ d'(u', v') \leq d(u, v) \tag{9.2}$$

Transformations (or mappings) that preserve this property are called
contractive transformations. It is easy to see how they are useful for
range searches. For a range query with radius r, if the distance between
a transformed object and the transformed query is more than r, it is
guaranteed that the distance between the original object and the original
query is also more than r and, hence, the object can be pruned.

A similarly useful property for kNN queries is the *proximity-
preserving* property which ensures that for any triplet of objects u, v, w,
if u were closer to w than v, the same relationship is maintained after
the transformation as well, i.e., u' will be closer to w' than v':

$$\forall u, v, w, \ d(u, w) \leq d(v, w) \Rightarrow d'(u', w') \leq d'(v', w') \tag{9.3}$$

Transformations that obey this property are useful for kNN searches
as the order of distances from the query is maintained in the transformed
space as well.

9.2 Quality Measures

To assess the usefulness of a particular dimensionality reduction
method for a practical task, it is important to measure its quality. The
two most important measures of quality are *distortion* and *stress*.

9.2.1 Distortion

Suppose, for a mapping f, it is guaranteed that for every pair of
objects u and v,

$$\frac{1}{c_1}.d(u, v) \leq d'(f(u), f(v)) \leq c_2.d(u, v) \tag{9.4}$$

where $f(u)$ and $f(v)$ denote the transformed objects.

The terms $c_1, c_2 \geq 1$ provide bounds on the distance after the
transformation. The maximum *contraction* is captured by c_1 while the
maximum *expansion* is captured by c_2.

DISTORTION is measured as the product of these two terms:

$$\text{Distortion} = c_1 . c_2 \tag{9.5}$$

Distortion measures the worst possible change in the ratio of two distances in the original space to that in the transformed space.

For certain mappings, it is analytically possible to compute the distortion. For others, the distortion is generally measured empirically as the product of the worst ratios of contraction and expansion seen for examples in the dataset:

$$\text{Distortion} = \max_{\forall u,v} \left\{ \frac{d(u,v)}{d'(f(u), f(v))} \right\} \times \max_{\forall u,v} \left\{ \frac{d'(f(u), f(v))}{d(u,v)} \right\} \tag{9.6}$$

An embedding that has $c_2 = 1$ is a *contractive* embedding while an embedding that has $c_1 = c_2 = 1$ is an *isometric* embedding. An isometric embedding is ideal as it preserves the distances exactly.

9.2.2 Stress

While distortion measures the worst-case behavior of a transformation, a useful quality metric that measures the average or overall behavior of an embedding is STRESS:

$$\text{Stress}_1 = \sqrt{\frac{\sum_{\forall u,v} \left(d'(f(u), f(v)) - d(u,v) \right)^2}{\sum_{\forall u,v} \left(d(u,v) \right)^2}} \tag{9.7}$$

Stress measures the average difference in the distances before and after the transformation (normalized by the original distance). Since the denominator is a constant for a given instance, sometimes the quality is measured by just using the numerator.

In an alternate definition of stress, the normalization is done before the summation:

$$\text{Stress}_2 = \sqrt{\sum_{\forall u,v} \frac{\left(d'(f(u), f(v)) - d(u,v) \right)^2}{\left(d(u,v) \right)^2}} \tag{9.8}$$

This imparts more relative weight to the smaller distances.

9.3   Embedding

EMBEDDING is a transformation from one space and distance function to another space and distance function. Generally, the target space is a vector space (see Section C.1) with the target distance being Euclidean. The characteristics of the embedding depend both on the nature of the space and the distance function.

For example, it is always possible to have a distance-preserving embedding (i.e., where distortion is 1) for an n-object dataset in a metric space with distance d onto an n-dimensional vector space with distance function $d' = L_\infty$ (see Section 5.2 for the definition). If the original n objects are denoted by $O_1, \ldots, O_n$, then the embedded object $O'_i = \{d(O_i, O_1), \ldots, d(O_i, O_n)\}$. Thus, in the embedded space, each dimension i represents the distance of every object to O_i.

Example 9.1 [Embedding]. Embed the following 3 objects

$$O_1 = (2, 3), O_2 = (1, 5), O_3 = (6, 4)$$

with a metric distance $d = L_1$ onto a 3-dimensional vector space with distance $d' = L_\infty$ such that the embedding is distance-preserving.

The embeddings are

$$O'_1 = d(O_1, O_1), d(O_1, O_2), d(O_1, O_3) = (0, 3, 5) \qquad (9.9)$$
$$O'_2 = d(O_2, O_1), d(O_2, O_2), d(O_2, O_3) = (3, 0, 6) \qquad (9.10)$$
$$O'_3 = d(O_3, O_1), d(O_3, O_2), d(O_3, O_3) = (5, 6, 0) \qquad (9.11)$$

The distances are

$$d'(O'_1, O'_2) = 3 = d(O_1, O_2) \qquad (9.12)$$
$$d'(O'_2, O'_3) = 6 = d(O_2, O_3) \qquad (9.13)$$
$$d'(O'_3, O'_1) = 5 = d(O_3, O_1) \qquad (9.14)$$

$\square$

Embedding is often very useful in applications that use statistical distance measures such as the quadratic form distance (QFD) (see Section 5.3). QFD does not allow indexing directly. However, since the QFD matrix is symmetric and positive definite, it can undergo *Cholesky decomposition* [Press et al., 2007]. Assume that the Cholesky decomposition of the QFD matrix A is $A = B^T B$, where B is an upper triangular (square) matrix. (Thus, B^T is a lower triangular matrix.) This allows the QFD distance to be embedded in a vector space having the same dimensionality but with the L_2 norm. For any two object vectors $\vec{u}, \vec{v}$,

$$
\begin{aligned}
QFD(\vec{u}, \vec{v}) &= \sqrt{(\vec{u} - \vec{v})^T A (\vec{u} - \vec{v})} \\
&\quad - \sqrt{(\vec{u} - \vec{v})^T B^T B (\vec{u} - \vec{v})} \\
&= \sqrt{(B\vec{u} - B\vec{v})^T (B\vec{u} - B\vec{v})} \\
&= L_2(B\vec{u}, B\vec{v})
\end{aligned}
\tag{9.15}
$$

Thus, the embedding is $(\vec{x}, QFD) \mapsto (B\vec{x}, L_2)$ where $A = B^T B$. This transformation allows further dimensionality reduction as well.

9.4 Singular Value Decomposition (SVD)

The SINGULAR VALUE DECOMPOSITION (SVD) technique uses the concept of matrix decomposition to reduce dimensionality [Golub and Reinsch, 1970]. The original dataset is represented as a matrix A of size $n \times k$ where n denotes the number of objects and k denotes the dimensionality. The SVD factorizes the matrix into three components:

$$
A_{n \times k} = U_{n \times n} \Sigma_{n \times k} V_{k \times k}^T
\tag{9.16}
$$

The columns of U, called the *left singular vectors*, are the eigenvectors (see Section C.3.2 for the definition) of the matrix AA^T. The matrix UU^T is the orthonormal matrix I_n of size $n \times n$. Similarly, the columns of V, called the *right singular vectors*, are the eigenvectors of $A^T A$. Also, VV^T is the orthonormal matrix I_k of size $k \times k$.

The Σ matrix is diagonal with only the σ_{ii} values being non-zero. The σ_{ii} values are called *singular values* which are the *positive square roots* of eigenvalues of AA^T or $A^T A$. The number of non-zero singular values is at most k (assuming $n > k$) and they are generally arranged in a descending order, i.e., $\sigma_{11} \geq \sigma_{22} \geq \cdots \geq \sigma_{kk}$.

The matrix V shows how each dimension can be represented as a linear combination of other dimensions, while U shows how each object can be represented as a linear combination of other objects. The columns of V are called *input basis vectors* and those of U are called *output basis vectors*.

9.4.1 Spectral Decomposition

If A is a real symmetric matrix of size $m \times m$, then since $A = A^T$, $U = V$ as $A^T A = A A^T = A^2$. Consequently, the decomposition of A can be expressed as

$$A = Q \Sigma Q^T \qquad (9.17)$$

This is called the *spectral decomposition* of A. The matrix Q is of size $m \times m$ and contains the eigenvectors of A^2. The m singular values of A are stored in Σ. The connection between the singular values and eigenvalues can be established using the above. The eigenvectors of A are the same as those of A^2, but the eigenvalues of A are the square roots of the eigenvalues of A^2. The singular values of A are its eigenvalues and are, thus, the square roots of the eigenvalues of A^2.

When A is not a square matrix, the eigenvalues are not defined. Instead, the singular values, which are the square roots of eigenvalues of $A A^T$ (or $A^T A$ as the number of non-zero singular values is at most the rank of the matrix A), represent the equivalent notion.

9.4.2 Transformation Using SVD

SVD can be used to transform the original space by

$$T = AV = U\Sigma \qquad (9.18)$$

The matrix V is, thus, called the *SVD transform matrix*. Essentially, T is a rotation of the original space where A resides, and has the same dimensionality k. The columns of V form the basis vectors in the new rotated space.

Example 9.2 [SVD]. Find the SVD and transformation of

$$A = \begin{bmatrix} 2 & 4 \\ 1 & 3 \\ 0 & 1 \\ -1 & 0.5 \end{bmatrix} \qquad (9.19)$$

$$A = U\Sigma V^T$$

$$\text{where } U = \begin{bmatrix} -0.80 & 0.22 & 0.05 & 0.54 \\ -0.56 & -0.20 & -0.34 & -0.71 \\ -0.16 & -0.31 & 0.90 & -0.21 \\ -0.01 & -0.89 & -0.22 & 0.37 \end{bmatrix}$$

$$\Sigma = \begin{bmatrix} 5.54 & 0 \\ 0 & 1.24 \\ 0 & 0 \\ 0 & 0 \end{bmatrix}$$

$$V = \begin{bmatrix} -0.39 & 0.92 \\ -0.92 & -0.39 \end{bmatrix} \tag{9.20}$$

$$T = AV$$

$$= \begin{bmatrix} 2 & 4 \\ 1 & 3 \\ 0 & 1 \\ -1 & 0.5 \end{bmatrix} \times \begin{bmatrix} -0.39 & 0.92 \\ -0.92 & -0.39 \end{bmatrix}$$

$$= \begin{bmatrix} -4.46 & 0.27 \\ -3.15 & -0.25 \\ -0.92 & -0.39 \\ -0.06 & -1.15 \end{bmatrix} \tag{9.21}$$

$\square$

Since SVD is just a rotation, it preserves the L_2 norm (i.e., the lengths) of the vectors (equivalently, the distances between points). Thus, SVD is an *isometric* embedding. For example, in Example 9.2, the length of any vector in A is the same as the length of the corresponding vector in T. For example, the length of the first vector in A is $\sqrt{2^2 + 4^2} = \sqrt{20}$ which is equal to $\sqrt{(-4.46)^2 + (0.27)^2}$.

The running time for SVD is $O(nkr)$ for a matrix A of size $n \times k$ and rank r. Assuming $r = k < n$, the time becomes $O(nk^2)$.

Also, as there are at most k non-zero singular values, retaining only the first k columns of U and the first k rows of Σ result in a more compact SVD with no loss of information.

The decomposition of A using SVD can be, thus, expressed as

$$A = U_{1...k}\Sigma_{1...k}V_{1...k}^T \tag{9.22}$$

or, equivalently,

$$A = \sum_{i=1}^{k} (\vec{u}_i \sigma_{ii} \vec{v}_i^T) \tag{9.23}$$

9.4.3 Dimensionality Reduction Using SVD

When the dimensionality is reduced to k', only the first k' terms are retained in the summation of Eq. (9.23):

$$A \approx \sum_{i=1}^{k'} (\vec{u}_i \sigma_{ii} \vec{v}_i^T) \tag{9.24}$$

The dimensionality reduction can be alternatively viewed in a matrix form. Only the first k' columns of U and V are used along with the first k' values from Σ. Thus,

$$A \approx U_{1...k'} \Sigma_{1...k'} V_{1...k'}^T \tag{9.25}$$

The transformed and reduced data can be expressed as

$$T' \approx A.V_{1...k'} \tag{9.26}$$

The first k' columns of V form the basis vectors of the transformed space with reduced dimensionality k'. This space produces the best rank k' approximation of the original space in terms of sum squared error.

Example 9.3 [Dimensionality Reduction Using SVD]. Find the SVD and transformation of

$$A = \begin{bmatrix} 2 & 4 \\ 1 & 3 \\ 0 & 1 \\ -1 & 0.5 \end{bmatrix} \tag{9.27}$$

after reducing the dimensionality to $k' = 1$.

$$A \approx A_{k'} = U_{k'} \Sigma_{k'} V_{k'}^T$$

$$\text{where } U_{k'} = \begin{bmatrix} -0.80 \\ -0.56 \\ -0.16 \\ -0.01 \end{bmatrix}$$

$$\Sigma_{k'} = \begin{bmatrix} 5.54 \end{bmatrix}$$

$$V_{k'} = \begin{bmatrix} -0.39 \\ -0.92 \end{bmatrix}$$

$$\therefore A \approx \begin{bmatrix} 1.74 & 4.10 \\ 1.23 & 2.90 \\ 0.35 & 0.84 \\ 0.02 & 0.06 \end{bmatrix} \tag{9.28}$$

Comparing $A_{k'}$ with the original A, it can be seen that the values are distorted a bit but not much. The transformed and reduced data is

$$T'_{k'} = A.V_{k'}$$

$$= \begin{bmatrix} 2 & 4 \\ 1 & 3 \\ 0 & 1 \\ -1 & 0.5 \end{bmatrix} \times \begin{bmatrix} -0.39 \\ -0.92 \end{bmatrix}$$

$$= \begin{bmatrix} -4.46 \\ -3.15 \\ -0.92 \\ -0.06 \end{bmatrix} \tag{9.29}$$

It can be seen from Example 9.2 that the reduced data is, in essence, the first k' columns of the original transformed data. □

The transformation that reduces the dimensionality using SVD is *contractive*. This can be understood from the fact that the new reduced data $T_{k'}$ contains a proper subset of the dimensions of the transformed space T, and, as discussed earlier, T preserves the length of the original data A since it is just a rotation. Therefore, the vectors in T' are shorter.

9.4.4 Dimensionality of Reduced Space

An important question that arises in the context of dimensionality reduction is how many dimensions to retain, i.e., what should be the reduced dimensionality? While there is no easy answer for this, the SVD uses the concept of *energy* (also known as *spread* or *variance*) for this.

The total energy of a dataset is the sum of the squares of its singular values, i.e.,

$$E = E_k = \sum_{i=1}^{k} \sigma_{ii}^2 \tag{9.30}$$

A useful heuristic is to reduce to k' dimensions such that $p\%$ of the energy is retained, i.e.,

$$\frac{E_{k'}}{E_k} \times 100 \geq p \tag{9.31}$$

Generally, p is assumed to be between 80% and 95% depending on the application. In Example 9.3, $k' = 1$ retains $(5.54^2)/(5.54^2 + 1.24^2) = 95.22\%$ of the energy.

9.5   Principal Component Analysis (PCA)

The PRINCIPAL COMPONENT ANALYSIS (PCA) method is a way of identifying patterns in a dataset [Jolliffe, 2002]. More precisely, it shows how the input basis vectors for a dataset are correlated, and then, transforms the data from this set of (possibly correlated) axes to a set of uncorrelated axes. The new axes are called the *principal components*. Similar to SVD, PCA is also an orthogonal linear transformation (i.e., a rotation) and, hence, the lengths of vectors are preserved by the transformation. It is equivalent to the DISCRETE KARHUNEN-LOÈVE TRANSFORM (KLT) [Fukunaga, 1990].

9.5.1   Algorithm

The procedure for PCA is very similar to that of SVD, and can be summarized as follows (assume that the data matrix B is of size $n \times k$):

1. Mean center the data (strictly speaking, this step is optional): For each dimension i, the mean $\mu(B_i)$ is first computed. Then this mean is subtracted from each column i to produce the new data matrix A, i.e., $A_i = B_i - \mu(B_i)$. The transformation guarantees that $\mu(A_i) = 0$.

2. Compute the covariance matrix of the dimensions: The covariance matrix C is of size $k \times k$. If data is mean centered, then the covariance matrix is simply $C = A^T A$.

3. Find eigenvectors and eigenvalues of the covariance matrix: There will be k such eigenvectors with the corresponding eigenvalues. Assume that they are denoted by $V = \{\vec{v}_1, \ldots, \vec{v}_k\}$ and $E = \{e_1, \ldots, e_k\}$ respectively. These eigenvectors are the *principal components*.

4. Sort the eigenvalues in descending order: Without loss of generality, assume that $e_1 \geq \cdots \geq e_k$.

5. Project the data onto the eigenvectors: Project the data matrix A onto the new axes $\vec{v}_1, \ldots, \vec{v}_k$ one by one.

Example 9.4 [PCA]. Compute the PCA and the corresponding transformation of

$$B = \begin{bmatrix} 2 & 4 \\ 1 & 3 \\ 0 & 1 \\ -1 & 0.5 \end{bmatrix} \tag{9.32}$$

The data is first mean-centered.

$$\mu(B) = \begin{bmatrix} 0.500 & 2.125 \end{bmatrix} \tag{9.33}$$

$$\therefore A = B - \mu(B) = \begin{bmatrix} 1.5 & 1.875 \\ 0.5 & 0.875 \\ -0.5 & -1.125 \\ -1.5 & -1.625 \end{bmatrix} \tag{9.34}$$

The correlation matrix is

$$C = A^T A = \begin{bmatrix} 5.000 & 6.250 \\ 6.250 & 8.187 \end{bmatrix} \tag{9.35}$$

The eigenvectors and eigenvalues of the correlation matrix are

$$\text{Eigenvectors } V = \begin{bmatrix} 0.613 & -0.789 \\ 0.789 & 0.613 \end{bmatrix} \tag{9.36}$$

$$\text{Eigenvalues } E = \begin{bmatrix} 13.043 \\ 0.143 \end{bmatrix} \tag{9.37}$$

The transformed data obtained by projecting onto the eigenvectors is

$$\text{Transformed data } T = A.V = \begin{bmatrix} 2.400 & -0.034 \\ 0.997 & 0.142 \\ -1.195 & -0.295 \\ -2.203 & 0.187 \end{bmatrix} \tag{9.38}$$

□

Again, it can be easily verified that the lengths of the vectors obtained *after* the mean-centering are preserved although the mean-centering process destroys this property. As an example, consider the first vector: $\sqrt{(1.5)^2 + (1.875)^2} = \sqrt{(2.4)^2 + (-0.034)^2}$ but $\sqrt{(2.4)^2 + (-0.034)^2} \neq \sqrt{2^2 + 4^2}$.

However, since every vector is first shifted using the mean of the original matrix, mean-centering still allows the neighborhood relationships among a set of points to be preserved, i.e., if point u were closer to point v than point w before the mean-centering, the same relationship exists after the process. In other words, mean-centering is a *proximity preserving* transformation.

Mean-centering is considered an important step as it enables computing the correlation matrix C much faster. More importantly, mean-centering actually allows bypassing the computation of the correlation matrix altogether as it can be observed that the eigenvector matrix V of $C = A^T A$ is really the matrix V obtained by the SVD of A. Thus, PCA can be computed much faster using SVD when the data is mean-centered. Note that the PCA of A is different from the SVD of the original matrix B.

The running time of PCA for a matrix B of size $n \times k$ is $O(nk^2 + k^3)$.

9.5.2   Dimensionality Reduction Using PCA

Dimensionality reduction using PCA is achieved in the same way as in SVD. If k' dimensions are required, then the first k' columns of the eigenvector matrix V are used.

Example 9.5 [Dimensionality Reduction Using PCA]. Reduce the dimensionality to $k' = 1$ of B in Example 9.4.

Retaining only the first column of V from Eq. (9.36), the reduced data is

$$
\begin{aligned}
T' &= A.V_{1\ldots k'} \\
&= \begin{bmatrix} 1.5 & 1.875 \\ 0.5 & 0.875 \\ -0.5 & -1.125 \\ -1.5 & -1.625 \end{bmatrix} \times \begin{bmatrix} 0.613 \\ 0.789 \end{bmatrix} \\
&= \begin{bmatrix} 2.400 \\ 0.997 \\ -1.195 \\ -2.203 \end{bmatrix}
\end{aligned}
\tag{9.39}
$$

This corresponds to the first k' columns of the transformed data T from Example 9.4.   □

9.5.3   Number of Reduced Dimensions

The number of dimensions to retain is again determined based on the same heuristic that uses the concept of *energy* of the dataset as in SVD. The energy is the sum of the eigenvalues. In this example, $k' = 1$ retains $(13.043)/(13.043 + 0.143) = 98.91\%$ of the energy.

9.6 Multi-Dimensional Scaling (MDS)

MULTI-DIMENSIONAL SCALING (MDS) tries to choose an embedding that aims to minimize the *stress* as defined by Eq. (9.7) [Kruskal, 1964, Kruskal and Wish, 1978]. The algorithm minimizes only the numerator, i.e., sum of the squared differences of the distances; the denominator, being a constant, plays no role in the minimization. Since the optimal minimization is a hard problem and requires impractical running time, the MDS method works according to a simple heuristic.

The points in the embedded space are first initialized randomly in the k-dimensional target Euclidean space. Then they are modified such that the stress reduces. This is achieved by computing the distance of the embedded point to all the other embedded points and then moving the point using the principle of steepest descent. The algorithm continues in iterations. In each iteration, it examines the points one by one till a stopping criterion is reached which can be either a fixed number of iterations or when the decrease in stress from one iteration to the next falls below a pre-defined threshold.

The important advantage of MDS is that it does not require a vector representation or a distance function definition of the original points; all it requires is a distance matrix between all pairs of points. The embedded distance is generally assumed to be Euclidean.

9.6.1 Variants

There are different important variations of MDS. The original formulation that reduces a quantity called *strain* is called the CLASSICAL MDS [Torgerson, 1952]. The strain works with the inner products of the object vectors. The more popular version uses the *stress* function of Eq. (9.7) [Kruskal, 1964]. This is called the METRIC MDS (or simply MDS). The strain can be shown to be equivalent to the stress formulation after suitable transformations [Buja et al., 2008]. If the original distances are Euclidean, then MDS is optimal. For other metric distances, there is no such guarantee.

The NON-METRIC MDS version works even when the distances are specified only qualitatively [Shepard, 1962a, Shepard, 1962b, Kruskal, 1964]. The most common way of specifying such qualitative information is by specifying only the order among the distances, but not their actual values. In other words, given two pairs of objects O_1, O_2 and O_3, O_4, it is only specified that $d(O_1, O_2) > d(O_3, O_4)$. The non-metric MDS method projects the objects onto a Euclidean space that respects this ranking among the distances. Thus, it is *proximity preserving*. However, the entire input ordering must be specified, i.e., no two distances can be left unordered.

9.6.2   Sammon Projection

An alternative version of MDS that aims to minimize the stress according to the definition given in Eq. (9.8) is SAMMON PROJECTION [Sammon, 1969]. Unlike MDS, Sammon projection gives more importance to smaller distances due to the normalization effect. The methodology remains the same, i.e., the points are initialized randomly in the k-dimensional target Euclidean space and are moved by steepest descent till the algorithm converges or a stopping criterion is reached.

9.7   IsoMap

ISOMAP [Tenenbaum et al., 2000] is a non-linear dimensionality reduction technique that builds upon both PCA and MDS. IsoMap aims to preserve the *geodesic* distances between the points in a lower dimensional space. The geodesic distance between two points is measured along the hyper-dimensional surface of the space, and not through the straight line connecting them. In many applications of high-dimensional spaces, geodesic distances more accurately represent the "true" dissimilarity between a pair of points. Thus, preserving the geodesic distances preserves the intrinsic geometry of the space.

For neighboring points, the geodesic distance is close to the Euclidean distance. However, for far-off points, the geodesic distance may require computing a path via the space and not across it as done by the Euclidean distance. An example of this is points on the surface of a sphere.

Consequently, IsoMap uses the concept of neighborhood graphs to estimate the geodesic distances. Each point in the graph is connected by an edge to its neighbors. In the ϵ-IsoMap, all points that are within a Euclidean distance of ϵ are being made neighbors, while in the k-IsoMap, only the k nearest neighbors are considered.

The edges in this graph are weighted by the corresponding Euclidean distances. The path length of the shortest weighted paths between all pairs of points form the distance matrix Δ. Assuming a total of n points, each point is represented as an n-length vector, each component of which is the distance to another point.

A lower dimensional subspace of this distance matrix Δ is found by

MDS. The resulting transformation is the IsoMap transformation. The dimensionality, d', of the output space is determined by choosing the d' eigenvectors corresponding to the top d' eigenvalues and projecting onto them.

IsoMap, thus, assumes the existence of a *manifold*. A manifold is a space that is locally Euclidean, i.e., it resembles a Euclidean space near each point.

9.8   FastMap

Most dimensionality reduction techniques require computation of $O(n^2)$ distances when there are n objects in the dataset. FASTMAP [Faloutsos and Lin, 1995] improves upon this by providing an efficient way of avoiding this quadratic cost. Although it works for any input vector space endowed with a metric distance, the embedded space it outputs is restricted to a vector space with the distance being Euclidean.

The basic idea of FastMap is the following:

1. Find the axis with the largest range or spread.

2. Obtain the first dimension by projecting the input points onto that.

3. Obtain the next dimensions by repeating the above two steps.

We next discuss each of these steps in detail.

9.8.1   Axis with Largest Range

Unlike SVD that mathematically finds the axis with the largest variance, FastMap approximates that by using the line that joins the two most distant points (called *pivots*) in the dataset. In some sense, this corresponds to the *diameter* of the dataset.

However, finding the most distant pair requires quadratic costs. FastMap, therefore, resorts to a heuristic. It first picks up a random point, P_1. It then picks the point, P_2, that is farthest from P_1. Next, it updates P_1 by choosing the point that is at the largest distance from P_2. It keeps updating the pair of points P_1 and P_2 until they converge, i.e., when they iterate only among themselves.

The convergence, however, is guaranteed only after $O(n)$ steps. Since each step requires $O(n)$ computations, this degrades the FastMap to a

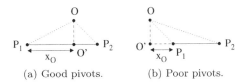

(a) Good pivots.   (b) Poor pivots.

Figure 9.1: Obtaining the first dimension in FastMap.

quadratic time algorithm. Thus, the updating of pivots stops after a few steps. This, of course, may not find the object pair with the largest distance. As we will see later, this may cause a problem for FastMap.

9.8.2 Projection

Assume that the pivots are P_1 and P_2 as shown in Figure 9.1a. Thus, the line joining them acts as the projection axis. The projection of a point O on this axis is O'. The distance, x_O, of O' from the first pivot, P_1, is the new *first* coordinate of O. Using Pythagorean geometry,

$$d(P_1,O)^2 - d(P_1,O')^2 = d(O,O')^2 = d(P_2,O)^2 - d(P_2,O')^2$$
$$\Rightarrow d(P_1,O)^2 - (x_O)^2 = d(P_2,O)^2 - (d(P_1,P_2) - x_O)^2$$
$$\Rightarrow x_O = \frac{d(P_1,P_2)^2 + d(P_1,O)^2 - d(P_2,O)^2}{2.d(P_1,P_2)} \qquad (9.40)$$

It is not guaranteed that the new coordinate value, x_O, will be always positive. Consider Figure 9.1b where the projection of O falls outside the line between P_1 and P_2. Ideally, this should not have happened as instead of P_1 and P_2, points O and P_2 should have been chosen as the pivots. However, since the pivot choosing method stops after a fixed number of steps, this situation cannot be ruled out.

9.8.3 Subsequent Dimensions

The above method of obtaining the first dimension needs a generalization. Assume an original dimensionality of k and a reduced target dimensionality of k'. The general idea that FastMap follows is to project the points onto a $(k-1)$-dimensional plane perpendicular to the line joining the two pivots. The original distance measure d is modified to a new distance d' that works on the resulting $(k-1)$-dimensional plane. The problem then changes to obtaining $(k'-1)$ dimensions from the new $(k-1)$-dimensional plane. The process is repeated k' times and the coordinates gathered in each step forms the final k' coordinates.

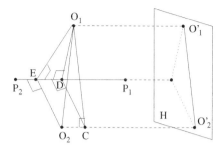

Figure 9.2: Obtaining subsequent dimensions in FastMap.

For any arbitrary original metric distance d, the new distance d', however, is not guaranteed to be a metric distance anymore. Thus, the subsequent projections can run into trouble as it depends on the input distance being a metric. However, if d is Euclidean to start with, every intermediate d' will be a metric distance.

Figure 9.2 shows the general scheme of reducing the dimensionality by 1. The $(k-1)$-dimensional hyperplane perpendicular to the line joining the two pivots, P_1 and P_2, is denoted by H. Assume that O_1' and O_2' respectively are the projections of two input points O_1 and O_2 onto the plane H. We need to compute the new distance measure $d'(O_1', O_2')$. Once this is achieved for any pair of objects O_1, O_2, the algorithm can proceed assuming H to be the original space and d' to be the original distance.

The projections of O_1 and O_2 onto the $P_1 P_2$ line are D and E respectively while the projection of O_1 onto the $O_2 O_2'$ line is C. Thus, $O_1' O_2'$ is of the same length as $O_1 C$. Again, using properties of right-angled triangles from Pythagorean geometry,

$$
\begin{aligned}
d(O_1, O_2)^2 &= d(O_1, C)^2 + d(O_2, C)^2 \\
&= d'(O_1', O_2')^2 + d(D, E)^2 \\
&= d'(O_1', O_2')^2 + (|d(D, P_1) - d(E, P_1)|)^2 \\
&= d'(O_1', O_2')^2 + (|x_{O_1} - x_{O_2}|)^2 \qquad (9.41) \\
\Rightarrow \ d'(O_1', O_2')^2 &= d(O_1, O_2)^2 - (|x_{O_1} - x_{O_2}|)^2 \qquad (9.42)
\end{aligned}
$$

The distance, $d_i(O_a, O_b)$, used at the ith step is obtained from the distance at the $(i-1)^{\text{th}}$ step using Eq. (9.42), i.e.,

$$
d_i(O_a, O_b)^2 = d_{i-1}(O_a, O_b)^2 - (|x_{O_a}^{i-1} - x_{O_b}^{i-1}|)^2 \qquad (9.43)
$$

At the 1st step, the distance $d_1(O_a, O_b)$ is the original distance, i.e., $d_1(O_a, O_b)^2 = d(O_a, O_b)^2$.

Table 9.1: Euclidean distance between points for FastMap.

d	O_1	O_2	O_3	O_4
O_1	0.00	4.58	6.16	4.06
O_2	4.58	0.00	6.71	5.10
O_3	6.16	6.71	0.00	6.56
O_4	4.06	5.10	6.56	0.00

The ith coordinate of a point O can be computed directly using the formula

$$x_O^i = \frac{d_i(P_1^i, P_2^i)^2 + d_i(P_1^i, O)^2 - d_i(P_2^i, O)^2}{2.d_i(P_1^i, P_2^i)} \tag{9.44}$$

The pivots chosen at the ith step are denoted by P_1^i and P_2^i.

Example 9.6 [FastMap]. Reduce the dimensionality of the following sets of points to 2 using FastMap:

$$O_1 = (2, 3, 5), \ O_2 = (4, 7, 6), \ O_3 = (8, 2, 4), \ O_4 = (5, 7, 1)$$

The Euclidean distance matrix between the points is given in Table 9.1.

Assume that the pivots chosen are $P_1 = O_3$ and $P_2 = O_2$. Using Eq. (9.40), the first coordinates obtained for all the points are:

$$O_1' : 4.62, \ O_2' : 6.71, \ O_3' : 0.00, \ O_4' : 4.62$$

The new distances in the next round, listed in Table 9.2, are obtained by applying Eq. (9.42). Note that since the distances are measured on a plane perpendicular to the line joining O_2 and O_3, these two points project to the same position on the plane and, consequently, their new distance becomes 0.

Assume that the pivots chosen this time are $P_1 = O_2$ and $P_2 = O_4$. Note that these points do not have the largest pairwise distance. Nevertheless, using Eq. (9.40) again, the next coordinates obtained are:

$$O_1'' : 2.34, \ O_2'' : 0.00, \ O_3'' : -0.01, \ O_4'' : 4.65$$

Thus, the reduced 2-dimensional representations are:

$$O_1 : (4.62, 2.34), \ O_2 : (6.71, 0.00), \ O_3 : (0.00, -0.01), \ O_4 : (4.62, 4.65)$$

□

Table 9.2: Transformed distance between points for FastMap.

d'	O'_1	O'_2	O'_3	O'_4
O'_1	0.00	4.08	4.07	4.06
O'_2	4.08	0.00	0.00	4.65
O'_3	4.07	0.00	0.00	4.66
O'_4	4.06	4.65	4.66	0.00

9.8.4 Discussion

The biggest asset of FastMap is its running time. In each step, the choice of pivots requires $O(n)$ time. The distance computation between any two vectors requires $O(k)$ time. When the reduced dimensionality is k', the number of steps is k'. The overall time complexity, therefore, is $O(n.k.k')$.

The crucial disadvantage of FastMap is that it may not work for non-metric distances as the distance squares produced by Eq. (9.42) may become negative. For Euclidean distances, the problem does not arise, and the resultant mapping can be shown to be necessarily *contractive* [Faloutsos and Lin, 1995].

9.9 Embedding Methods

We next discuss the important embedding methods.

9.9.1 Lipschitz Embeddings

A particular class of embeddings, called the LIPSCHITZ EMBEDDINGS, map a dataset D with metric distance d onto a k-dimensional vector space, where k is an input parameter [Bourgain, 1985, Johnson and Lindenstrauss, 1984]. The strategy is similar to that in Example 9.1, but more general.

First, k random subsets of D are chosen. These subsets are called the *reference sets*. The distance of an object O to a reference set $\mathcal{A}$ is defined as the minimum distance to any element of the set, i.e.,

$$d(O, \mathcal{A}) = \min_{A \in \mathcal{A}} d(O, A) \qquad (9.45)$$

The embedded feature vector for the object O is then defined using this

notion of distance. The value in a particular dimension is the distance
to the corresponding reference set:

$$O' = f(O) = \{d(O, \mathcal{A}_1), \ldots, d(O, \mathcal{A}_k)\} \qquad (9.46)$$

The embedding is contractive when the new distance is $d' = \frac{1}{k}L_1$.

Consider a reference set $\mathcal{A}$ and two objects O_1 and O_2. Assume,
without loss of generality, that the minimum distance of O_1 to $\mathcal{A}$ is due
to A_1 and that of O_2 is due to A_2, i.e.,

$$A_1 = \underset{A \in \mathcal{A}}{\operatorname{argmin}}\, d(O_1, A) \qquad (9.47)$$

$$A_2 = \underset{A \in \mathcal{A}}{\operatorname{argmin}}\, d(O_2, A) \qquad (9.48)$$

Consider the dimension of O_1 and O_2 corresponding to $\mathcal{A}$. The difference in the values is

$$
\begin{aligned}
|d(O_1, \mathcal{A}) - d(O_2, \mathcal{A})| &= |d(O_1, A_1) - d(O_2, A_2)| \\
&= \max \begin{cases} d(O_1, A_1) - d(O_2, A_2) \\ d(O_2, A_2) - d(O_1, A_1) \end{cases} \\
&\leq \max \begin{cases} d(O_1, A_1) - d(O_2, A_1) & [\text{using Eq. (9.47)}] \\ d(O_2, A_2) - d(O_1, A_2) & [\text{using Eq. (9.48)}] \end{cases} \\
&\leq d(O_1, O_2) \qquad (9.49)
\end{aligned}
$$

Summing all the differences due to k such reference sets and then scaling
the sum by $\frac{1}{k}$ shows that the Lipschitz embedding is *contractive*.

No guarantee can be given about the distortion, though. The general
Lipschitz embedding method, therefore, is not so useful practically.

9.9.2   LLR Embedding

A variant of Lipschitz embedding that guarantees a distortion of
at most $O(\log_2 n)$ for n objects is LLR EMBEDDING [Linial et al.,
1994, Linial et al., 1995] (named after Linial, London, and Rabinovich).
However, the guarantee comes at a cost: the embedded space must have
a dimensionality of $k = O(\log_2^2 n)$.

The $O(\log_2^2 n)$ reference sets are organized into $O(\log_2 n)$ groups,
where each reference set in the ith group is of size 2^i for $i =
1, \ldots, O(\log_2 n)$. Assume that the distance in the embedded space is
$d' = L_p$. Then, the embedding of object O is

$$O' = f(O) = k^{-1/p}\{d(O, \mathcal{A}_1), \ldots, d(O, \mathcal{A}_k)\} \qquad (9.50)$$

where $\mathcal{A}_j$ are the reference sets. The scaling factor $k^{-1/p}$ is needed to make the embedding *contractive*.

It was proved by [Linial et al., 1995] that with high probability, for any two objects O_i, O_j,

$$\frac{c}{\lceil \log_2 n \rceil} d(O_i, O_j) \le d'(O_i', O_j') \le d(O_i, O_j) \tag{9.51}$$

where c is a constant. Hence, the distortion is $O(\log_2 n)$.

Even though LLR embedding guarantees the distortion, the practical utility of it is limited due to the extremely high dimensionality of the embedded space. For example, even with a very small $n = 1000$, $\lceil \log_2^2 \rceil = 100$. Also, for a large sized reference set $\mathcal{A}_j$, the time to compute the minimum distance of an object to this set is impractical (when j is, say, $\log_2 n$).

9.9.3 SparseMap

In order to make the LLR embedding method practical, SPARSEMAP was proposed [Hristescu and Farach-Colton, 1999]. It uses two efficient heuristics:

1. Instead of computing the exact minimum distance $d(O, \mathcal{A}_j)$ from an object O to a reference set $\mathcal{A}_j$, it computes $\widehat{d}(O, \mathcal{A}_j)$ by considering only some (and not all) of the objects in $\mathcal{A}_j$ and, thus, avoids all $|\mathcal{A}_j|$ computations. Necessarily, $\widehat{d}(O, \mathcal{A}_j)$ is an upper bound of $d(O, \mathcal{A}_j)$.

2. Instead of retaining all the $\mathcal{A}_k$ reference sets, it retains only some (say k') of them. This reduces the dimensionality to k' instead of $k = O(\log_2^2 n)$. The strategy used to select the k' reference sets is called *greedy resampling* where the $\mathcal{A}_j$'s that contribute the largest amount to the stress are deleted. However, note that since calculating the stress itself requires a lot of computations (to be precise, $O(n^2)$), only some of the object pairs are sampled to estimate the stress.

As a result of these changes, although SparseMap can run much faster, the embedding may *not* remain *contractive* anymore. Further, the properties of bounded distortion are lost. Nevertheless, for most practical datasets the results are acceptable and can be better than FastMap in terms of both quality and number of distance computations [Hristescu and Farach-Colton, 1999], especially for non-Euclidean distances.

9.9.4 JL Lemma

The JOHNSON-LINDENSTRAUSS LEMMA (JL LEMMA) proposes an embedding method from an original vector space of dimensionality m with n points to another vector space that can control the distortion, albeit with an increase in the reduced dimensionality [Johnson and Lindenstrauss, 1984]. If the distortion is required to be bounded by $(1 + \epsilon)$ where ϵ is a parameter, the reduced dimensionality k should be $> (8 \ln n)/\epsilon^2 = O(\log_2 n/\epsilon^2)$.

Similar to LLR embedding, the construction for this mapping is also randomized. This is, thus, a randomized algorithm. A set of k vectors $\{r_1, \ldots, r_k\}$ of dimensionality m are constructed where each component r_{ij} of a vector is sampled from the standard normal distribution $N(0, 1)$.

An object O is then mapped to

$$O' = f(O) = (1/\sqrt{k})\{\langle O, r_1 \rangle, \ldots, \langle O, r_k \rangle\} \tag{9.52}$$

where $\langle \cdot, \cdot \rangle$ denotes the inner product (or the dot product).

For any two object vectors $\vec{u}, \vec{v}$ and their respective embeddings $\vec{u'}, \vec{v'}$, it can be shown that, with very high probability

$$(1 - \epsilon)||\vec{u} - \vec{v}||_2^2 \leq ||\vec{u'} - \vec{v'}||_2^2 \leq (1 + \epsilon)||\vec{u} - \vec{v}||_2^2$$

$$\Rightarrow (1 - \epsilon)d^2(\vec{u}, \vec{v}) \leq d'^2(\vec{u'}, \vec{v'}) \leq (1 + \epsilon)d^2(\vec{u}, \vec{v})$$

$$\Rightarrow \sqrt{(1 - \epsilon)}d(\vec{u}, \vec{v}) \leq d'(\vec{u'}, \vec{v'}) \leq \sqrt{(1 + \epsilon)}d(\vec{u}, \vec{v}) \tag{9.53}$$

The distortion, therefore, is $\sqrt{(1 + \epsilon)(1 - \epsilon)^{-1}} = 1 + \epsilon + O(\epsilon^2) + \cdots$. When ϵ is small, the quadratic and higher order terms can be ignored.

9.9.4.1 Efficient Construction

A particularly remarkably efficient way of embedding was described in [Achlioptas, 2001, Achlioptas, 2003] where the construction of the projection matrix did not require sampling from a normal distribution. For a data matrix D of size $n \times m$, a projection or embedding matrix R of size $m \times k$ is constructed by choosing the independent and identically distributed (i.i.d.) random variables r_{ij} in either of the following ways:

$$r_{ij} = \begin{cases} +1 & \text{with probability } 1/2 \\ -1 & \text{with probability } 1/2 \end{cases} \tag{9.54}$$

$$r_{ij} = \sqrt{3} \times \begin{cases} +1 & \text{with probability } 1/6 \\ 0 & \text{with probability } 2/3 \\ -1 & \text{with probability } 1/6 \end{cases} \tag{9.55}$$

The embedded data is then represented as

$$E = (1/\sqrt{k})D.R \tag{9.56}$$

When $k = \log_2 n(4+2\beta)/(\epsilon^2/2 - \epsilon^3/3) = O(\log_2 n/\epsilon^2)$, it was proved by [Achlioptas, 2001, Achlioptas, 2003] that with probability $1 - (1/n^\beta)$, for any two object vectors $\vec{u}, \vec{v}$ and their corresponding embeddings $\vec{u'}, \vec{v'}$, Eq. (9.53) holds. Since sampling according to Eq. (9.54) and Eq. (9.55) are much more efficient operations, the overall embedding is much faster as well.

9.9.5 Locally Linear Embedding (LLE)

LOCALLY LINEAR EMBEDDING (LLE) is an embedding technique that takes the view that although the global space is non-linear, locally linear patches of the surface exist [Roweis and Saul, 2000]. Thus, within the neighborhood of every point, the space is linear and, hence, each point is modeled as a *linear* combination of its neighbors.

Two important constraints are followed. First, every point is reconstructed as a weighted linear sum of *only* its neighbors. In other words, the contribution of every non-neighbor point is 0. Second, the weights of the neighbors add up to 1.

Consider a point x_i in an m-dimensional space. Its neighborhood, denoted by $\mathcal{N}(x_i)$, consists of either the k nearest points or all points within a range of r. The point x_i is represented by a linear combination of the points $x_j \in \mathcal{N}(x_i)$. If the weights are denoted by $\vec{w}$, the total *error* in the reconstruction of all the points is

$$\text{Error}(w) = \sum_{\forall x_i} \left(x_i - \sum_{x_j \in \mathcal{N}(x_i)} (w_j . x_j) \right)^2 \tag{9.57}$$

The optimal weight vector $\hat{w}$ that minimizes the total error over all the points is found by least squares regression.

The next step is the actual dimensionality reduction. The high-dimensional vector x_i is reduced to a lower dimensional vector y_i using the weights obtained by the linear regression. The aim is to again reconstruct y_i from its neighbors. However, this time, a set $S \subset \mathcal{N}(y_i)$ of only m' neighbors (equivalently, weights) are used. The quantity m' is, thus, the reduced dimensionality. The *error* for this reconstruction step is

$$\text{Error}(m') = \sum_{\forall y_i} \left(y_i - \sum_{y_j \in S \subset \mathcal{N}(y_i), |S|=m'} (w_j . y_j) \right)^2 \tag{9.58}$$

Representing the above formulation as a matrix problem and choosing the lowest m' eigenvalues and their corresponding eigenvectors yields the solution.

9.10   Bounds on Distortion

If the original distance d is not a metric, it is advisable to embed the dataset into a metric distance d' such that similarity search queries can be answered more efficiently. However, if d does not follow certain *relaxed metric properties*, then any embedding of this space into a metric space *cannot* have a low distortion [Bhattacharya et al., 2009].

The metric properties of symmetry and triangular inequality are relaxed in the following way:

- γ-relaxed symmetry ($\gamma \geq 0$):

$$\forall p, q, \ |d(p,q) - d(q,p)| \leq \gamma \tag{9.59}$$

- α-relaxed triangular inequality ($\alpha \leq 1$):

$$\forall p, q, r, \ d(p,r) + d(r,q) \geq \alpha.d(p,q) \tag{9.60}$$

The first relaxed property states that even if the distance is not symmetric, the difference is not more than a constant γ. The second relaxed property states that while the sum of two distances is not necessarily larger than the third distance, it is at least greater than a constant fraction α of it. Putting $\gamma = 0$ and $\alpha = 1$ gives back the original metric distance properties.

In [Bhattacharya et al., 2009], it was proved that

- If d does *not* obey γ-relaxed symmetry, then any embedding into a metric space d' must have a distortion of at least $(1 + \gamma/M)$ where the largest pairwise distance is M, i.e., $\forall u, v, \ d(u,v) \leq M$.

- If d does *not* obey α-relaxed triangular inequality, then any embedding into a metric space d' must have a distortion of at least $(1/\alpha)$.

Chapter 10

Data Representation Techniques

In many applications, it is necessary and useful to represent data in a standard format. This enables comparing the feature values of an object from one dataset directly to another object from another dataset. A common example is images where two feature vectors produced from two different images may need to be compared. The dimensionality reduction techniques such as PCA (Section 9.5) and SVD (Section 9.4) project on basis vectors that are produced from the datasets themselves. Thus, two datasets will have different projection vectors. The DATA REPRESENTATION techniques described in this chapter use a consistent set of basis vectors for projection. As a side effect, these methods can be used as dimensionality reduction tools as well. We first describe three discrete signal processing methods before concluding with a histogram representation technique. The signal processing methods work well for time-series data.

10.1 Discrete Fourier Transform (DFT)

FOURIER ANALYSIS is a way to analyze the frequency components in a signal. It represents a periodic wave as a sum of (infinite) sine and cosine waves. Given a signal in the time domain $f(x)$, the FOURIER TRANSFORMATION transforms it into the frequency domain $g(u)$:

$$g(u) = \int_{-\infty}^{\infty} f(x)e^{-2\pi uxi}\, dx \qquad (10.1)$$

Here, i denotes the *imaginary* number $\sqrt{-1}$. Fourier transformation can be easily inverted to get the time domain signal from the wave domain:

$$f(x) = \int_{-\infty}^{\infty} g(u)e^{+2\pi uxi}\, du \qquad (10.2)$$

Together, $f(x)$ and $g(u)$ form a *Fourier transform pair*. (Note the symmetry in the equations.)

The above general definition of Fourier transformation assumes the signals in both time and frequency domains to be continuous. The transformation, when used for discrete data, is called DISCRETE FOURIER TRANSFORMATION (DFT) [Oppenheim et al., 1999].

Assume that the discrete data is represented in the form of a vector x of dimensionality N. The *discrete Fourier transform (DFT)* of x, denoted by X, is another vector of the same dimensionality N:

$$X_k = 1. \sum_{n=0}^{N-1} x_n e^{-(2\pi/N)kni} \quad k = 0, \ldots, N-1 \qquad (10.3)$$

The inverse discrete Fourier transform (IDFT) of X produces the original vector x:

$$x_n = \frac{1}{N}. \sum_{k=0}^{N-1} X_k e^{(2\pi/N)kni} \quad n = 0, \ldots, N-1 \qquad (10.4)$$

The above equations use two different scaling factors, $s_1 = 1$ and $s_2 = 1/N$. To avoid using separate scaling factors, sometimes both of them are considered to be $1/\sqrt{N}$.

10.1.1   Properties

When both the scaling factors are $1/\sqrt{N}$, an important property of the Fourier transformation is given by *Parseval's theorem* [Oppenheim et al., 1999] which states that the lengths of the original and the transformed vectors remain the same, i.e.,

$$||x||_2 = ||X||_2 \text{ or, } \sum_{n=0}^{N-1} |x_n|^2 = \sum_{k=0}^{N-1} |X_k|^2 \qquad (10.5)$$

Thus, the DFT (and IDFT) is an invertible, linear mapping, and is essentially a rotation in an N-dimensional space.

10.1.2   Coefficients

Using the expansion $e^{\theta i} = \cos\theta + i\sin\theta$, the DFT can be expressed as:

$$X_k = \frac{1}{\sqrt{N}}. \sum_{n=0}^{N-1} x_n e^{-(2\pi/N)kni}$$

$$= \frac{1}{\sqrt{N}}. \sum_{n=0}^{N-1} x_n \left(\cos\left(\frac{2\pi}{N}kn\right) - i\sin\left(\frac{2\pi}{N}kn\right)\right) \qquad (10.6)$$

Using Eq. (10.6), the first coefficient is the (scaled) sum

$$X_0 = \frac{1}{\sqrt{N}} \cdot \sum_{n=0}^{N-1} x_n \left(\cos 0 - \mathbf{i} \sin 0 \right) = \frac{1}{\sqrt{N}} \cdot \sum_{n=0}^{N-1} x_n \qquad (10.7)$$

The other coefficients define the frequency components (cosine and sine) at frequencies $2\pi(k/N)$ for $k = 0, 1, \ldots, N-1$.

10.1.3 Dimensionality Reduction

For a continuous signal, generally, the high frequency components are dropped as they pertain more to noise. Consequently, if k components are required, the lowest k frequency coefficients are retained.

The same idea can be used for DFT to reduce the dimensionality of a vector from N to k. Since DFT (or IDFT) is essentially a rotation in the N-dimensional space, the above way of dimensionality reduction guarantees a contractive mapping.

However, for a database of N-dimensional vectors, the concept of high frequency noise makes little sense. Thus, an alternate way of reducing the dimensionality is to use the k components for which the variances are the highest. This helps in retaining the largest amount of variation for that dataset.

10.2 Discrete Cosine Transform (DCT)

A particularly problematic aspect of DFT (and IDFT) is the set of sine components which are imaginary. The DISCRETE COSINE TRANSFORMATION (DCT) is a similar method of data transformation that represents a signal (which is a vector in the discrete sense) in terms of different cosine components only [Oppenheim et al., 1999]. The exact definition of DCT varies and there are at least two commonly used formulations:

$$X_k^{(1)} = \frac{1}{\sqrt{N}} x_0 \left[x_n \cos \left[\frac{\pi.k}{2.N} \right] \right] + \sqrt{\frac{2}{N}} \sum_{n=1}^{N-1} \left[x_n \cos \left[\frac{\pi}{N} \left(n + \frac{1}{2} \right) k \right] \right]$$

$$k = 0, \ldots, N - 1 \qquad (10.8)$$

$$X_k^{(2)} = \sqrt{\frac{2}{N}} \sum_{n=0}^{N-1} \left[x_n \cos \left[\frac{\pi}{N} \left(n + \frac{1}{2} \right) \left(k + \frac{1}{2} \right) \right] \right]$$

$$k = 0, \ldots, N - 1 \qquad (10.9)$$

The inverse DCT (IDCT) functions remain the same. Similar to DFT, the DCT (and IDCT) are length-preserving functions as well and are, again, essentially rotations in an N-dimensional space. Hence, the dimensionality reduction can also be achieved in the same manner by either retaining the k lowest frequency coefficients or the k highest variance components.

10.3 Discrete Wavelet Transform (DWT)

10.3.1 Wavelets

The Fourier transformation analyzes a signal only in terms of frequency. It, however, ignores the time resolution. WAVELETS analyze a signal in both time and frequency domains [Rao and Bopardikar, 1998]. In general, it has good time resolution but poor frequency resolution at high frequencies and good frequency resolution but poor time resolution at low frequencies. Therefore, wavelets are very useful for short duration signals of high frequency and long duration signals of short frequency.

The wavelets are generated from a *mother wavelet function* ψ. The function ψ should follow two important properties. First, it should have a zero mean, i.e., $\oint_x \psi(x) \, dx = 0$. This ensures the oscillatory or wave nature of the function. Second, it should have a unit length, i.e., $\oint_x \psi^2(x) \, dx = 1$. This guarantees that the transformed signal has the same scale as the original signal.

The *basis functions* that transform a signal are generated by *scaling* and *shifting* the mother wavelet function ψ. If the scaling factor is s and the shifting factor is l, the corresponding basis function is

$$\psi_{s,l}(t) = \frac{1}{\sqrt{s}} \psi \left(\frac{t - l}{s} \right) \qquad (10.10)$$

where t denotes time.

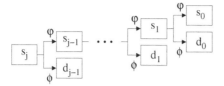

Figure 10.1: DWT basis vectors.

10.3.2 Discrete Wavelets

The DISCRETE WAVELET TRANSFORMATION (DWT) is the discrete version of the wavelets [Fleet, 2008]. Similar to its counterparts such as DFT or DCT, it also transforms a vector into a new space by using a set of basis vectors generated by the wavelet function.

Instead of a single mother wavelet function as in the case of continuous signals, the DWT works with two sets of functions:

1. *Wavelet* functions ψ

2. *Scaling* functions ϕ

The basis vectors for these two functions are generated at different *levels*. At level j, there are $n = 2^j$ wavelet basis vectors. These n vectors can be spanned by the two sets of basis vectors ψ and ϕ at level $j - 1$. The ψ vectors at level $j - 1$ can again be constituted by basis vectors at level $j - 2$, etc. This continues till level 0 is reached at which point there is only 1 wavelet and 1 scaling function. Figure 10.1 shows how the break-up progresses.

10.3.3 Haar Wavelets

The simplest and very commonly used wavelet transform for discrete datasets is the HAAR WAVELET. Given a vector of size n (assume for the time being that n is a power of 2), the Haar wavelet transformation consists of the following steps:

1. Compute the *sum* and *difference* between each consecutive pairs of values.

2. Scale the new values by a factor of $1/\sqrt{2}$.

3. Repeat the steps for the sum coefficients till only one value is left.

The Haar wavelet transformation preserves the *length* of the vector. Moreover, it is an *invertible* function, i.e., given a transformed vector v', the original vector v can be obtained in a lossless manner from v'.

Example 10.1 [Haar Wavelets]. Compute the Haar wavelets for the vector

$$v = \{2, 5, 8, 9, 7, 4, -1, 1\}$$

Since the vector v contains $2^3 = 8$ values, it can be thought of to be a wavelet at level 3. Therefore, let it be denoted by $v = f_3$. Following the Haar wavelet transformation steps, we get

$$f_3 = \{2, 5, 8, 9, 7, 4, -1, 1\} \tag{10.11}$$

$$f_2 = \frac{1}{\sqrt{2}} \{2 + 5, 8 + 9, 7 + 4, -1 + 1\}, \frac{1}{\sqrt{2}} \{2 - 5, 8 - 9, 7 - 4, -1 - 1\}$$

$$= \left\{ \frac{7}{\sqrt{2}}, \frac{17}{\sqrt{2}}, \frac{11}{\sqrt{2}}, \frac{0}{\sqrt{2}} \right\}, \left\{ \frac{-3}{\sqrt{2}}, \frac{-1}{\sqrt{2}}, \frac{3}{\sqrt{2}}, \frac{-2}{\sqrt{2}} \right\} \tag{10.12}$$

$$f_1 = \frac{1}{\sqrt{2}} \left\{ \frac{7 + 17}{\sqrt{2}}, \frac{11 + 0}{\sqrt{2}} \right\}, \frac{1}{\sqrt{2}} \left\{ \frac{7 - 17}{\sqrt{2}}, \frac{11 - 0}{\sqrt{2}} \right\},$$

$$\left\{ \frac{-3}{\sqrt{2}}, \frac{-1}{\sqrt{2}}, \frac{3}{\sqrt{2}}, \frac{-2}{\sqrt{2}} \right\}$$

$$= \left\{ \frac{24}{2}, \frac{11}{2} \right\}, \left\{ \frac{-10}{2}, \frac{11}{2} \right\}, \left\{ \frac{-3}{\sqrt{2}}, \frac{-1}{\sqrt{2}}, \frac{3}{\sqrt{2}}, \frac{-2}{\sqrt{2}} \right\} \tag{10.13}$$

$$f_0 = \frac{1}{\sqrt{2}} \left\{ \frac{24 + 11}{2} \right\}, \frac{1}{\sqrt{2}} \left\{ \frac{24 - 11}{2} \right\},$$

$$\left\{ \frac{-10}{2}, \frac{11}{2} \right\}, \left\{ \frac{-3}{\sqrt{2}}, \frac{-1}{\sqrt{2}}, \frac{3}{\sqrt{2}}, \frac{-2}{\sqrt{2}} \right\}$$

$$= \left\{ \frac{35}{2\sqrt{2}} \right\}, \left\{ \frac{13}{2\sqrt{2}} \right\}, \left\{ \frac{-10}{2}, \frac{11}{2} \right\}, \left\{ \frac{-3}{\sqrt{2}}, \frac{-1}{\sqrt{2}}, \frac{3}{\sqrt{2}}, \frac{-2}{\sqrt{2}} \right\}$$

$$= \left\{ \frac{35}{2\sqrt{2}}, \frac{13}{2\sqrt{2}}, \frac{-10}{2}, \frac{11}{2}, \frac{-3}{\sqrt{2}}, \frac{-1}{\sqrt{2}}, \frac{3}{\sqrt{2}}, \frac{-2}{\sqrt{2}} \right\} \tag{10.14}$$

The vector $v' = f_0$ is the Haar wavelet transformed version of $v = f_3$. The lengths of both the vectors are the same: $||f_0||_2 = 15.52 = ||f_3||_2$. □

The inverse Haar wavelet transformation follows the same steps in the reverse fashion, i.e., it starts with only one sum and one difference coefficient, computes their (scaled) sum and difference to get the two sums at the previous level, then computes the (scaled) sums and differences of those sums, and so on.

10.3.4 Haar Wavelet Functions

The wavelet (ψ) and scaling (ϕ) functions for the Haar discrete wavelet transform are respectively

$$\psi(x) = \begin{cases} +1 & \text{if } 0 \le x < \frac{1}{2} \\ -1 & \text{if } \frac{1}{2} < x \le 1 \\ 0 & \text{otherwise} \end{cases} \tag{10.15}$$

$$\phi(x) = \begin{cases} 1 & \text{if } 0 \le x \le 1 \\ 0 & \text{otherwise} \end{cases} \tag{10.16}$$

The basis functions after applying *shifting* at level i and *scaling* at level j are

$$\psi_{j,i}(x) = 2^{\frac{j}{2}}.\psi(2^j.x - i); \quad j = 0,\ldots; \quad i = 0,\ldots,2^j - 1 \tag{10.17}$$

$$\phi_{j,i}(x) = 2^{\frac{j}{2}}.\phi(2^j.x - i); \quad j = 0,\ldots; \quad i = 0,\ldots,2^j - 1 \tag{10.18}$$

Thus, scaling corresponds to *binary dilation* while shifting corresponds to *dyadic translation*. The coefficients corresponding to $\psi_{j,i}$ are *averages* and are called the *sum* coefficients while the coefficients corresponding to $\phi_{j,i}$ are *differences* and are called the *detail* coefficients.

10.3.5 Basis Functions for Haar Wavelets

The coefficients $\psi_{j,i}$ and $\phi_{j,i}$ form the basis vectors for the Haar discrete wavelet transform. Since the sum coefficients can be expressed in terms of the sum and detail coefficients at the lower levels, only the $\psi_{0,0}$ function is needed; the others are expressed in terms of $\phi_{.,.}$.

For a vector of dimensionality $n = 2^j$, j levels of basis vectors are needed. Of these, the number of basis vectors corresponding to the detail coefficients (i.e., the ψ component) is $2^{j-1} + 2^{j-2} + \cdots + 2^0 = 2^j - 1$ while that for the sum coefficients (i.e., the ϕ component) is 1.

The DWT using Haar can be thought of in matrix terms. A data vector v is rotated using the Haar transformation matrix H to yield the transformed data $v' = v.H$. The matrix H has the $(2^j - 1)$ ψ and 1 ϕ basis vectors as the columns. Thus, H is *orthonormal* (see Section C.3 on properties of matrices). Therefore, the inverse Haar wavelet transform is easy to obtain as it is just the transpose, i.e., $H^{-1} = H^T$.

Each step of the Haar transformation at any level can be defined in terms of a matrix multiplication step. Thus, given a data vector f_3 having $2^3 = 8$ dimensions, the next transformed vector f_2 can be obtained as $f_2 = f_3.H_2$ where H_2 denotes the transformation matrix for Haar at level 2. Similarly, the next levels f_1 and f_0 can be obtained by applying the subsequent Haar DWT matrices H_1 and H_0 on f_2 and f_1 respectively:

$$f_2 = f_3.H_2 \tag{10.19}$$
$$f_1 = f_2.H_1 \tag{10.20}$$
$$f_0 = f_1.H_0 \tag{10.21}$$
$$\therefore \ f_0 = f_3.H_2.H_1.H_0 \tag{10.22}$$

Denoting the entire transformation matrix at level 3 by $H_{(3)}$,

$$f_0 = f_3.H_{(3)} \text{ where } H_{(3)} = H_2.H_1.H_0 \tag{10.23}$$

The inverse transformation is simply the transposed matrix. Thus,

$$f_3 = f_0.H_{(3)}^{-1} \text{ where } H_{(3)}^{-1} = H_{(3)}^{T} \tag{10.24}$$

10.3.6   Dimensionality Reduction

The Haar wavelets can be used for dimensionality reduction in the following way. The sum coefficient contains the scaled average of the entire vector. Hence, if only 1 dimension needs to be retained, it is the best choice. The first detail coefficient in addition to the sum coefficient produces the average values in the two halves of the vector. Thus, it is the natural choice for the second reduced dimension. In this way, it can be seen that the next 2 detail coefficients allow the vector to be re-constructed in 4 parts. Thus, the sum and detail coefficients allow a natural dimensionality reduction technique when the reduced dimensionality is in a power of 2. Similar to DFT and DCT, the coefficients with the largest variances can also be retained.

10.3.7   Discussion

An important question to ponder is what happens when the original dimensionality of the vector is not a power of 2? The basis functions for the Haar wavelets are not defined properly for such cases. The solution is to pad up the vector with additional dimensions having values 0 such that the length becomes a power of 2.

If the padding is done only at the end of the original vector, the importance of the latter half becomes less. The detailed coefficients for the latter half are mostly wasted. Hence, it is better to pad equal amounts of zeroes in both halves. Within each half, however, the same argument holds true and, hence, the distribution of zeroes should be done equally in a recursive manner in each half.

10.4 V-Optimal Histogram

Histograms remain one of the main ways of representing data. Formally, a HISTOGRAM is an ordered list of tuples $\langle I_1, f_1 \rangle, \ldots, \langle I_n, f_n \rangle$ where the values in the interval $I_i = [l_i, r_i)$ have frequency f_i. Generally, the intervals are adjacent, i.e., $r_i = l_{i+1}$.

In many situations, the interval is replaced by the middle value $v_i = (l_i + r_i)/2$ and the histogram is denoted as a list of values and their frequencies: $\langle v_1, f_1 \rangle, \ldots, \langle v_n, f_n \rangle$. For example, the histogram

$$\langle [0.5, 1.5), 3 \rangle, \ \langle [1.5, 3.5), 5 \rangle, \ \langle [3.5, 6.5), 1 \rangle, \ \langle [6.5, 7.5), 3 \rangle \qquad (10.25)$$

can be represented as

$$\langle 1.0, 3 \rangle, \ \langle 2.5, 5 \rangle, \ \langle 5.0, 1 \rangle, \ \langle 7.0, 3 \rangle \qquad (10.26)$$

10.4.1 Optimal Partitioning

The partitioning problem for histograms can be stated as follows. Assume a sorted list V of n values $v_1, \ldots, v_n$ in ascending order having frequencies $f_1, \ldots, f_n$ respectively. Thus, V can be considered as a histogram with n bins. The aim is to output another histogram H having $b < n$ bins. The quantity b is generally much smaller than n, i.e., $b \ll n$. The bins are *non-overlapping* but *contiguous* intervals on V where each interval I_i, $i = 1, \ldots, b$ is of the form $[l_i, r_i)$ and has a value (or frequency) h_i. The frequency h_i is the average of the frequencies of the values that fall in the interval I_i:

$$h_i = \text{avg}\{f_j \in [l_i, r_i)\} \qquad (10.27)$$

The *estimate* $e(f_j)$ of the old frequency f_j in its corresponding interval I_i is the new frequency h_i computed using Eq. (10.27). The *error* for these estimates is measured using the *sum squared error (SSE)* which is the L_2 norm of the frequencies. Hence, for a range $[l, r)$, the SSE is

$$\text{SSE}\{[l, r)\} = \sum_{\forall f_j \in [l,r)} (f_j - e(f_j))^2$$

$$= \sum_{\forall f_j \in [l,r)} (f_j - h_i)^2 \ \text{ where } f_j \in I_i \qquad (10.28)$$

The problem is to choose the *optimal partitioning* of the range $[v_1, v_n]$ that *minimizes* the SSE according to Eq. (10.28).

The usual ways of constructing *equi-width* histograms where the bins are equally spaced apart, or *equi-height* histograms where each bin is constrained to have the same frequency, do not achieve the optimal error.

10.4.2   Algorithm

The V-OPTIMAL HISTOGRAMS were originally proposed by [Ioannidis and Poosala, 1995] to optimize the *variance* measured using Eq. (10.28). It thus acquired the name *V-optimal*. The concept was adopted for space-bounded problems by [Jagadish et al., 1998].

The algorithm is based on the dynamic programming (DP) paradigm. The overall problem is to place n values in b bins. Denoting the optimal SSE of this by $SSE^*(n, b)$, the problem can be broken down into smaller sub-problems in the following manner.

Consider the placement of i values into k bins. For any j where $1 \leq j \leq i$, assume that $k - 1$ bins have already been placed optimally. Then, the last bin covers all the values from j to i. Hence, the combined error for a particular j is $SSE^*(j, k - 1) + SSE([l_{j+1}, r_i])$. Now, the choice for j is any of the i places. Hence, the optimal partitioning of i values into k bins can be found out by the following recurrence:

$$SSE^*(i, k) = \min_{1 \leq j \leq i} \{SSE^*(j, k - 1) + SSE([l_{j+1}, r_i])\} \qquad (10.29)$$

Of course, this assumes that the optimal partitioning of any j into $k - 1$ bins can be computed. Using the recurrence principle, $SSE^*(j, k - 1)$ can be again broken into simpler terms as in Eq. (10.29). The base case is when there is only one value and one partition (the SSE in this case is 0).

The above formulation can be efficiently implemented using a dynamic programming table having n rows (corresponding to values) and b columns (corresponding to bins). The last entry $SSE^*(n, b)$ gives the optimal error and the backtracking pointers produce the solution.

The computation starts from the cell $(1, 1)$ and proceeds in a column-scan order. This ensures that the entries $(j, k - 1)$, $\forall 1 \leq j \leq i$ required for the cell (i, k) are available when $SSE^*(i, k)$ is computed.

Example 10.2 [V-Optimal Histogram]. Find the V-optimal histogram using 3 bins for the following set of data:

$$48, 60, 24, 72, 96$$

The base cases are $SSE^*(1, 1) = 0$, $SSE^*(2, 2) = 0$ and $SSE^*(3, 3) = 0$. The three corner cases $SSE^*(1, 2)$, $SSE^*(1, 3)$, and $SSE^*(2, 3)$ do not make sense physically as they have more buckets

Table 10.1: Computation of V-optimal histogram: base cases.

	1	2	3
$v_1 = 48$	$SSE^* = 0$ $BACK = \varnothing$	$SSE^* = 0$ $BACK = \varnothing$	$SSE^* = 0$ $BACK = \varnothing$
$v_2 = 60$	$SSE^* = 72$ $BACK = \varnothing$		$SSE^* = 0$ $BACK = \varnothing$
$v_3 = 24$	$SSE^* = 672$ $BACK = \varnothing$		
$v_4 = 72$	$SSE^* = 1260$ $BACK = \varnothing$		
$v_5 = 96$	$SSE^* = 2880$ $BACK = \varnothing$		

than data points (i.e., $b > n$); nevertheless, they can be treated as 0 for uniformity.

The error for a single bucket, i.e., $SSE^*(\cdot, 1)$ is the cost of substituting all the values by their average. For example,

$$
\begin{aligned}
SSE^*(2,1) &= SSE^*\{48,60\} \\
&= (48 - \text{avg}(48,60))^2 + (60 - \text{avg}(48,60))^2 \\
&= 72 \tag{10.30}
\end{aligned}
$$

After computing all such values, the initial table is displayed in Table 10.1.

Consider the computation of the value $SSE^*(2,2)$ which finds the cost of putting the first 2 values in 2 buckets. Using Eq. (10.29), it is the minimum of

$$
\begin{aligned}
SSE^*(2,2) &= \min \left\{ \begin{array}{l} SSE^*(1,1) + SSE^*\{60\}, \\ SSE^*(2,1) + 0 \end{array} \right. \\
&= \min \left\{ \begin{array}{l} 0 + 0, \\ 72 + 0 \end{array} \right. \\
&= 0 \tag{10.31}
\end{aligned}
$$

The zero error is intuitive as two values can be always put in two bins without any error. The back pointer $BACK(2,2)$ shows how the breakup is done. The value $(1,1)$ indicates that the first value is put in bin 1 and the rest in bin 2.

Table 10.2: Computation of V-optimal histogram: partial.

	1	2	3
$v_1 = 48$	$SSE^* = 0$ $BACK = \varnothing$	$SSE^* = 0$ $BACK = \varnothing$	$SSE^* = 0$ $BACK = \varnothing$
$v_2 = 60$	$SSE^* = 72$ $BACK = \varnothing$	$SSE^* = 0$ $BACK = (1,1)$	$SSE^* = 0$ $BACK = (1,2)$
$v_3 = 24$	$SSE^* = 672$ $BACK = \varnothing$	$SSE^* = 72$ $BACK = (2,1)$	$SSE^* = 0$ $BACK = (2,2)$
$v_4 = 72$	$SSE^* = 1260$ $BACK = \varnothing$	$SSE^* = 672$ $BACK = (3,1)$	$SSE^* = 72$ $BACK = (3,2)$
$v_5 = 96$	$SSE^* = 2880$ $BACK = \varnothing$	$SSE^* = 960$ $BACK = (3,1)$	

Next, consider the computation of $SSE^*(3, 2)$:

$$SSE^*(3, 2) = \min \begin{cases} SSE^*(1,1) + SSE^*\{60, 24\}, \\ SSE^*(2,1) + SSE^*\{24\}, \\ SSE^*(3,1) + 0 \end{cases}$$

$$= \min \begin{cases} 0 + (60 - \text{avg}(60, 24))^2 + (24 - \text{avg}(60, 24))^2, \\ 72 + 0, \\ 672 + 0 \end{cases}$$

$$= 72 \tag{10.32}$$

Since $BACK = (2, 1)$, the optimal partitioning of the first 3 values into 2 bins is to put the first 2 values in bin 1 and the rest in bin 2.

Similarly, after filling up the rest of the entries except the last, the state of the table is shown in Table 10.2.

The computation of $SSE^*(5, 3)$ requires finding the minimum over the entire previous column:

$$SSE^*(5, 3) = \min \begin{cases} SSE^*(2,2) + SSE^*\{24, 72, 96\}, \\ SSE^*(3,2) + SSE^*\{72, 96\}, \\ SSE^*(4,2) + SSE^*\{96\}, \\ SSE^*(5,2) + 0 \end{cases}$$

$$= \min \begin{cases} 0 + 2688, \\ 72 + 288, \\ 672 + 0, \\ 2880 + 0 \end{cases}$$

$$= 360 \tag{10.33}$$

Table 10.3: Computation of V-optimal histogram: complete.

	1	2	3
$v_1 = 48$	$SSE^* = 0$ $BACK = \varnothing$	$SSE^* = 0$ $BACK = \varnothing$	$SSE^* = 0$ $BACK = \varnothing$
$v_2 = 60$	$SSE^* = 72$ $BACK = \varnothing$	$SSE^* = 0$ $BACK = (1,1)$	$SSE^* = 0$ $BACK = (1,2)$
$v_3 = 24$	$SSE^* = 672$ $BACK = \varnothing$	$SSE^* = 72$ $BACK = (2,1)$	$SSE^* = 0$ $BACK = (2,2)$
$v_4 = 72$	$SSE^* = 1260$ $BACK = \varnothing$	$SSE^* = 672$ $BACK = (3,1)$	$SSE^* = 72$ $BACK = (3,2)$
$v_5 = 96$	$SSE^* = 2880$ $BACK = \varnothing$	$SSE^* = 960$ $BACK = (3,1)$	$SSE^* = 360$ $BACK = (3,2)$

The overall error is, therefore, 360, and the back pointer $BACK(5,3) = (3,2)$. Thus, the break-up is to put the first 3 values into 2 bins and then the rest in bin 3. Recursively, going backwards on the $BACK$ pointers reveals that the break-up of 3 values into 2 bins is by putting the first 2 values in bin 1 and the third in bin 2. Hence, the final break-up is

$$
\begin{aligned}
[(5,3)] &= [(3,2)] \cup \{72, 96\} \\
&= \{[(2,1)] \cup \{24\}\} \cup \{72, 96\} \\
&= \{48, 60\} \cup \{24\} \cup \{72, 96\} \quad\quad (10.34)
\end{aligned}
$$

Table 10.3 shows the complete table. □

10.4.3 Discussion

Each computation of a cell requires computing the minimum of 1 column and all rows before it, which is $O(n)$. This, of course, assumes that the computation of $SSE([l_{j+1}, r_i))$ requires a constant amount of time. To ensure that, all such possible $SSE([l_{j+1}, r_i))$ values for every j and i are computed beforehand using the dynamic programming table. Since the total number of cells is $n.b$, the total computation time, therefore, is $O(n^2.b)$. When n is very large, this is not a very efficient solution as far as running time is concerned. However, the fact that it produces the optimal answer makes the algorithm useful and appealing.

Appendices

Appendix A

Memory and Disk Accesses

In this appendix, we describe the modes of accessing data from various storage devices including main memory, hard disk, and flash memory.

A.1 Memory Access

To process any data item, it must be first made available in the main memory of the system. It is then brought to the cache and finally accessed through the CPU registers.

With the increasing gap between the CPU speed and the main memory access speed, well-written programs aim to exploit the *locality* in data as much as possible. The locality is both spatial and temporal. To enable exploitation of this data locality, memory and storage systems are organized as a *memory hierarchy*.

Memory that allows faster access is costly and is, hence, employed in lesser capacity and utilized less than slower, less expensive memory. Different types of memory are, thus, stored in a hierarchical manner with the costliest and least capacity memory sitting at the top and the cheapest and largest capacity memory forming the bottom-most layer. This is called a *memory hierarchy*. The reason why it works is two-fold:

1. Programs tend to access data higher up in the hierarchy much more often due to spatial and temporal *locality of access*.

2. Data access algorithms employ intelligent *caching* techniques that exploit the locality.

The net effect of a memory hierarchy, thus, is to give the program a sense of a large amount of memory with very fast access.

Nevertheless, in database applications, the size of data is extremely large and it mostly resides on disk. For a single query, it is assumed that none of the data is in the cache or in the memory and, consequently,

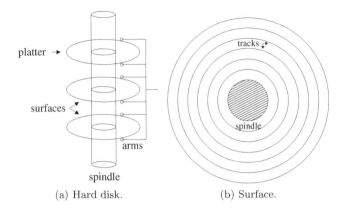

(a) Hard disk.   (b) Surface.

Figure A.1: A hard disk.

the entire dataset has to be accessed from the disk. Thus, the memory hierarchy is not very effective.

For multiple queries, however, the memory hierarchy does play a role by caching data that is used more often. However, the searching methods studied in this book ignore the effect and assume that no data is available in the memory.

A.2   Disks

A HARD DISK is a mechanical device that is accessed using mechanical motions of a read-write head called the *arm*. Due to this mechanical property, the speed of accessing information from a hard disk is limited by the physical laws of mechanical components.

The layout of a typical disk is shown in Figure A.1a. A single disk consists of multiple *platters*. In the center lies the *spindle* which enables the platters to rotate. Generally, both *surfaces* of a platter can be accessed. A surface (Figure A.1b) consists of concentric *tracks* which are divided into *sectors* separated by *gaps* (Figure A.2a). Aligned tracks from all the surfaces form a *cylinder*. The *arm* has multiple read-write heads corresponding to each surface. The arm can physically move back and forth from the outermost track to the innermost one (Figure A.2b). Tracks on the same cylinder can be accessed without moving the arm head.

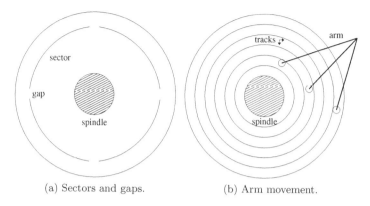

(a) Sectors and gaps.   (b) Arm movement.

Figure A.2: Accessing data from a hard disk.

A.2.1 Disk Capacity

The *storage capacity* of a disk is computed directly using the number of platters, etc.:

$$
\text{Capacity} = (\text{bytes/sector}) \times (\text{sectors/track}) \times (\text{tracks/surface})
$$
$$
\times (\text{surfaces/platter}) \times (\text{platters/disk}) \qquad (\text{A.1})
$$

Example A.1 [Disk Capacity]. Find the total storage capacity of a disk with 1024 bytes per sector, 500 sectors per track, 50000 tracks per surface, 2 surfaces per platter, and 5 platters.

Using Eq. (A.1), the capacity is $1024 \times 500 \times 50000 \times 2 \times 5$ bytes $= 250\,\text{GB}$. □

A.2.2 Disk Access

The *smallest* unit of information that can be read from or written to disk is a *sector*. The smallest unit of information that an operating system can access is a *block* or *page*. Generally, a block is larger in size and consists of a contiguous sequence of sectors.

A.2.2.1 Random I/O

The time to access a particular random block or page in a disk is called the RANDOM ACCESS TIME or time for RANDOM I/O. It consists of three components:

1. *Seek time* T_{seek}: The time to position the arm head over the cylinder that contains the first sector of the target block.

2. *Rotational latency* T_{rotation}: The time to rotate the arm head to the first bit of the sector.

3. *Transfer time* T_{transfer}: The time to read all the bits from the block.

The total access time is a combination of these three components:

$$T_{\text{access}} = T_{\text{seek}} + T_{\text{rotation}} + T_{\text{transfer}} \qquad (A.2)$$

For a typical disk, the rotational speeds are 60, 90, 120, or 250 revolutions per second. The sector size is typically 512 or 1024 bytes. Generally, the inner tracks are smaller with about 500 sectors per track and the outer tracks are larger with about 1000 sectors per track. Therefore, data that is accessed more often is stored on the outer tracks. Typically, there are about 50,000 to 100,000 tracks per platter and 1-5 platters per disk.

The average seek times are between 2-10 ms. The rotational latency for a full revolution varies from 17 ms to 4 ms with the average being about half of this. The aggregate is, thus, between 4-18 ms.

A.2.2.2 Sequential I/O

The time to access the next block or disk page in a disk is called the SEQUENTIAL ACCESS TIME or time for SEQUENTIAL I/O. Since the disk head is already placed in the beginning of the first sector corresponding to the block, the sequential I/O enjoys zero seek time and zero rotational latency. It needs to pay only the transfer time and is, therefore, much faster than random I/O.

Example A.2 [Disk Access Times]. Find the random and sequential I/O times of a block of size 4 KB for a disk having a rotational speed of 7200 rpm (revolutions per minute) and an average seek time of 6 ms. Assume that the average number of sectors per track is 500 and the size of a sector is 1024 bytes.

The seek time, T_{seek}, is 6 ms.

The average rotational latency is the time taken for a half revolution and is equal to $T_{\text{rotation}} = \frac{1}{2} \times (60/rpm) \times 10^3 = 4.17$ ms.

The transfer time for a block, which is equivalent to 4 sectors, is $T_{\text{transfer}} = \frac{4}{500} \times (60/rpm) \times 10^3 = 0.07$ ms.

The average random access time, therefore, is $T_{\text{access}} = 6 + 4.17 + 0.07 = 10.24$ ms.

On the other hand, the average sequential access time is only $T_{\text{transfer}} = 0.07$ ms.   □

The time to access a set of B blocks is, however, computed differently. The random access time for accessing B blocks is simply the random

I/O time for a single block multiplied by B. On the other hand, if the B blocks are placed sequentially on the disk, only the first block requires a random I/O. The next $B - 1$ blocks require sequential I/O times.

Example A.3 [Block Access Times]. Find the random and sequential access times of a set of 4 blocks for Example A.2.

The random I/O time for a block is 10.24 ms. Thus, for 4 blocks, the total time is $4 \times 10.24 = 40.96$ ms.

The sequential I/O time for a block is 0.07 ms. The total time for for accessing 4 sequential blocks, therefore, is $10.24 + (4 - 1) \times 0.07 = 10.45$ ms.

Therefore, the ratio of access times is $40.96/10.45 = 3.9$. □

A.3 Flash

FLASH MEMORY is a non-volatile memory based on SSD (solid-state device) technology. There are two main types of flash memory: NOR and NAND. The NOR type allows word-level access and is costlier while the NAND type allows block-level access and is cheaper and more ubiquitous.

There is a considerable asymmetry in the read-write access performance for flash memory with reads being much faster than writes. The writes (in NAND flash) happen in blocks which can be as large as 256 KB or 512 KB. Hence, to modify even a single bit, first the entire block needs to be copied to the memory before the bit is changed and the entire block is written back.

Typical flash memory read speeds are around 310 MB/s. While fresh writes can progress at 180 MB/s, updates require much more time and can proceed at a *data transfer rate* of only 80 MB/s [Awasthi et al., 2012]. In contrast, the typical read speeds for disk are about 160 MB/s. This is about half that of a flash memory. Writes to disks require a bit more time due to verification and can operate at speeds of 128 MB/s for sequential accesses and 64 MB/s for random accesses [Awasthi et al., 2012]. The comparative advantage of flash memory over disks is, therefore, more for reads.

Flash memory generally shows a mechanical degradation after about 10^6 read-write cycles. Hence, the blocks are written in a round-robin fashion across the flash to increase the lifetime.

A flash drive has faster access than a disk (especially for reads) but is slower than main memory. The costs are also in the middle. Hence, it is a nice candidate to fit in the memory hierarchy between main memory and hard disk. The algorithms that leverage flash memory must handle the special write modality, though.

Appendix B

Distances of Bounding Boxes

In this appendix, we describe how the minimum and maximum distances between two geometric shapes (points, rectangles, and spheres) can be computed. We assume that the figures lie in a vector space of dimensionality t and the distance measure is Euclidean (i.e., L_2).

A point P is represented as

$$P \equiv (p_1, p_2, \ldots, p_t)$$

A hyper-rectangle R is represented by the lowest and highest coordinates in each of the t dimensions:

$$R \equiv (l, h); \quad l = (l_1, \ldots, l_t), \ h = (h_1, \ldots, h_t)$$

A hyper-sphere S is represented by its center point and the radius:

$$S \equiv (c, r); \quad c = (c_1, \ldots, c_t)$$

B.1 Distance of a Point from a Rectangle

The minimum Euclidean distance of a point P from a hyper-rectangle R is

$$d_{min}(P, R) = \sqrt{\sum_{i=1}^{t} \Delta_i^2} \tag{B.1}$$

$$\text{where } \Delta_i = \begin{cases} l_i - p_i & \text{when } p_i < l_i \\ p_i - h_i & \text{when } p_i > h_i \\ 0 & \text{otherwise} \end{cases} \tag{B.2}$$

For every dimension, the first case occurs when P is before the lower end-point of R, the second case occurs when P is after the higher end-point, and the third case occurs when P is in between.

The maximum Euclidean distance of a point P from a hyper-rectangle R is

$$d_{max}(P, R) = \sqrt{\sum_{i=1}^{t} \Delta_i^2} \tag{B.3}$$

$$\text{where } \Delta_i = \max\left\{|p_i - l_i|, |h_i - p_i|\right\} \tag{B.4}$$

The two cases correspond to when P is farther from the lower end-point of R and the higher end-point of R respectively.

B.2 Distance of a Point from a Sphere

The minimum Euclidean distance of a point P from a hyper-sphere S is

$$d_{min}(P, S) = \min\{d(P, c) - r, \ 0\} \tag{B.5}$$

$$\text{where } d(P, c) = \sqrt{\sum_{i=1}^{t} (p_i - c_i)^2} \tag{B.6}$$

The first case happens when P is outside the hyper-sphere. In the second case, when P is inside, the minimum distance is 0.

The maximum Euclidean distance of a point P from a hyper-sphere S is

$$d_{max}(P, S) = d(P, c) + r \tag{B.7}$$

$$\text{where } d(P, c) = \sqrt{\sum_{i=1}^{t} (p_i - c_i)^2} \tag{B.8}$$

B.3 Distance of a Sphere from a Rectangle

The distance of a sphere S from a rectangle R can be computed by using the distance of the center of the sphere from the rectangle as described in Section B.1.

The minimum distance is

$$d_{min}(S, R) = \min\left\{d_{min}(c, R) - r, \ 0\right\} \tag{B.9}$$

The maximum distance is

$$d_{max}(S, R) = d_{max}(c, R) + r \qquad \text{(B.10)}$$

B.4 Distance of a Sphere from a Sphere

The minimum distance of a hyper-sphere $S^{(1)} \equiv (c^{(1)}, r^{(1)})$ from another hyper-sphere $S^{(2)} \equiv (c^{(2)}, r^{(2)})$ is computed using the distances between the centers

$$d_{min}(S^{(1)}, S^{(2)}) = \min \left\{ d(c^{(1)}, c^{(2)}) - (r^{(1)} + r^{(2)}), \, 0 \right\} \qquad \text{(B.11)}$$

The first case happens when the hyper-spheres do not intersect while in the second case, they intersect.

The maximum distance is

$$d_{max}(S^{(1)}, S^{(2)}) = d(c^{(1)}, c^{(2)}) + (r^{(1)} + r^{(2)}) \qquad \text{(B.12)}$$

B.5 Distance of a Rectangle from a Rectangle

The minimum distance of a hyper-rectangle $R^{(1)} \equiv (l^{(1)}, h^{(1)})$ from another hyper-rectangle $R^{(2)} \equiv (l^{(2)}, h^{(2)})$ is

$$d_{min}(R^{(1)}, R^{(2)}) = \left(\sum_{i=1}^{t} \Delta_i^2 \right)^{1/2} \qquad \text{(B.13)}$$

$$\text{where } \Delta_i = \begin{cases} l_i^{(1)} - h_i^{(2)} & \text{when } h_i^{(2)} < l_i^{(1)} \\ l_i^{(2)} - h_i^{(1)} & \text{when } h_i^{(1)} > l_i^{(2)} \\ 0 & \text{otherwise} \end{cases} \qquad \text{(B.14)}$$

For every dimension, the first case occurs when the first hyper-rectangle $R^{(1)}$ is completely before the second one $R^{(2)}$, the second case happens in the reverse situation, and the third case is when the two hyper-rectangles overlap.

The maximum distance is

$$d_{max}(R^{(1)}, R^{(2)}) = \left(\sum_{i=1}^{t} \Delta_i^2 \right)^{1/2} \tag{B.15}$$

$$\text{where } \Delta_i^{max} = \max \left\{ |h_i^{(2)} - l_i^{(1)}|, |h_i^{(1)} - l_i^{(2)}| \right\} \tag{B.16}$$

The two cases correspond to the two maximum possible distances: the lower end-point of $R^{(1)}$ to the higher end-point of $R^{(2)}$, and vice versa.

Appendix C

Vectors and Matrices

This appendix discusses the various definitions and properties related to vectors and matrices.

C.1 Vector Spaces

Informally, a VECTOR SPACE is a collection of vectors that can be *added* together and *scaled* by a scalar quantity. A vector space $\mathcal{V}$ over a field $\mathcal{F}$ defines the following two operations:

1. *Vector addition*: $\mathcal{V} \times \mathcal{V} \to \mathcal{V}$, denoted as $\vec{x} + \vec{y}$

2. *Scalar multiplication*: $\mathcal{F} \times \mathcal{V} \to \mathcal{V}$, denoted as $c\vec{x}$

If the scalars are real numbers, then $\mathcal{V}$ forms a *real vector space*. Examples of vector spaces are $\mathcal{R}^n$, $m \times n$ matrices, etc.

A SUBSPACE is a non-empty subset that is closed under the vector addition and the scalar multiplication operations. Examples of subspaces are lower triangular matrices and symmetric matrices, but not the first quadrant, or the first and third quadrants taken together.

When the vector space is endowed with a Euclidean distance between any two vectors, it is referred to as a EUCLIDEAN SPACE.

The L_p NORM of a vector is the L_p norm distance of it from the origin $(0, 0, \ldots, 0)$. Thus, the L_2 norm of a vector is its *length*.

C.2 Matrices

A set of vectors with equal dimensionality may be considered as a matrix where the rows represent the vectors and the columns represent the dimensionality.

C.3 Properties of Matrices

The *transpose* of a matrix A, denoted by A^T, is the matrix obtained by interchanging the rows and columns. Thus, if A is of size $n \times m$, the size of A^T is $m \times n$.

A matrix is *square* if the number of rows is equal to the number of columns. It is *symmetric* if every $(i, j)^{\text{th}}$ entry is equal to the $(j, i)^{\text{th}}$ entry. It is *diagonal* if only the diagonal entries, i.e., the $(i, i)^{\text{th}}$ entries are non-zero. A square diagonal matrix is called an *identity* matrix if all the diagonal entries are 1. It is generally denoted by I (or I_n to indicate the size $n \times n$ of the matrix). A matrix is *lower triangular* if all the entries above the main diagonal are 0. Similarly, it is *upper triangular* if all the entries below the main diagonal are 0.

The *inverse* of a matrix A is another matrix, denoted by A^{-1}, such that the multiplication of them produces the identity matrix, i.e., $A.A^{-1} = I$.

A matrix is *orthogonal* if all its columns are linearly independent of each other. If the L_2 norm of each column (i.e., its length) of an orthogonal matrix is 1, it is called an *orthonormal* matrix. Thus, an identity matrix is orthonormal. The inverse of an orthonormal matrix is its transpose, i.e., if A is orthonormal, $A^{-1} = A^T$.

A matrix A is *positive semi-definite* if $\vec{z}^T A \vec{z} \geq 0$ for all non-zero vectors $\vec{z}$. It is *positive definite* if $\vec{z}^T A \vec{z} > 0$ for all $\vec{z} \neq \vec{0}$.

C.3.1 Rank of a Matrix

The COLUMN RANK of a matrix A is the largest number of linearly independent columns of A. Similarly, the ROW RANK is the largest number of linearly independent rows. Since both the values are the same, it is simply called the RANK of the matrix.

C.3.2 Eigenvectors and Eigenvalues

Given a square matrix A, consider the equation

$$A\vec{x} = \lambda \vec{x} \tag{C.1}$$

The solution vector $\vec{x}$ for the above equation is called the EIGENVECTOR of A, the corresponding EIGENVALUE for which is λ. For a matrix A with rank r, there are r eigenvectors with non-zero eigenvalues.

In general, multiplying a vector by a matrix rotates the vector. The specialty of eigenvectors is that the matrix A does not rotate it; it simply stretches it by a fraction, which is the eigenvalue.

C.4 Dimensionality

A set of k vectors $\vec{v_1}, \vec{v_2}, \ldots, \vec{v_k}$ are *linearly independent* if and only if the linear combination $c_1 \vec{v_1} + c_2 \vec{v_2} + \cdots + c_k \vec{v_k} = \vec{0}$ implies that $c_1 = c_2 \cdots = c_k = 0$. In other words, no vector can be expressed as a linear combination of the others.

The SPAN of a set of vectors is the vector space generated by their *linear* combinations. A BASIS of a vector space $\mathcal{V}$ is a set of vectors that is linearly independent and that spans $\mathcal{V}$.

The cardinality of the basis of a vector space $\mathcal{V}$, i.e., the number of linearly independent vectors needed to span V, is called its DIMENSION-ALITY. The bases (i.e., the set of basis vectors) for a vector space may vary, but their cardinality remains the same, i.e., the dimensionality is constant.

Appendix D

Probability and Statistics

In this appendix, we review the different concepts related to probability and statistics.

D.1 Random Variable

An outcome of a statistical experiment is called a RANDOM VARIABLE. A random variable can assume values from the possible outcomes of the experiment. Each value of the random variable is associated with a probability with which the random variable assumes that particular value. Thus, for a random variable X, if the value is x, the probability is denoted by $P(X = x)$.

The SAMPLE SPACE of a random experiment is the set of all possible outcomes of that experiment. A subset of the sample space is an EVENT. Thus, in an event, the random variable can obtain a subset of the possible values. A COMPLEMENT of an event is the complement of the subset of outcomes associated with the event. Thus, the probability of the complement of an event is the total probability (which is 1) minus the probability of the event.

D.2 Probability Distribution

A PROBABILITY DISTRIBUTION is an assignment of each value of a random variable to a probability. If the random variable can assume *continuous* values, it is called a PROBABILITY DENSITY FUNCTION (PDF); if, on the other hand, the random variable assumes only *discrete* values, it is often called a PROBABILITY MASS FUNCTION (PMF). For many cases, however, the name "probability density function" is used for both. Valid probability distribution functions follow two important properties:

1. The probability of each value of the random variable is between 0 and 1, i.e., $0 \leq P(X = x) \leq 1$.

2. The sum of probabilities of all values of the random variable adds up to 1, i.e., $\oint_x P(X = x)\, dx = 1$.

The CUMULATIVE DENSITY FUNCTION (CDF) specifies the probability of a random variable for all values up to a particular value. In other words, it is the sum of the probabilities of all values of the random variable that is less than or equal to the specified value. The *cumulative probability* is computed by

$$C(X = y) = \int_{-\infty}^{y} P(X = x)\, dx \tag{D.1}$$

D.3 Statistical Parameters

Assume a dataset containing n objects, $\{O_1, O_2, \ldots, O_n\}$ where each object has d attributes. The jth attribute of the ith object is denoted by O_{ij}.

The MEAN of the jth attribute over all the n objects is

$$\mu_j = \frac{\sum_{i=1}^{n} O_{ij}}{n} \tag{D.2}$$

The VARIANCE of the jth attribute is the squared difference from the mean:

$$var_j = \sigma_j^2 = \frac{\sum_{i=1}^{n} (O_{ij} - \mu_j)^2}{n} \tag{D.3}$$

The STANDARD DEVIATION σ_j is the positive square root of the variance.

The COVARIANCE between two attributes measures how much one attribute varies with respect to the other. Between two attributes j and k, it is defined as

$$cov_{j,k} = \frac{\sum_{i=1}^{n} \left[(O_{ij} - \mu_j) \cdot (O_{ik} - \mu_k) \right]}{n} \tag{D.4}$$

The variance of an attribute is, thus, the covariance of the attribute with itself.

The CORRELATION COEFFICIENT normalizes the covariance by the standard deviations of the two attributes:

$$corr_{j,k} = \frac{cov_{j,k}}{\sigma_j \sigma_k} \tag{D.5}$$

$$= \frac{\sum_{i=1}^{n} \left[(O_{ij} - \mu_j).(O_{ik} - \mu_k)\right]}{\sum_{i=1}^{n}(O_{ij} - \mu_j).\sum_{i=1}^{n}(O_{ik} - \mu_k)} \tag{D.6}$$

The correlation coefficient is always between -1 and $+1$.

The COVARIANCE MATRIX for the dataset is a $d \times d$ matrix C where each C_{jk} entry ($\forall j, k = 1, \ldots, d$) denotes the covariance between the attributes j and k. The matrix is symmetric and the diagonals contain the variances.

Bibliography

[Achlioptas, 2001] Achlioptas, D. (2001). Database-friendly random projections. In *ACM Symposium on Principles of Database Systems (PODS)*, pages 274–281. (Page 198), (Page 199)

[Achlioptas, 2003] Achlioptas, D. (2003). Database-friendly random projections: Johnson-Lindenstrauss with binary coins. *Journal of Computer and System Sciences*, 66(4):671–687. (Page 198), (Page 199)

[Adelson-Velskii and Landis, 1962] Adelson-Velskii, G. and Landis, E. M. (1962). An algorithm for the organization of information. *Proceedings of USSR Academy of Sciences*, 146:263–266. (Page 39)

[Agarwal et al., 1998] Agarwal, P. K., de Berg, M., Matoušek, J., and Schwarzkopf, O. (1998). Constructing levels in arrangements and higher order Voronoi diagrams. *SIAM Journal of Computing*, 27(3):654–667. (Page 51)

[Aggarwal et al., 1987] Aggarwal, A., Guibas, L. J., Saxe, J. B., and Shor, P. W. (1987). A linear-time algorithm for computing the Voronoi diagram of a convex polygon. In *ACM Symposium on Theory of Computing (STOC)*, pages 39–45. (Page 51)

[Aoe et al., 1992] Aoe, J. I., Morimoto, K., and Sato, T. (1992). An efficient implementation of trie structures. *Software – Practice and Experience*, 22:695–721. (Page 51)

[Aurenhammer, 1991] Aurenhammer, F. (1991). Voronoi diagrams – a survey of a fundamental geometric structure. *ACM Computing Surveys (CSUR)*, 23(3):345–405. (Page 47)

[Aurenhammer and Edelsbrunner, 1984] Aurenhammer, F. and Edelsbrunner, H. (1984). An optimal algorithm for constructing the weighted Voronoi diagram in the plane. *Pattern Recognition*, 17(2):251–257. (Page 50)

[Awasthi et al., 2012] Awasthi, A., Nandini, A., Bhattacharya, A., and Sehgal, P. (2012). Hybrid HBase: Leveraging flash SSDs to improve cost per throughput of HBase. In *International Conference on Management of Data (COMAD)*, pages 68–79. (Page 221)

[Bayer, 1972] Bayer, R. (1972). Symmetric binary B-trees: Data structure and maintenance algorithms. *Acta Informatica*, 1(4):290–306. (Page 39)

[Beckmann et al., 1990] Beckmann, N., Kriegel, H.-P., Schneider, R., and Seeger, B. (1990). The R*-tree: An efficient and robust access method for points and rectangles. In *ACM Special Interest Group on Management of Data (SIGMOD)*, pages 322–331. (Page 78)

[Bentley, 1975] Bentley, J. L. (1975). Multidimensional binary search trees used for associative searching. *Communications of the ACM (CACM)*, 18(9):509–517. (Page 35), (Page 42)

[Bentley, 1979] Bentley, J. L. (1979). Decomposable searching problems. *Information Processing Letters*, 8(5):244–251. (Page 44)

[Berchtold et al., 2000] Berchtold, S., Böhm, C., Jagadish, H. V., Kriegel, H.-P., and Sander, J. (2000). Independent quantization: An index compression technique for high-dimensional data spaces. In *IEEE International Conference on Data Engineering (ICDE)*, pages 577–588. (Page 172), (Page 174)

[Berchtold et al., 1997] Berchtold, S., Böhm, C., Keim, D. A., and Kriegel, H.-P. (1997). A cost model for nearest neighbor search in high-dimensional data space. In *ACM Symposium on Principles of Database Systems (PODS)*, pages 78–86. (Page 145)

[Berchtold et al., 1998a] Berchtold, S., Böhm, C., and Kriegel, H.-P. (1998a). Improving the query performance of high-dimensional index structures by bulk-load operations. In *International Conference on Extending Database Technology (EDBT)*, pages 216–230. (Page 91)

[Berchtold et al., 1998b] Berchtold, S., Böhm, C., and Kriegel, H.-P. (1998b). The pyramid-technique: Towards breaking the curse of dimensionality. In *ACM Special Interest Group on Management of Data (SIGMOD)*, pages 142–153. (Page 154), (Page 158)

[Berchtold et al., 1996] Berchtold, S., Keim, D., and Kriegel, H. P. (1996). The X-tree: An index structure for high-dimensional data. In *International Conference on Very Large Data Bases (VLDB)*, pages 28–39. (Page 149), (Page 151), (Page 153)

[Bhattacharya et al., 2010] Bhattacharya, A., Bhowmick, A., and Singh, A. K. (2010). Finding top-k similar pairs of objects annotated with terms from an ontology. In *International Conference on Scientific and Statistical Database Management (SSDBM)*, pages 214–232. (Page 101)

[Bhattacharya et al., 2009] Bhattacharya, A., Kar, P., and Pal, M. (2009). On low distortion embeddings of statistical distance measures into low dimensional spaces. In *International Conference on Database and Expert Systems Applications (DEXA)*, pages 164–172. (Page 200)

[Bhattacharyya, 1943] Bhattacharyya, A. (1943). On a measure of divergence between two statistical populations defined by their probability distributions. *Bulletin of Calcutta Mathematical Society*, 35:99–110. (Page 100)

[Bourgain, 1985] Bourgain, J. (1985). On Lipschitz embedding of finite metric spaces in Hilbert space. *Israel Journal of Mathematics*, 52(1-2):46–52. (Page 195)

[Brin, 1995] Brin, S. (1995). Near neighbor search in large metric spaces. In *International Conference on Very Large Data Bases (VLDB)*, pages 574–584. (Page 118)

[Buja et al., 2008] Buja, A., Swayne, D. F., Littman, M. L., Dean, N., Hofmann, H., and Chen, L. (2008). Data visualization with multidimensional scaling. *Journal of Computational and Graphical Statistics*, 17(2):444–472. (Page 189)

[Burkhard and Keller, 1973] Burkhard, W. A. and Keller, R. M. (1973). Some approaches to best-match file searching. *Communications of the ACM (CACM)*, 16(4):230–236. (Page 135)

[Ciaccia et al., 1997] Ciaccia, P., Patella, M., and Zezula, P. (1997). M-tree: An efficient access method for similarity search in metric spaces. In *International Conference on Very Large Data Bases (VLDB)*, pages 426–435. (Page 120), (Page 124)

[Comer, 1979] Comer, D. (1979). The ubiquitous B-tree. *ACM Computing Surveys (CSUR)*, 11(2):121–137. (Page 35), (Page 61), (Page 62)

[Cormen et al., 2009] Cormen, T. H., Leiserson, C. E., Rivest, R. L., and Stein, C. (2009). *Introduction to Algorithms*. MIT Press. (Page 35), (Page 36), (Page 39), (Page 69), (Page 70)

[Datar et al., 2004] Datar, M., Immorlica, N., Indyk, P., and Mirrokni, V. S. (2004). Locality-sensitive hashing scheme based on p-stable distributions. In *Symposium on Computational Geometry (SCG)*, pages 253–262. (Page 26)

[de Berg et al., 2008] de Berg, M., Cheong, O., van Kreveld, M., and Overmars, M. (2008). *Computational Geometry: Algorithms and Applications*. Springer. (Page 47), (Page 48), (Page 50)

[Edelsbrunner, 1987] Edelsbrunner, H. (1987). *Algorithms in Combinatorial Geometry*. Springer-Verlag. (Page 51)

[Endres and Schindelin, 2003] Endres, D. M. and Schindelin, J. E. (2003). A new metric for probability distributions. *IEEE Transactions on Information Theory*, 49(7):1858–1860. (Page 100)

[Fagin et al., 1979] Fagin, R., Nievergelt, J., Pippenger, N., and Strong, H. R. (1979). Extendible hashing—A fast access method for dynamic files. *ACM Transactions on Database Systems (TODS)*, 4(3):315–344. (Page 18)

[Faloutsos and Lin, 1995] Faloutsos, C. and Lin, K.-I. (1995). Fastmap: A fast algorithm for indexing, data-mining and visualization of traditional and multimedia datasets. In *ACM Special Interest Group on Management of Data (SIGMOD)*, pages 163–174. (Page 191), (Page 195)

[Faloutsos and Roseman, 1989] Faloutsos, C. and Roseman, S. (1989). Fractals for secondary key retrieval. In *ACM Symposium on Principles of Database Systems (PODS)*, pages 247–252. (Page 30), (Page 82)

[Ferhatosmanoglu et al., 2000] Ferhatosmanoglu, H., Tuncel, E., Agrawal, D., and Abbadi, A. E. (2000). Vector approximation based indexing for non-uniform high dimensional data sets. In *ACM International Conference on Information and Knowledge Management (CIKM)*, pages 202–209. (Page 168)

[Finkel and Bentley, 1974] Finkel, R. and Bentley, J. L. (1974). Quad trees: A data structure for retrieval on composite keys. *Acta Informatica*, 4(1):1–9. (Page 35), (Page 36), (Page 39)

[Fleet, 2008] Fleet, P. J. V. (2008). *Discrete Wavelet Transformations: An Elementary Approach with Applications*. Wiley. (Page 205)

[Fortune, 1986] Fortune, S. J. (1986). A sweepline algorithm for Voronoi diagrams. In *Symposium on Computational Geometry (SCG)*, pages 313–322. (Page 48), (Page 50)

[Fredkin, 1960] Fredkin, E. (1960). Trie memory. *Communications of the ACM (CACM)*, 3(9):490–499. (Page 51)

[Fukunaga, 1990] Fukunaga, K. (1990). *Introduction to Statistical Pattern Recognition.* Academic Press. (Page 186)

[Golub and Reinsch, 1970] Golub, G. H. and Reinsch, C. (1970). Singular value decomposition and least squares solutions. *Numerische Mathematik*, 14(5):403–420. (Page 181)

[Gusfield, 1997] Gusfield, D. (1997). *Algorithms on Strings, Trees, and Sequences.* Cambridge University Press. (Page 54), (Page 55), (Page 56)

[Guttman, 1984] Guttman, A. (1984). R-trees: A dynamic index structure for spatial searching. In *ACM Special Interest Group on Management of Data (SIGMOD)*, pages 47–57. (Page 35), (Page 36), (Page 73)

[Hamming, 1950] Hamming, R. W. (1950). Error detecting and error correcting codes. *Bell System Technical Journal*, 29(2):147–160. (Page 107)

[Hjaltason and Samet, 1999] Hjaltason, G. R. and Samet, H. (1999). Distance browsing in spatial databases. *ACM Transactions on Database Systems (TODS)*, 24(2):265–318. (Page 70), (Page 72)

[Hristescu and Farach-Colton, 1999] Hristescu, G. and Farach-Colton, M. (1999). Cluster-preserving embedding of proteins. Technical Report 99-50, Department of Computer Science, Rutgers University. (Page 197)

[Indyk and Motwani, 1998] Indyk, P. and Motwani, R. (1998). Approximate nearest neighbors: Towards removing the curse of dimensionality. In *ACM Symposium on Theory of Computing (STOC)*, pages 604–613. (Page 23), (Page 25)

[Ioannidis and Poosala, 1995] Ioannidis, Y. E. and Poosala, V. (1995). Balancing histogram optimality and practicality for query result size estimation. In *ACM Special Interest Group on Management of Data (SIGMOD)*, pages 233–244. (Page 210)

[Jagadish, 1990] Jagadish, H. V. (1990). Spatial search with polyhedra. In *IEEE International Conference on Data Engineering (ICDE)*, pages 311–319. (Page 88)

[Jagadish et al., 1998] Jagadish, H. V., Koudas, N., Muthukrishnan, S., Poosala, V., Sevcik, K., and Suel, T. (1998). Optimal histograms with quality guarantees. In *International Conference on Very Large Data Bases (VLDB)*, pages 275–286. (Page 210)

[Johnson and Lindenstrauss, 1984] Johnson, W. and Lindenstrauss, J. (1984). Extensions of Lipschitz mappings into a Hilbert space. *Contemporary Mathematics*, 26:189–206. (Page 195), (Page 198)

[Jolliffe, 2002] Jolliffe, I. T. (2002). *Principal Component Analysis*. Springer. (Page 186)

[Kamel and Faloutsos, 1993] Kamel, I. and Faloutsos, C. (1993). On packing R-trees. In *ACM International Conference on Information and Knowledge Management (CIKM)*, pages 490–499. (Page 89)

[Kamel and Faloutsos, 1994] Kamel, I. and Faloutsos, C. (1994). Hilbert R-tree: An improved R-tree using fractals. In *International Conference on Very Large Data Bases (VLDB)*, pages 500–509. (Page 30), (Page 82)

[Katayama and Satoh, 1997] Katayama, N. and Satoh, S. (1997). The SR-tree: An index structure for high-dimensional nearest neighbor queries. In *ACM Special Interest Group on Management of Data (SIGMOD)*, pages 369–380. (Page 85)

[Klee, 1980] Klee, V. (1980). On the complexity of d-dimensional Voronoi diagrams. *Archiv der Mathematik*, 34(1):75–80. (Page 51)

[Kruskal, 1964] Kruskal, J. B. (1964). Multidimensional scaling by optimizing goodness of fit to a nonmetric hypothesis. *Psychometrika*, 29(1):1–27. (Page 189)

[Kruskal and Wish, 1978] Kruskal, J. B. and Wish, M. (1978). *Multidimensional scaling*. SAGE Publications. (Page 189)

[Kullback, 1959] Kullback, S. (1959). *Information Theory and Statistics*. John Wiley and Sons. (Page 100)

[Larson, 1978] Larson, P.-Å. (1978). Dynamic hashing. *BIT*, 18(2):184–201. (Page 17)

[Larson, 1988] Larson, P.-Å. (1988). Dynamic hash tables. *Communications of the ACM (CACM)*, 31(4):446–457. (Page 20)

[Lee and Wong, 1977] Lee, D. T. and Wong, C. K. (1977). Worst-case analysis for region and partial region searches in multidimensional binary search trees and balanced quad trees. *Acta Informatica*, 9:23–29. (Page 41), (Page 43)

[Lee and Wong, 1980] Lee, D. T. and Wong, C. K. (1980). Quintary trees: A file structure for multidimensional database systems. *ACM Transactions on Database Systems (TODS)*, 5(3):339–353. (Page 45)

[Leuker, 1978] Leuker, G. S. (1978). A data structure for orthogonal range queries. In *IEEE Symposium on Foundations of Computer Science (FOCS)*, pages 28–34. (Page 44)

[Leutenegger et al., 1997] Leutenegger, S. T., Edgington, J. M., and Lopez, M. A. (1997). STR: A simple and efficient algorithm for R-tree packing. In *IEEE International Conference on Data Engineering (ICDE)*, pages 497–506. (Page 89), (Page 90)

[Levenshtein, 1965] Levenshtein, V. I. (1965). Binary codes capable of correcting spurious insertions and deletions of ones. *Problems in Information Transmission*, 1:8–17. (Page 106)

[Linial et al., 1994] Linial, N., London, E., and Rabinovich, Y. (1994). The geometry of graphs and some of its algorithmic applications. In *IEEE Symposium on Foundations of Computer Science (FOCS)*, pages 577–591. (Page 196)

[Linial et al., 1995] Linial, N., London, E., and Rabinovich, Y. (1995). The geometry of graphs and some of its algorithmic applications. *Combinatorica*, 15:215–245. (Page 196), (Page 197)

[Litwin, 1980] Litwin, W. (1980). Linear hashing: A new tool for file and table addressing. In *International Conference on Very Large Data Bases (VLDB)*, pages 212–223. (Page 20)

[Ljosa et al., 2006] Ljosa, V., Bhattacharya, A., and Singh, A. K. (2006). Indexing spatially sensitive distance measures using multi-resolution lower bounds. In *International Conference on Extending Database Technology (EDBT)*, pages 865–883. (Page 102), (Page 104)

[Mahalanobis, 1936] Mahalanobis, P. C. (1936). On the generalised distance in statistics. *Proceedings of the National Institute of Science of India*, 2:49–55. (Page 97)

[Maly, 1976] Maly, K. (1976). Compressed tries. *Communications of the ACM (CACM)*, 23(2):262–271. (Page 53)

[Manning et al., 2008] Manning, C. D., Raghavan, P., and Schütze, H. (2008). *An Introduction to Information Retrieval*. Cambridge University Press. (Page 98), (Page 101)

[Manolopoulos et al., 2006] Manolopoulos, Y., Nanopoulos, A., Papadopoulos, A. N., and Theodoridis, Y. (2006). *R-Trees: Theory and Applications*. Springer-Verlag. (Page 73), (Page 78)

[McCreight, 1976] McCreight, E. M. (1976). A space-economical suffix tree construction algorithm. *Journal of ACM*, 23(2):262–272. (Page 55)

[Micó et al., 1994] Micó, M. L., Oncina, J., and Vidal, E. (1994). A new version of the nearest-neighbour approximating and eliminating search algorithm (AESA) with linear preprocessing time and memory requirements. *Pattern Recognition Letters*, 15(1):9–17. (Page 133), (Page 135)

[Motwani and Raghavan, 1995] Motwani, R. and Raghavan, P. (1995). *Randomized Algorithms*. Cambridge University Press. (Page 23)

[Munkres, 1999] Munkres, J. (1999). *Topology*. Prentice Hall. (Page 102)

[Navarro, 2001] Navarro, G. (2001). A guided tour to approximate string matching. *ACM Computing Surveys (CSUR)*, 33(1):31–88. (Page 106)

[Navarro, 2002] Navarro, G. (2002). Searching in metric spaces by spatial approximation. *VLDB Journal*, 11(1):28–46. (Page 125)

[Nievergelt et al., 1984] Nievergelt, J., Hinterberger, H., and Sevcik, K. C. (1984). The grid file: An adaptable, symmetric multikey file structure. *ACM Transactions on Database Systems (TODS)*, 9(1):38–71. (Page 27)

[Ooi et al., 2000] Ooi, B. C., Tan, K.-L., Yu, C., and Bressan, S. (2000). Indexing the edges – a simple and yet efficient approach to high-dimensional indexing. In *ACM Symposium on Principles of Database Systems (PODS)*, pages 166–174. (Page 159), (Page 163)

[Oppenheim et al., 1999] Oppenheim, A. V., Schaffer, R. W., and Buck, J. R. (1999). *Discrete-Time Signal Processing*. Prentice Hall. (Page 202), (Page 203)

[Österreicher and Vajda, 2003] Österreicher, F. and Vajda, I. (2003). A new class of metric divergences on probability spaces and its applicability in statistics. *Annals of the Institute of Statistical Mathematics*, 55(3):639–653. (Page 100)

[Peleg et al., 1989] Peleg, S., Werman, M., and Rom, H. (1989). A unified approach to the change of resolution: Space and gray-level. *IEEE*

Transactions on Pattern Analysis and Machine Intelligence (PAMI), 11:739–742. (Page 105)

[Press et al., 2007] Press, W. H., Teukolsky, S. A., Vetterling, W. T., and Flannery, B. P. (2007). *Numerical Recipes: The Art of Scientific Computing*. Cambridge University Press. (Page 180)

[Puech and Yahia, 1985] Puech, C. and Yahia, H. (1985). Quadtrees, octrees, hyperoctrees: A unified analytical approach to tree data structures used in graphics, geometric modeling and image processing. In *Symposium on Computational Geometry (SCG)*, pages 272–280. (Page 42)

[Ramasubramanian and Paliwal, 1992] Ramasubramanian, V. and Paliwal, K. K. (1992). An efficient approximation-elimination algorithm for fast nearest neighbour search based on a spherical distance coordinate formulation. *Pattern Recognition Letters*, 13(7):471–480. (Page 136)

[Rao and Bopardikar, 1998] Rao, R. M. and Bopardikar, A. S. (1998). *Wavelet Transforms: Introduction to Theory and Applications*. Addison-Wesley. (Page 204)

[Robinson, 1981] Robinson, J. T. (1981). The K-D-B-Tree: A search structure for large multidimensional dynamic indexes. In *ACM Special Interest Group on Management of Data (SIGMOD)*, pages 10–18. (Page 35), (Page 64), (Page 65)

[Roussopoulos and Leifker, 1985] Roussopoulos, N. and Leifker, D. (1985). Direct spatial search on pictorial databases using packed R-trees. In *ACM Special Interest Group on Management of Data (SIGMOD)*, pages 17–31. (Page 89)

[Roweis and Saul, 2000] Roweis, S. T. and Saul, L. K. (2000). Nonlinear dimensionality reduction by locally linear embedding. *Science*, 290:2323–2326. (Page 199)

[Rubner et al., 2000] Rubner, Y., Tomasi, C., and Guibas, L. J. (2000). The earth mover's distance as a metric for image retrieval. *International Journal of Computer Vision*, 40(2):99–121. (Page 102)

[Ruiz, 1986] Ruiz, E. V. (1986). An algorithm for finding nearest neighbors in (approximately) constant average time. *Pattern Recognition Letters*, 4(3):145–157. (Page 129), (Page 130)

[Sakurai et al., 2000] Sakurai, Y., Yoshikawa, M., Uemura, S., and Kojima, H. (2000). The A-tree: An index structure for high-dimensional spaces using relative approximation. In *International Conference on Very Large Data Bases (VLDB)*, pages 516–526. (Page 169)

[Samet, 1990] Samet, H. (1990). *The Design and Analysis of Spatial Data Structures*. Addison-Wesley. (Page 42)

[Samet, 2006] Samet, H. (2006). *Foundations of Multidimensional and Metric Data Structures*. Morgan Kaufmann. (Page 36), (Page 41), (Page 43)

[Sammon, 1969] Sammon, J. W. J. (1969). A nonlinear mapping for data structure analysis. *IEEE Transactions on Computers*, C-18(5):401–409. (Page 190)

[Schütze and Manning, 1999] Schütze, H. and Manning, C. D. (1999). *Foundations of Statistical Natural Language Processing*. MIT Press. (Page 100)

[Sedgewick and Wayne, 2011] Sedgewick, R. and Wayne, K. (2011). *Algorithms*. Addison-Wesley. (Page 39)

[Sellis et al., 1987] Sellis, T. K., Roussopoulos, N., and Faloutsos, C. (1987). The R+-Tree: A dynamic index for multi-dimensional objects. In *International Conference on Very Large Data Bases (VLDB)*, pages 507–518. (Page 80)

[Shepard, 1962a] Shepard, R. N. (1962a). The analysis of proximities: Multidimensional scaling with an unknown distance function. I. *Psychometrika*, 27(2):125–140. (Page 189)

[Shepard, 1962b] Shepard, R. N. (1962b). The analysis of proximities: Multidimensional scaling with an unknown distance function. II. *Psychometrika*, 27(3):219–246. (Page 189)

[Silberschatz et al., 2010] Silberschatz, A., Korth, H. F., and Sudarshan, S. (2010). *Database System Concepts*. McGraw-Hill. (Page 56)

[Tenenbaum et al., 2000] Tenenbaum, J. B., de Silva, V., and Langford, J. C. (2000). A global geomteric framework for nonlinear dimensionality reduction. *Science*, 290:2319–2323. (Page 190)

[Torgerson, 1952] Torgerson, W. S. (1952). Multidimensional scaling: I. Theory and method. *Psychometrika*, 17(4):401–419. (Page 189)

[Uhlmann, 1991a] Uhlmann, J. K. (1991a). Metric trees. *Applied Mathematics Letters*, 4(5):61–62. (Page 112), (Page 113)

[Uhlmann, 1991b] Uhlmann, J. K. (1991b). Satisfying general proximity/similarity queries with metric trees. *Information Processing Letters*, 40(4):175–179. (Page 116)

[Ukkonen, 1995] Ukkonen, E. (1995). On-line construction of suffix-trees. *Algorithmica*, 14(3):249–260. (Page 55)

[van Rijsbergen, 1979] van Rijsbergen, C. J. (1979). *Information Retrieval*. Butterworth. (Page 10)

[Vidal, 1994] Vidal, E. (1994). New formulation and improvements of the nearest-neighbour approximating and eliminating search algorithm (AESA). *Pattern Recognition Letters*, 15(1):1–7. (Page 129), (Page 130), (Page 132)

[Weber et al., 1998] Weber, R., Schek, H.-J., and Blott, S. (1998). A quantitative analysis and performance study for similarity-search methods in high-dimensional spaces. In *International Conference on Very Large Data Bases (VLDB)*, pages 194–205. (Page 148), (Page 164)

[Weiner, 1973] Weiner, P. (1973). Linear pattern matching algorithms. In *IEEE Symposium on Switching and Automata Theory (SWAT)*, pages 1–11. (Page 54), (Page 55)

[Werman et al., 1985] Werman, M., Peleg, S., and Rosenfeld, A. (1985). A distance metric for multi-dimensional histograms. *Computer, Vision, Graphics, and Image Processing*, 32(3):328–336. (Page 105)

[White and Jain, 1996] White, D. A. and Jain, R. (1996). Similarity indexing with the SS-tree. In *IEEE International Conference on Data Engineering (ICDE)*, pages 516–523. (Page 83)

[Willard, 1979] Willard, D. E. (1979). The Super-B-tree algorithm. Technical Report TR-03-79, Harvard University. (Page 44)

[Yianilos, 1993] Yianilos, P. N. (1993). Data structures and algorithms for nearest neighbor search in general metric spaces. In *ACM-SIAM Symposium on Discrete Algorithms (SODA)*, pages 311–321. (Page 113), (Page 115)

Index

A-tree, 169–173
accuracy, 9, 11
AESA, 129–136
    fixed anchor point, *see*
        FAP-AESA
    linear, *see* LAESA
    vector space, *see* FAP-AESA
anchor point, 136
angular
    distance, 99
    similarity, 99
average pairwise distance, 101
AVL tree, 39

B+-tree, 35, 61–64, 73, 74, 82,
        154–156, 159, 161
B-tree, 61–64
base prototype, 133
basis, 229
best-first search, 70–72, 122
Bhattacharyya
    coefficient, 100
    distance, 100
binary search tree, *see* BST
bit interleaving curve, 30
bitmap indexing, 33, 56–58
bounding
    box, 61, 65–68, 70, 73, 74, 88,
        170, 173
    polyhedron, 88
    rectangle, 74, 85–87, 171
    sphere, 84–87
breadth-first search, 69
BST, 35–39
    balanced, 38, 39

bucket
    overflow, *see* overflow bucket
    primary, *see* primary bucket
bulk-loading, 89, 173

cdf, 232
chaining, 16
Cholesky decomposition, 180
city-block distance, 96
closed addressing, 16
closed hashing, 16
collision, 15
column curve, 30
column-prime curve, 30
compact trie, 53
compressed trie, 53, 54
confusion matrix, 7, 8
contractive, 178, 179, 185,
        195–197, 203
correlation coefficient, 233
cosine
    distance, 99
    similarity, 98, 99
covariance, 232
covariance matrix, 186, 233
cumulative density function, *see*
        cdf
curse of dimensionality, 75, 91,
        141, 148, 149, 154

data-partitioning method, 35, 147
DCT, 203–205, 208
dead space, 35, 74, 76, 80, 123
Delaunay
    graph, 48, 125, 126, 128

For Product Safety Concerns and Information please contact our EU
representative GPSR@taylorandfrancis.com Taylor & Francis Verlag GmbH,
Kaufingerstraße 24, 80331 München, Germany

Printed and bound by CPI Group (UK) Ltd, Croydon, CR0 4YY
01/05/2025
01858338-0002